THE
SEASON
AFTER

THE SEASON AFTER

ARE SPORTS DYNASTIES DEAD?

Peter King

WARNER BOOKS

A Warner Communications Company

Warner Books, Inc., 666 Fifth Avenue, New York, NY 10103

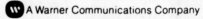 A Warner Communications Company

Printed in the United States of America
First printing: August 1989
10 9 8 7 6 5 4 3 2 1

Library of Congress Cataloging-in-Publication Data

King, Peter, 1957–
    The season after : are sports dynasties dead? / Peter King.
      p. cm.
    ISBN 0-446-51413-6
    1. Professional sports—United States.   2. Professional sports—
Economic aspects—United States.   3. Professional sports—Canada.
4. Professional sports—Economic aspects—Canada.   I. Title.
GV583.K49   1989
338.4'7796'0973—dc20   89-9202
                                                                CIP

Designed by Giorgetta Bell McRee

To my mom and dad, Phyllis and the late Kenneth "Lefty" King, who gave me integrity and a work ethic, and who took me to Fenway Park. I miss you, Dad.

And to my wife, Ann, who—and I know I'll get some arguments on this—is the best woman in the world.

Contents

Acknowledgments

I'd like to thank:

Sparky Anderson, Mel Blount, Bob Bourne, Terry Bradshaw, Pat Calabria, Frank Cashen, Michael Cooper, Bob Cousy, Ron Darling, Mike Ditka, Helene Elliott, Jim Finks, Tom Friend, Phil Garner, Joe Greene, an airsick Wayne Gretzky, Jack Ham, Dan Hampton, Chick Hearn, Tom Heinsohn, Sam Huff, Harry Hulmes, Davey Johnson, Ann King, Laura King, Mary Beth King, KLAC-AM radio, Jerry Kramer, Tom Lasorda, Jim Matheson, Phil McConkey, Doug Moe, John Muckler, Ray Nitschke, Marty Noble, Bill Parcells, Johnny Parker, Sam Pollock, Pat Riley, Phil Rizzuto, Dan Rooney, Pete Rose, Glen Sather, Bill Sharman, Phil Simms, Mike Singletary, Vito Stellino, Tom Verducci, George Young, an editor named Jim Frost, and an agent named David Black.

And a sports editor named Dick Sandler.

Voices

"If a team can be in the playoffs every year and in the Super Bowl every three or four years, that's the closest you can come to a dynasty today."
—*Former San Francisco 49ers coach*
BILL WALSH, 1986

"Boy, I was wrong about the Mets. After 'eighty-six, I thought for sure they'd be a dynasty."
—*Detroit Tigers manager*
SPARKY ANDERSON, 1988

"Greed has just about destroyed every great team in sports. And it looks like we're not going to escape."
—*Edmonton Oilers coach and general manager*
GLEN SATHER, 1987

"The question is more and more an economic one: Can anyone afford to have a dynasty?"
—*Former major-league infielder*
PHIL GARNER, 1989

"We have left the field of competitive sports. We're in show business. The players are entrepreneurs, individual entrepreneurs, out not only for top billing but for top dollar. The TV and the media make these players into something they really aren't—franchise players, the best there ever was, superstars. All those words are just buzzwords. They create an image about this business that really was never intended to be. You and I know it's a game. It's just that it's not allowed to be a game anymore."
—*New Orleans Saints general manager*
JIM FINKS, 1989

"I suppose we could have another true dynasty someday. Maybe. It's a matter of odds. The planets may align correctly again, and everything might go right for a team for a few years.

"But I doubt it."

—Former Green Bay Packers guard
JERRY KRAMER, 1989

Introduction

In 1986, the New York Giants of the National Football League and a rookie for the club, defensive back Greg Lasker from Arkansas, couldn't agree to contract terms. The Giants were offering a four-year contract worth a total of $860,000. In the first year of the contract, the Giants proposed, they would pay Lasker $345,000 in salaries and bonuses, with that amount to be increased depending on where Lasker finished on the team and in the league in tackles and interceptions.

Linebacker Harry Carson, who at this point in his career had been a league all-star in seven different years with the Giants, was due to make $350,000 in 1986.

But Lasker and his agent, Tom Selakovich of Chicago, thought the Giants' offer was slightly low. So Selakovich held Lasker out of training camp for several days. Lasker stayed in a hotel near the camp, waiting for the contract to get done. Reporters went to his room one day and found him reading the *Wall Street Journal*. "I just want what's fair," Lasker said. After a five-day stalemate, the Giants improved some language in the contract, added $5,000 to it, and Lasker signed.

For four years Greg Lasker had played good football at Arkansas. But he was never very good in pro football. The Giants never had him in the starting lineup in his two years and two months with the team—when the Giants tried to work him into the starting lineup in training camp in 1987, he made more mental errors than the rest of the defensive secondary combined—and Lasker never seemed very interested in playing the game. He talked sometimes about how he couldn't wait to go home to Arkansas in the off-season. He made $540,750 while hanging around with the Giants.

Greg Lasker illustrates a vicious sporting cycle, and the cycle is a part of why extended greatness in sports is nearly impossible today.

The player knew he had some power. He knew he could force management to pay him a little bit more because all the other draft choices in the second round were sharing financial information from the other teams in the league, and the Giants' offer was slightly below the market. The Giants knew they could afford to pay the player slightly more because of their solid base of income: they sold 76,891 tickets to every game at Giants Stadium in New Jersey, and they made $16 million that year from the league's network television contract. The player knew he would get some small concession from the team. The team knew it had invested lots of time and effort in scouting and acquiring the player. Other teams gave in slightly to other players; the Giants gave in slightly to this one.

Before Lasker ever put on the pads, the Giants handed him a check for $225,000, as a signing bonus. By the end of the four-month regular season, he had made $120,000 in salary. By the end of the one-month playoffs, he had made an extra $64,000, which is what each Giant earned for winning Super Bowl XXI.

In five and a half months, a fairly insignificant member of the New York Giants had earned $409,000.

What you have here is this: a player getting used to sudden and fabulous wealth as he tries to make a quantum leap from college to pro sports; a team impatient for him to grow and disbelieving when his effort isn't consistently high; veteran teammates angry at the system that rewards rookies more than most proven journeymen; and a coaching staff that has to take all of these things into account—and more, like drug temptations, like monitoring the agents and portfolio managers trying to get pieces of the players, like how to create motivation and desire.

"It's human nature to let down emotionally a little after you've made some money, and not to be as sky-high and not to want it as much," Giants quarterback Phil Simms says. "It's like the guy who has ten dollars and who's out working to make more. He's working his ass off. Then, one day, all of a sudden he's a millionaire. He says, 'Oh, I'll continue to work as hard as I did before.' Oh, sure he will. 'My life won't change,' he'll say. Sure. Hey, it happens. Even though we might not see it ourselves, it does happen. You try to always go back to what you did the year before. It's impossible. You're just different."

You didn't have this a generation ago, when truly big money hadn't hit sports yet. Exactly twenty years earlier, in 1966, Minnesota drafted a defensive tackle named Jerry Shay from Purdue, and he started for six years in the NFL. His approximate career take: $203,000. "Each year when we went to camp, our attitude was, 'Whip me, beat me, abuse me. Just don't let me go,' " Shay said. In the space of two decades, the National Football League had gone from paying a first-round draft choice who started for six years a total of $203,000 to paying an above-average prospect $225,000 for signing his name to a contract.

There are many other things you didn't have in sports a generation ago. Money is the root of some evil in sports, not all.

A generation ago—not quite thirty something years ago, in 1960—the Boston Celtics of the National Basketball Association had just won their second of eight straight league championships. The Montreal Canadiens had just become the first team ever to win five consecutive National Hockey League championships. The New York Yankees won their tenth American League pennant in twelve seasons of baseball. In the National Football League, the Green Bay Packers won their first of six Western Conference titles over an eight-year stretch; after five of those six titles, the Packers would win the league championship.

From 1969 to 1989, one pro basketball team, the Los Angeles Lakers, won titles in succession.

From 1960 to 1989, one major-league baseball team, the Oakland Athletics, won more than two World Series in succession; there hasn't been a repeat winner since 1978.

From 1967 to 1989, no pro football team won more than two National Football League championships in succession.

In hockey, exceptions—and three great recent teams—reign. Since the Canadiens started sharing the Cup with the rest of the league in the sixties, Montreal, the Islanders, and Edmonton have all had a recent run at greatness. But Montreal and the Islanders both fell after they rose.

The point is, the dynasty is comatose. It is on a respirator. This book is about why.

It is because incredible sums of money at young ages, especially for players who have never had money before, often satisfy athletic hunger.

It is because of expansion evening out competition. There were 43 teams in the four major sports a generation ago. There are 102 today.

It is because every sport has a sophisticated system of making sure the bad teams aren't bad for long. The draft, especially, drags down the great and lifts up the poor, and baseball and hockey didn't have drafts a generation ago.

It is because ownership, with the cost of buying and operating franchises now a matter of tens of millions instead of tens of thousands, is more impatient with losing today and will spend more than ever to try to win.

It is because of free agency, which has not built superteams, only superrich ones.

It is because minor-league systems are a fraction of what they once were, because of cost and dilution due to expansion. So an injury or bad trade or star succumbing to drugs can cripple a team today instead of merely detouring it.

It is because scouting and coaching, like the guts of all late-twentieth-century businesses, have entered the computer and video age, flooding sports teams with so much information about the competition that there's not much chance that innovations will surprise anybody.

It is because the crush of celebrity, the crush of outside forces, can inflate heads and bank accounts much more than a generation ago.

It is because of all these things. And it is because, in many ways, it *has* to be this way.

Dynasties have to be dormant because other teams must have hope. There's so much money involved in running a sports franchise today that there are very few sportsman owners left, running teams primarily to try to win—and if they didn't win, they didn't have to sell. John Galbreath and Tom Yawkey are gone. The Tribune Corporation and Labatt's Breweries Limited are here, and they want to show a profit. They want to put fans in the stands and numbers on the Arbitron books. So they have to win. Some year soon, they have to win. In very few cases—Wrigley Field in baseball, Giants Stadium and Lambeau Field in football, Boston Garden in basketball, Madison Square Garden and The (Montreal) Forum in hockey—will consistently bad teams be consistently supported at the box office and on TV.

"Sports is one of the few businesses set up so that the victor doesn't get the spoils," says General Manager George Young of the football Giants.

"It's important that the fan in the franchise city have a hope. Football, and all sports, are created needs. We have to have a system to hold the fans, to hold the ratings. Our product is close games. It has to be. We have to have an entertaining game for our fans and for television, or the money's not going to be there."

This book will follow the New York Giants for two years as they try to repeat their January 1987 Super Bowl title. In lesser depth, it will follow the Los Angeles Lakers, Edmonton Oilers, and New York Mets as they try to win after winning once.

You will read reason, and you will read opinion. Such as these:

• The former Pro Bowl cornerback of the Pittsburgh Steelers, Mel Blount, is sitting in his Manhattan office. He works for the National Football League now, as its director of player relations. Blount talks about how society has changed in the last decade or so.

He says: "We're living in a different time, even from the time of the seventies. They say the more things change, the more they stay the same. Well, people are the same. Society's different. We've got a different kind of athlete today because society is different, and sports are different. I don't think it's very helpful to the sport to be giving $500,000 bonuses to rookies who never played a play for you. What does that say to the veterans who never got that kind of money but have helped build your team? What's happened, I think, is we've created a different kind of ballplayer today. I'm not sure the toughness is there anymore."

• The manager of the Cincinnati Reds, Pete Rose, is sitting in the lobby restaurant of the Grand Hyatt in Manhattan in the middle of the 1988 summer. He is talking about parity.

He says: "You give me any team out of the twenty-six in the major leagues today, and you give me the chance to make three changes—I don't mean really major things necessarily—and you'll have one of the best teams in the game. How many teams have won the last eight World Series? Eight. How many teams have won the American League in the last six years? Six. And Cleveland's the seventh, and a lot of people think they're close."

• The veteran defenseman of the Montreal Canadiens, Larry Robinson, is leaving Madison Square Garden after a dispiriting 1988 loss. There are more and more of those these days for the Canadiens, the class of the league for two decades but one of several teams annually in the hunt as the nineties beckoned. Robinson talks about obstacles to continued greatness.

He says: "You can't have dynasties now, not the way there used to be. Look at the Islanders. They built a great core, and after they got into the Stanley Cup Finals for the fifth time, they looked around and saw all their guys were twenty-eight, twenty-nine, thirty years old, on the downside of their careers. They've got to draft people to replace them, but when you pick at the bottom of the draft every year, it doesn't matter how great your scouts are. You just won't get the great players. They're not there."

• Tom Landry, then the coach of the Dallas Cowboys, is sitting in his office, and the question of the late eighties in the National Football League is posed to him: What has happened to the Cowboys—and to Chuck Noll's Steelers and to Don Shula's Dolphins, for that matter?

He says: "The Dallas Cowboys are proof that the NFL system works. The NFL system knocks down the good teams. Look at Buffalo, Indianapolis, New Orleans. They've been down for so long, and they've been able to build their teams up with the best college players. We've been drafting low for quite a while. Everybody says Chuck and Don and I are too old or whatever. That's foolishness. Coaching doesn't kick in until your team's quality and ability matures."

• Boomer Esiason, the quarterback of the Cincinnati Bengals, is riding in the back of a limousine to the studios of the ABC affiliate in Cincinnati to appear live on *Good Morning America*. It is 6:35 A.M. on a January Monday in 1989. Cincinnati sleeps. Esiason, the day after the Bengals beat Buffalo to win the American Football Conference championship and qualify for the Super Bowl against San Francisco, yawns. He is whipped. He talks about repeating.

He says: "Let me tell you something. They ought to give us next year off. They ought to give us and the Forty-niners next year off. Do you have any idea how beat up we are, and how long it takes to recover from a football season? We've been in training camp since July tenth. That's longer than everybody else because we had to play an early exhibition game. We're going to play twenty-four football games this year, and we'll have less time off in the off-season than anyone. God, I feel like crap."

• Bill Sharman, the former Celtics player and Los Angeles Lakers president, is sitting in his Los Angeles office. He doesn't speak anymore, the result of a larynx operation. But he writes. He is answering a question about the difficulty of one team sustaining excellence.

He writes: "With the increase in popularity and publicity in most sports, it has enhanced the salaries of players to unbelievable highs, which has encouraged more kids to participate than ever before. Look at golf, as an example. In the forties and fifties and earlier years, there were only about twelve to fifteen players who were capable of winning on the PGA golf tour. Today there are hundreds of players out there that are now skilled enough to win any golf tournament. This also applies to other sports because of the same reasons. Therefore, with so many outstanding players available, it naturally helps the weaker teams more."

• Los Angeles Dodgers manager Tom Lasorda is holding court with some writers in a Miami hotel lobby before the 1989 Super Bowl. He is talking about winning today versus winning yesterday.

He says: "Because the talent is spread so well, in order for you to win, practically everybody has to be healthy, and practically everyone has to have peak years. This isn't just baseball. I don't care how good you are, if you lose one or two key guys during the year, your chances of winning are slim. Depth isn't what it used to be."

• The assistant general manager of the Cincinnati Bengals, Mike Brown, is sitting high above Miami, in his Omni International Hotel suite, days before Super Bowl XXIII against San Francisco. He is talking about the new breed of ownership in the NFL, the ultrarich breed; there are eight league owners who appeared on *Forbes* magazine's list of the wealthiest Americans, with net worths of at least $225 million.

He says: "The league is different today. It used to be that we had gentlemen's agreements about things. But that's not the case now. This used to be the family business for a lot of people, but that's not the case now. To some owners, money is absolutely no object."

• The point guard of the Boston Celtics' glory years, Bob Cousy, is sitting in Runyon's, the Manhattan sporting bar/restaurant, doing a national sports talk show with Bob Costas. The subject is dynasties, and why they don't happen anymore in sports.

He says: "We were basically motivated by fear. We didn't have no-cut guaranteed contracts. Red Auerbach basically motivated us by throwing out a few four-letter words and we went out and overachieved. Nothing works for long periods of time anymore. You can't motivate people the same way. It's impossible. There's too much money, and there's too many other things in these athletes' lives."

Players, very naturally, think differently with a million dollars in the bank in their late twenties.

• Glen Sather, the coach and general manager of the Edmonton Oilers, pours himself into a cushy chair in the lounge adjacent to the club's locker room. He talks about money.

"Greed has just about destroyed every great team in sports. Look at how many players on this team want to renegotiate every year. Priorities change."

Priorities have changed.

*   *   *

There are several factors that won't be addressed in this book, the biggest one being the them-against-the-world theory of nonrepeating. "You won't believe what it's like to be the Bears every week," Chicago defensive end Dan Hampton said in 1987. "It's like the Super Bowl for teams that play us." But when the Celtics went anywhere in the late fifties and the early sixties, they were the objects of incredible scorn. And the Yankees and Canadiens are still paying for years of greatness an era ago; fans in every road city still come to see legends fall, regardless of who currently wears the legendary uniform. Also, collegiate dynasties—such as UCLA's ten basketball championships in twelve seasons—won't be analyzed because the team-building rules in college are so much different than those governing professionals. Similar factors then and now in professional sports won't be discussed much. Marked differences will. And there are plenty of those.

The bottom-line question herein, naturally, is this: Can it happen again? Will anyone ever win eight National Basketball Association titles in succession, or fourteen baseball pennants in sixteen seasons? Will any hockey team dominate like the Canadiens of the fifties, or a football team like the Packers of the sixties?

Read on and you'll learn the answer.

Football: Land O'Parity

Euphoria

January 1987
Costa Mesa, California

The lobby of the Westin South Coast Plaza was just about clean now.

It was 7:30 A.M., half a day after the New York Giants won their first National Football League championship in thirty years, beating Denver 39–20 in Super Bowl XXI. Four hours earlier, this same ultramodern lobby with the piano bar and the plush chairs and the backgammon boards and the potted plants and the exhausted football players was a mess. Confetti everywhere. Beer cans and bottles strewn on the carpet. Grown men and women poured into the furniture, totally spent, partially from the game, partially from a party featuring Tom Cruise and Donna Rice (Gary Hart's Donna Rice). Gary Reasons, a linebacker for the Giants, barely awake, nearly motionless in one of the chairs, so bushed he could barely raise his voice and his hand for one last beer.

In the middle of it all, TV crews from ABC, CBS, and NBC had set up the lights and cameras for their morning news shows. On these shows, members of the Giants, who hadn't been to bed yet (linebacker Harry Carson showed up in his bathrobe and pajamas), told America what it felt like to be on the best football team in the world.

Now, all that lobby lacked was Bill Parcells. Parcells, the forty-five-year-old head coach of the Giants, was uncharacteristically late for his last date of Super Bowl week. This lobby had been Parcells's early-morning hangout all through the previous week. Every day at 6:00 A.M., Parcells would sit with friends or reporters, drinking coffee and reading the papers, far from the maddening crowd that would mob the hotel later in the day. Waiting for him now were National Football League Director of Security Charles Jackson and an NFL security officer, John Murphy, who would take Parcells in a limousine to his final Super Bowl obligation, the morning-after press conference twelve miles away in Anaheim. They glanced at their watches. They paced, because traffic crawled outside. At 7:40, Parcells, with his wife, Judy, stepped off the elevator to begin The Day After.

This was the happiest Bill Parcells had looked all season.

Parcells, a guarded, often-brooding man, looked different now because there wasn't another problem to solve, another opponent to break down, another film to watch. In the winter before the 1986 season, he had to supervise and monitor the rehabilitation of star linebacker Lawrence Taylor, who had abused far too many chemicals. In the spring before the 1986 season, he had to mesh his team's needs with the strengths of the annual NFL draft, and the fit had been a bad one: In a year of defensive brilliance among college players, the Giants needed a wide receiver quite badly, and they failed to get one. So Parcells fretted about that all season. In the summer, Parcells was angered by the holdouts of draft choices and star running back Joe Morris, frustrated by the loss of incumbent fullback George Adams to a hip injury, and peeved by the constant news media questioning about Taylor. In the fall, he worried constantly about his offensive shortcomings, and he spent more time than he would have liked trying to engineer trades to bolster the offense. He was thirty pounds overweight. He smoked far too many Marlboros. He felt the pressure of growing up a few football fields from the Giants' home—Giants Stadium, in East Rutherford, New Jersey—and turning a perennial loser into a champion.

That's why, on the morning after Super Bowl XXI, he looked like a kid sitting through the end of midnight mass on Christmas. That's why, the night before, he burst into the coaches' locker room after the victory and said: "This is better than sex!"

In the lobby, he tried to keep a serious look on his face, but every time he saw someone familiar, he'd break into a grin and say something like, "This is great. Isn't this great?"

Parcells saw a reporter who had been publicly skeptical of the team two months earlier, whispered in his ear, "Put away those funeral stories; can't use 'em," and smiled a wide smile.

Parcells saw a sleepy Lawrence Taylor and tried to pump some effervescence into him. "How do you feel?" he asked Taylor. Tired, Taylor said. "Doesn't it feel great?" Parcells asked. It will, Taylor said, after a little more sleep. "Hey," Parcells said, chiding him, "now that I know you're up at this hour, we're going to have all our meetings at this time next year."

Taylor left, and Parcells turned to a reporter to talk about the type of players he had on his team, competitive players like Taylor, quarterback Phil Simms, and nose tackle Jim Burt. All had been heroes the day before. "They had some obligations at the Rose Bowl," Parcells said, "so they took a limo back to the hotel last night. You know one of the things they talked about? They were talking about winning it again. Like, 'Let's win it just one more time. You know how special that would make us?' A lot of teams win it once. Not many teams win it again."

Parcells dispatched his wife in a car to the airport; she would fly back with other wives and families in a charter, separate from the team plane. Then he went to his limo, Murphy driving, Jackson sitting in the passenger seat,

Parcells in back, coffee in hand. On the drive, Parcells paid no attention to the traffic on the San Diego freeway. He paid no attention to anything but the joy he felt.

"Let me tell you something," he said to Jackson. "This is great. Isn't this great? What a feeling this is. Last night, I told the team that nobody could ever tell them they couldn't do it, for the rest of their lives."

He paused for a few minutes, staring out at the traffic, drinking the coffee. Breaking the silence, he said, "Hey Charlie. Was Ditka as happy last year as I am right now?"

"No," Jackson said. Jackson had escorted the winning coach of Super Bowl XX, Mike Ditka of the Chicago Bears, to the final press conference in New Orleans a year earlier. "It didn't register with him yet, what had happened."

In Anaheim, the two men escorted Parcells to a side entrance of the Marriott Hotel, but he drew the stares of strangers anyway. The voices came at him from the potted plants and the columns and the shoe-shine chair, and he never broke stride.

"Way to go, coach."

"Thank you."

"I just wanted to shake your hand, Coach Parcells. Congratulations."

"Thank you."

"I've been a Giants' fan for thirty years, and I was never happier than yesterday."

"That's good. Thank you."

"Go Giants! Do it again!"

"We'll try."

Even with the late start he was a few minutes early for the press conference, so he sat on the side of a makeshift stage in the large ballroom and tried to look happily inconspicuous. From the other side of the room, one of the sponsors of the Super Bowl Most Valuable Player Award was pushing his shy kid toward Parcells. He pushed and he pushed, and finally the kid—ten or eleven years old—was close enough to Parcells to stretch out a pen and ask for an autograph.

"Let me ask you one question," Parcells said before signing. "How you doing in school?"

"Good," the kid said quietly.

"Keep it that way," Parcells said, writing. He handed the kid the signature.

There was applause as he stepped to the microphone, a greeting that rarely welcomes a sports figure to a press conference. In his opening statement to four hundred reporters, fourteen still photographers, and twelve Minicams on the rear podium, Parcells said: "I think I know what euphoria is now."

Later in the press conference, he was asked about some of the good players on his team who weren't playing very much because the team was so good. Parcells said, "There's not one unhappy guy on the New York Giants right now."

In thirty-six hours there would be.

For now, back at the Westin, there was talk of perspective. George Young, the team's general manager, sat in the lobby and accepted the same kind of gratitude Parcells had heard all morning. Young's expression didn't change much. He said: "What the players have to realize is what their business is. I hope they don't lose sight of the fact that their careers are short and they have to keep this success in perspective."

In thirty-six hours, perspective would be detoured. After flying home a champion, after lifting the Super Bowl trophy aloft to a celebrating mob at Giants Stadium, Parcells and the Giants would experience the pain that almost invariably follows great sporting joy today.

Winning the Super Bowl means money and prestige. The Giants would soon find out it also buys anger.

The Game's Over

January 1987
Upper Saddle River, New Jersey

Know a few things about George Young. He's smart. He knows people. He's a businessman. It's hard to surprise him. All of this comes from his fifteen years as a high school football coach and history teacher, two master's degrees, and nineteen years in the NFL as an assistant coach, general manager, personnel scout, and personnel director. A half-hour after the end of the Super Bowl, Young stood outside, detached. How detached? Like Hawaii to the continental forty-eight. A part of it, but removed. Everybody was talking about how Young, the fifty-six-year-old general manager who was so often boisterous and demonstrative and challenging, looked so grim after the most triumphant moment of his NFL career. One writer said, "George looks like he's in a dentist's chair."

Deep down, Young was thinking: "The game's over. It's next year. It's 1987."

So Young had steeled himself for some turbulence, win or lose. When the most controversial phone call of the off-season came two nights later to his home in the wealthiest county in the United States (Bergen), Young was taken aback but not stunned.

On the other end of the line was Robert Fraley, the agent for Parcells. Fraley wanted to get Parcells out of the final two years of his Giants contract.

As is protocol in the NFL, a team or agent must ask the club with contractual rights to a coach for permission to get him free from his existing contract. Parcells was to be paid $300,000 in 1987 and $325,000 in 1988 under his Giants contract. There was a head coach/director of football operations position open in Atlanta, and Fraley had already spoken at length with the Falcons about putting Parcells in it. Including perks, Atlanta was willing to offer Parcells at least $4.5 million over five years to run the football end of the franchise and coach the team. The Falcons' stance with Parcells had been a hands-off one, because negotiating with Parcells while he was under contract to the Giants would have been tampering, a serious offense by NFL standards. Atlanta could have been fined heavily (in dollars and perhaps by forfeiting a high college draft choice) by Commissioner Pete Rozelle if found guilty of tampering with Parcells.

Privately, some people in the Giants front office were certain Parcells or Fraley was in contact with the Falcons before the Super Bowl about a move to Atlanta. It's obvious why, if this was true, it was covered up very neatly by the Falcons, Fraley, and Parcells. Football teams preach single-minded loyalty and dedication, especially before the game for the championship of their sport. How would it look if Parcells or his agent were negotiating with another team the week before the Super Bowl?

Young didn't like most agents. He felt they cheapened the game, prostituted themselves to acquire unsophisticated clients and cared nothing about football. But he was smart enough to know they weren't going to go away. Young also didn't like Fraley's relationship with the Giants. He represented some players on the Giants (quarterback Jeff Rutledge and tight end Zeke Mowatt), and Young felt an agent shouldn't represent a coach and players on the same team. Fraley had represented Parcells since 1982, when Parcells succeeded Ray Perkins as the Giants' coach. Parcells in some ways resented having to employ an agent—he once checked Fraley into a New Jersey hotel under an assumed name because he didn't want people to know he had an agent—but he knew modern-day sport necessitated one. When Parcells's first head-coaching contract with the Giants had been torn up and renegotiated after a winning season in 1984, Parcells had to do the negotiating on the four-year, $1.25-million deal himself; Young thought it unethical for a coach to face firing one of his agent's clients someday.

Young's relationship with Fraley, however, had nothing to do with what was said on the telephone forty-eight hours after Parcells was carried from the Rose Bowl turf in triumph. Young told Fraley he wouldn't free Parcells from his contract. Young would not allow such instant disintegration.

When early editions of the *Boston Globe* and *Atlanta Constitution* broke the story in early January 30 editions, Parcells denied it. But the story was true. The *Globe*'s Will McDonough, America's top football journalist, knew Parcells better than any reporter. And the *Constitution*'s tuned-in beat writer on the Falcons, Chris Mortensen, was told by a highly placed source in the organization that Parcells was the club's top candidate for the dual job. An hour later, the *Constitution* was on the phone with Parcells. A furious Parcells railed at the writer: "I don't want to see my name in the paper connected with that!" But it was, and now the issue would come to a head. Would Commissioner Pete Rozelle overrule the Giants and allow Parcells to negotiate with the Falcons?

There was some reason to think Parcells would be allowed to go. In 1982, when Giants coach Ray Perkins went to management to ask out of his contract, the Giants said yes and Perkins became the head coach of his alma mater, Alabama. And Rozelle sometimes allows coaches and executives to leave their jobs if they are significantly bettering themselves. Moving from coach to coach/director of football operations, it seemed, was a significant betterment.

This is what Fraley told Rozelle. Rozelle didn't agree. Rozelle said moving from one team to another as coach—regardless of the other titles that went along with it—was a lateral move and could not be allowed. So he blocked Fraley's talks with Atlanta. "Our rules say permission (for a coach to negotiate with another team) cannot be unreasonably denied," said NFL Director of Communications Joe Browne. "I don't see anything unreasonable about this."

The Falcons were crushed. One of their front-office men said that when the news came down from Rozelle, club president Rankin Smith, Jr., "looked totally deflated." The Falcons had supported what Fraley was doing all along. As the plane carrying Atlanta executives returned home from the Super Bowl, they smiled and told reporters privately that something big was cooking. "Wait until you hear this," Atlanta vice president Taylor Smith said. The big news, the Falcons hinted, would come later in the week, when, not so coincidentally, Fraley hoped to have Parcells free from the Giants.

The Falcons weren't the only deflated party. Privately, Parcells seethed. Not because he had to stay with the Giants; he loved the area, the team, and the players. He had some professional differences with Young, but this wasn't the megaproblem some members of the press thought it was. They had always been able to work together, though they never socialized. In 1983, after a 3-12-1 Giants season beset by injuries, Young inquired about the availability of a very popular college coach, Howard Schnellenberger of the University of Miami. Parcells's agent was Fraley. Schnellenberger's agent was Fraley. Young didn't know about this daily double. Parcells's parents, an assistant coach, and his dog had all died during the disastrous season; the news that Young was feeling out Schnellenberger deflated Parcells further. "How would you feel?" linebacker Harry Carson said. "Your parents die, one of your best friends dies, you've worked your ass off, and your boss tries to fire you." Young to this day claims he was seeking out Schnellenberger only to protect himself in the event that a distraught Parcells quit. Days after the inquiry, the Giants announced Parcells would be back for the 1984 season.

Now, Parcells seethed because the Giants in 1982 let Perkins pursue a great opportunity and in 1987 refused to let Parcells do the same thing.

The story was packaged so neatly. Parcells didn't comment. The Falcons denied most of it. Rozelle blamed it on an overzealous agent. The story line in the papers went something like this: Aggressive agent seeks big-money savior for struggling franchise; tries to pillage Super Bowl champion; fails; Parcells, Giants live happily ever after. Afterward, the story just seemed to die because none of the principals had any definitive comment. A week later, the Falcons gave their coach/director of football operations job to Marion Campbell, who had never had a winning pro season as an NFL head coach.

The Giants, really, came out of the whole thing lucky. The players seemed insulated from the news and never felt there was any threat of Parcells's leaving. "I never took it seriously," said Phil Simms, their star quarterback. "I didn't pay any attention to it."

The Giants admitted quietly they would renegotiate Parcells's contract, if he would agree to do it. Stung by the Giants' refusal to let him out of his contract, Parcells wondered about his market value. Here he was, not far from being a coaching nomad, at forty-five just having finished a three-year, on-field overhaul of a sordid franchise, with the chance to be financially secure for the rest of his life by signing just one more contract. Those were all strong considerations. In his twenty-two years in the coaching business, Parcells had moved his family ten times. Was there one move—and only one—left in him? Apparently so. At least the potential was there for one. On his way to work one morning in early January, Parcells had talked openly of a friend, a head coach of another NFL team, who told him: "When the time comes, you will be willing to move." Not "should." "Will." Parcells heard.

Another friend, Denver coach Dan Reeves, had worried when the aluminum magnate who hired him to coach the Broncos, Edgar Kaiser, sold the team at a huge profit in 1984, leaving everyone in the organization leery about his job. The new owner, Canadian oilman Patrick Bowlen, had spared Reeves and his staff. The message, though, was clear to anyone in the coaching business. Loyalty lasts as long as you win, and sometimes not that long.

Truthfully, the money in coaching was getting to be so good that it rivaled what the league's best players were making. Lawrence Taylor, the league's MVP, earned $850,000 in 1986, and at least two coaches—San Francisco's Bill Walsh and Miami's Don Shula—were making more, approximately $900,000 or $1 million a year. Ditka of the Bears was also clearing approximately $1 million, though about $700,000 of that came from his own off-field business ventures. NFL coaches were the highest-paid ones in sports, mostly because executives felt, correctly, that great coaches in football had more to do with their teams' successes than did managers or coaches of great teams in other sports.

The coaching market was exploding, it seemed. Two weeks before the Super Bowl, Perkins, who everyone thought had taken his dream job with Alabama, signed an incredible contract as Tampa Bay's coach/director of football operations. The base salaries over the five-year term of Perkins's contract averaged $660,000 a year, guaranteed even if Perkins was fired by the Bucs. But the extras turned this into an extraordinary contract. Perkins was given a luxury box atop Tampa Stadium and one hundred season tickets, a hefty loan at below-market interest, two expensive cars, two American Express cards with a line of credit backed by the team, and a bonus system of payments. If the Buccaneers were to win eight games in 1987, 1988, or 1989, Perkins would earn an additional $50,000. If they were to win nine, he would earn an extra $100,000. Ten, $150,000. If they made it to the first round of the playoffs, he would earn $200,000. If they made it to the conference championship game, he would earn $250,000. A Super Bowl trip would net Perkins $300,000.

Parcells wasn't governed totally by money. In 1986, he turned down a $100,000 offer from Con Edison, the New York utilities giant, to be its commercial spokesman. He did it, in part, because he's not a speechmaker, and he doesn't particularly like the limelight. He also did it, in part, because he remembered something his father told him when he took the Giants coaching job in 1982. The people who had been fired from coaching jobs in New York sports, his father told him, often left on the same road, Madison Avenue. In other words, just coach. Don't endorse. Unless it didn't take very much time. But now, the incredible money had to be a factor in Parcells's decision about his future.

The other factor was competitive. A few days after the Super Bowl, an executive of another team and a friend of Parcells's called him and said: "I know you, and you're the type of guy who might need another challenge. You'd love to build something again." Parcells wondered if he would. He wondered about the chance he would be taking if he chose not to sign with the Giants again, if he chose to become a coaching free agent, if he chose to risk the $700,000 or so a year the Giants would offer him annually to sign again for a possible moon shot in 1988. Would coaches' salaries keep climbing? If the Giants won ten or twelve games and made the playoffs in each of the next two seasons, that would give Parcells five consecutive seasons as a playoff coach. Such consistency as a coach might be handsomely rewarded ($1 million per year?) by some megamillionaire in Detroit or Kansas City or San Diego or Houston.

Parcells was making things sticky for the Giants in the days after his disappointment. Four times in nine days after the Atlanta story broke, he refused to answer a question about whether he would be the coach of the Giants in 1987. And he didn't accompany the Giants to meet President Reagan at a White House reception on February 13, saying he had a family commitment. Everyone denied there was friction between the club and Parcells. But there was some, and it was undeniable.

Before the team left to see Reagan, Parcells, in his office at Giants Stadium, finally confirmed he would coach the Giants in 1987. "I have two years remaining on my contract," Parcells said. "I will honor my contract."

He would stay. Fine. But his relationship with the front office wouldn't be the same.

"Don't I have a wonderful life?" asked Young, sitting in his office during the Parcells affair. "I get home at three A.M. Tuesday from the Super Bowl, and all this starts that night. You think I had time to enjoy this? It's a shame. Sometimes people lose their perspective. It just happened a little faster than usual here."

"Last year," punter Sean Landeta said, "at least the Bears waited a few months before all their controversial stuff happened. We waited a few hours."

3

Hey, Repeat

Two nights after the Super Bowl, the Madison Square Garden cable-TV network invited Giants wide receiver Stacy Robinson to the Garden to take in Knicks-76ers game, have dinner, and appear on a postgame talk show. Robinson, an engaging talker and basketball lover, agreed. Near the start of the second half, a man in his twenties a few seats away from Robinson recognized him.

In the middle of Madison Square Garden, the man said: "STACY ROBINSON!!!"

Heads turned everywhere. "Hi," said Robinson. "How you doing?"

"Hey," the guy said, pulling out a business card and leaning across a few seats. "Can I have an autograph? Sign it to Kenneth Butts. He works in my office and he loves you guys. I can't believe it! Stacy Robinson! You're great! He'll go nuts. Kenneth Butts. B-U-T-T-S."

Robinson, who is hardly a household name in his own household, obliged. He watched most of the rest of the game in peace, talking basketball and talking Giants with a friend.

"Do you think we can repeat?" Robinson asked out of the blue.

He was serious. This had been the one constant question—annoyingly so —to most of the Giants since they dominated the Broncos so convincingly in the second half of the Super Bowl. It was a heck of a question. Only four times in the twenty-one-year history of the Super Bowl had a team defended its championship successfully. Only once in the previous seven seasons had the defending champ made it to the Super Bowl the next year.

This is why Robinson asked the question. And this is why, when Robinson had to leave, the autograph guy rose to shake his hand and give him a final message.

"Hey," the autograph guy said. "Repeat."

In the days following the game, every Giant had a reasonable-sounding theory about repeating. Defensive end Leonard Marshall said the Giants had their collective head on straight and wouldn't let success change them. This was the most common thought. The Giants also kept trying to distance themselves from the Bears, who won Super Bowl XX by 36 points, lost quarterback Jim McMahon to Taco Bell commercials and a shoulder injury, went 14-2, and were beaten in the first round of the National Football Conference playoffs.

"We're not like the Bears," said Marshall, back in town after appearing in the Pro Bowl in Hawaii. "They lost the idea of being hungry. They pulled apart. Their leading player pulled away from the team. I talked to (defensive tackle) Steve McMichael and (offensive tackle) Jimbo Covert at the Pro Bowl, and they were talking about how McMahon pulled away from the team. I don't think that'll happen with us at all. We don't have the inflated egos." McMahon, a fiesty competitor, battled with everyone on the Bears at some time, it seemed. He clashed with Ditka over the rehabilitation of injuries and over team rules. He ripped club president Mike McCaskey in 1986, saying the players on the team had no respect for him and laughed at him. He had a feud with his most talented receiver, Willie Gault, and Gault's wife claimed McMahon purposely didn't throw to her husband because of their private feelings for each other.

The comparisons to the Bears—the most controversial team west of the Yankees in 1986—were probably not good ones. Even without McMahon, their acknowledged leader and great clutch quarterback, the Bears won fourteen games, the same as the Giants. Had McMahon been healthy, Chicago —not Washington—could very well have been playing for the NFC championship two weeks before the Super Bowl. Who knows what would have happened? Everyone raved about the Giants' defense in 1986, but it was second to the Bears' in the NFL statistics. Only twice in sixteen games did Chicago's defense allow more than one touchdown in a game. McMahon pulling away from the team? He was the same guy in 1985, and the Bears won eighteen of nineteen games.

Chicago's respected middle linebacker, Mike Singletary, listened to all the theories about why the Bears didn't repeat. Watching the Giants line up in Honolulu for the Pro Bowl team picture, Singletary explained why he couldn't buy any of the theories.

"As the next season unfolds, you realize how difficult it is to get back there," Singletary said. "You can point to this and that, but there isn't any one reason teams have a difficult time doing it again the next season. We had a great season in 1986, but there are variables you can never account for that can happen. Repeating isn't easy, and dynasties are a figment of the media's imagination. This league is too tough to be dominated by any one team."

"Seven of our games [actually nine] were won by a touchdown or less," Harry Carson said. "Can you call that a dynasty?"

Indeed, the Giants' season had turned on an incredible streak of six games. After losing at Seattle October 19, the Giants beat Washington by 7 points, Dallas by 3, Philadelphia by 3, Minnesota by 2, Denver by 3, and San Francisco by 4. Each game was decided in the final three minutes.

In so many ways, 1986 just seemed to be the Giants' year. Vague? Yes. Inexplicable? Yes. They were a huge snowball rolling down Everest. After their six-game streak of narrow victories, they steamrolled every team they played. They won by 10, 20, 31, 46, 17, and 19. Nothing would go wrong for them. Nothing significant, anyway.

"Look at them," Los Angeles Raiders tight end Todd Christensen said, admiring from afar. "Everything's gone their way."

At Los Angeles September 21, Raiders defensive backs Mike Haynes and Vann McElroy tipped a Phil Simms pass into the hands of wide receiver Lionel Manuel for the winning New York touchdown. At St. Louis October 5, a replay official couldn't judge whether Cardinals wide receiver J.T. Smith was in or out of bounds on a disputed late-afternoon touchdown because of the deep shadows in the end zone; it was ruled no touchdown, and the Giants won by 7 points. At Giants Stadium October 27, Washington was called for a critical offsides penalty when the crowd, monitoring the seventh game of the World Series on hand-held TV sets, shrieked after a Mets home run and drew Redskins tackle Joe Jacoby into the critical penalty. Against Dallas November 2, wily defensive end George Martin head-faked a Dallas offensive tackle, Phil Pozderac, into an illegal-procedure call, negating a potential game-tying 30-yard pass play.

"That's it," *Newsday* columnist Joe Gergen said in the press box after the Martin play. "I'm calling God for comment."

At Minnesota November 16, on fourth down and 17 late in the fourth quarter, Simms completed a 21-yard pass to Bobby Johnson after the Vikings inexplicably dropped their double coverage on Johnson; the Giants won on a last-second field goal. Against Denver the next week, Martin stuck a huge paw in front of a pass and ran 78 yards for a touchdown, a very rare play for a defensive lineman. On December 1 at San Francisco, the usually conservative Parcells abandoned his staid game plan on fourth down and 2 late in the third quarter; the gamble worked, the Giants rallied from a 17–0 deficit to win, and Parcells was emboldened. Later in that same game, San Francisco's Jerry Rice, the NFL's leading receiver, dropped the potential game-winning touchdown pass. Rice, in the Giants' opening playoff victory, duplicated that drop on the first series of the game. A week later, in the NFC championship game, Pro Bowl receiver Gary Clark dropped what would have been the touchdown pass to put Washington back in the game.

"My guys wouldn't let us lose," Parcells said.

So often the Giants' season could have turned sour in 1986. It didn't. It wouldn't. Seemingly, it couldn't.

As NFL minds turned to 1987, there were two schools of thought on the Giants. School No. 1: The Giants couldn't be as good as they seemed in December and January, when they won their final five games by an average of 26.6 points. School No. 2: The Giants could be that good, and better, and for a long time. They were young enough, and unaffected enough.

Dallas president Tex Schramm was in school No. 1. "It was the Giants' year to lead a charmed life," Schramm said.

Player agent Leigh Steinberg was in school No. 2. "The Giants are the next dynasty in football," Steinberg said.

No one could know which man was correct. But there were two major reasons to think the Giants, without major injury, could repeat:

1. The work ethic was good. The offensive leadership—Simms, running back Joe Morris, tight end Mark Bavaro, a talented and devoted offensive line—was good enough to win consistently in the league and played with almost grim determination. They would not let down, Parcells thought. The defense would not either. Two more key players—linebacker Andy Headen and cornerback Perry Williams—were moving from their homes in the South to live full-time in New Jersey, which meant better attendance in the Giants' off-season training program. Parcells considered the off-season program a crucial part of the Giants' success. The weight-training and conditioning series of workouts had about thirty-nine full-time participants in this off-season— the most in Parcells's four years as coach.

2. The Giants had such a threatening defense, with a young core ready to take over for aging stars, that it was hard to imagine the team's getting blown out of many games in 1987. The defense had already intimidated the quarterbacks in its own division, the NFC East, to the point that they hated playing the Giants.

Parcells had developed what rapidly became a cliché toward the end of the season. He said he had blue-collar guys on his team, guys who came to work every day with a lunch-pail mindset. "That's funny," said Reeves of the Broncos during the Super Bowl. "I don't know a lot of guys in football who aren't blue-collar guys." Perhaps. Maybe Parcells just emphasized it more than other coaches did.

"I've got guys," he said, "who'd play anywhere, at any time. If I said to them, 'We've got a practice Saturday morning in the parking lot at Paramus Mall,' they'd be there. Taylor, Burt, Bavaro, Simms . . . those are the types of guys you need on a team."

Parcells loved Simms. "Parcells has his favorites," one of the offensive players said. "Simms is number one. That's his boy." This didn't manifest itself in easier practices for Simms, or shorter wind sprints after practice. When Simms made a mistake, most often Parcells would ride him, but everyone knew it was okay. It was a mistake because he was trying to make something good happen. If he threw a ball into coverage, something he saw made him think he could thread the ball in there. Parcells rarely screamed at Simms for the little mistakes. The team didn't begrudge Simms for his place with Parcells because, at thirty-one, he had worked so hard to get where he was. "Phil deserves this," said the often-irreverent Lawrence Taylor after the Super Bowl. "I'd rather have him on my side than anyone."

Simms learned New York fandom the hard way. Drafted in the first round by the then-inept Giants in 1979 from a small college in Kentucky, Morehead State, Simms was booed immediately because the fans felt the Giants had made a stupid pick. At the time, Wellington Mara told George Young and Ray Perkins—in jest—that they'd better erect barricades at the Lincoln Tunnel because the fans would be coming to New Jersey from New York furious over the choice. What the fans didn't know is that Bill Walsh, the San Francisco coach, was waiting to pick Simms in the draft after the Giants' choice if he was still available.

How football history would have been changed if the Giants hadn't picked Simms. If San Francisco had taken Simms, the 49ers wouldn't have taken a quarterback from Notre Dame named Joe Montana in the third round of that draft. Maybe Montana would have become a second- or third-string quarterback and not gotten off the bench yet. And maybe Simms would be considered one of the best quarterbacks of our time—in the 49ers' short-passing offense, a scheme more suited to the quarterback.

Simms, raised in Louisville, learned his work ethic early. One of eight children in a lower-middle-class family, he had to work for whatever spending money he had, so he took to delivering papers. In the morning, before school, he delivered the *Louisville Courier-Journal*; in the afternoon, the *Louisville Times*. He'd walk along the narrow streets of his Okolona suburb, balancing a pile of papers on his head, folding them and throwing them porchward.

He decided in high school that he wanted to be a football player, so he began lifting weights to improve his strength. Soon, the basement of the little house on Sarah Drive was full of weights. In college, the 210-pound Simms was judged to be the team's strongest player. His mother knew.

"One night when Phil was home from college," Barbara Simms said, "I was washing dishes after dinner. Phil came up behind me to give me a squeeze, and he broke one of my ribs. He really broke one of my ribs. I told him he had strength he didn't know he had."

The fans didn't know much about his work habits. Fans judged him only by what he did on the field with a bad team. Quarterbacks on bad teams with poor pass protection usually aren't very good. They can't be. With Simms, there was also the injury factor. Four of his first five seasons ended prematurely due to injuries, which led a skeptical press and public to wonder if Simms was injury-prone. When he did play, the Giants stunk, so he was booed. In 1983, a borderline player named Scott Brunner beat Simms out for the quarterback job—perhaps Parcells's biggest decision-making mistake as head coach—and Simms said he wanted to be traded. He hoped to go to Houston. He would go anywhere. "I gave the reporters lots to write about in those days," said Simms.

After the disaster (3-12-1) of 1983, Simms got a pleasant surprise one day. Parcells called him into his office and told him he was the Giants' quarterback of the future. And Simms would not be the quarterback of a predictable, maudlin offense that tried unsuccessfully to establish a running game on every first down. This would be an exciting offense, a wide-open offense, Parcells and offensive coordinator Ron Erhardt decided.

"I want you to work on throwing nothing but go patterns and twenty- and twenty-five-yard incuts," Parcells told Simms after the '83 season. Translation: Throw deep, and then throw deep some more.

Simms set a Giants record with 4,044 passing yards in 1984; the Giants went 9-7 and made the playoffs. Simms threw for 3,829 yards in 1985; the Giants went 10-6 and made the playoffs. With a depleted receiving corps in 1986, Simms threw for 3,487 yards (more than noted bombers John Elway of Denver and Dan Fouts of San Diego); the Giants went 14-2 and won the Super Bowl.

Still, in the middle of 1986 Simms was booed. The Giants were 6-2, tied for the NFC East lead before playing Dallas on November 2, 1986, and when the offense was introduced at Giants Stadium, Simms heard more boos than cheers. "Terrible, terrible. Ridiculous, ridiculous," said Erhardt. "These fans would boo Fouts." That week, CBS-TV analyst John Madden, who lived in an apartment near Central Park, was sitting in the park reading the paper when an ambulance driver stopped near his bench. "Hey, John," the driver said. "You're too nice to Phil Simms." All of this infuriated Parcells, who couldn't believe the people who watched the Giants games couldn't see Simms's talent. "Some of you guys who don't think this guy can play ought to be covering another sport," he told reporters in November.

Few saw the working-class side of Phil Simms. The fans read his responses to the public criticism, which meant there wasn't a love affair going on between the two sides. "Fuck the fans," Simms said late in 1986. "I don't give a shit what they think."

The fans didn't see this side of Simms: On the Friday before the Giants played Washington for the NFC championship, Simms was due in Manhattan for a 5:00 P.M. NFL news conference hyping the game. Before he left the locker room that afternoon, he told strength and conditioning coach Johnny Parker, "Wait for me. I haven't lifted yet." Friday was one of Simms's days to lift weights. This would be no exception. At 7:15, Simms returned to the locker room and Parker was waiting. He went through his ninety-minute routine—the locker room, except for Parker and the equipment guys, had been empty for three hours—with no one else around.

On January 20, the players' day off at the Super Bowl, Simms, Taylor, backup quarterback Jeff Rutledge, and close Parcells friend Mickey Corcoran scheduled eighteen holes of golf at the Anaheim Hills Country Club. But because of a press obligation all morning, Simms figured he wouldn't be able to play golf and get his regularly scheduled weight-lifting session in. So on his day off, he canceled the golf game. The Giants lifted only free weights —Parker didn't believe in Nautilus or any of the other trendy weight-training programs, at least for football players—and they didn't know of any southern California gyms with free weights. Parker went and found one. That afternoon, Simms lifted. "He's a rare person," Parker said that day.

It was fitting, then, that Simms came up big in the biggest game of his life. He completed 22 of 25 passes in the Super Bowl, earning the most valuable player award. Not only had a quarterback never had such a great game in Super Bowl history, a quarterback had never had such an accurate day in a playoff game in the sixty-seven-year history of the league. "It's still unbelievable," Simms said, getting the keys to his MVP car two weeks after the game. "My wife [Diana] and I still sit at the dinner table sometimes and say, 'Can you believe it?' "

After the game, a stoic Charlie Conerly, the man whose Giants passing records continue to be broken by Simms, sidled up to Parcells and started crying. Parcells was stunned.

"I'm so happy for Simms," Conerly said. "No one knows how hard it is to play in New York. No one knows how hard it was for him." Except, perhaps for Conerly. The weak quarterbacks couldn't take the heat.

Simms, then, would be a good barometer to see which way this team would go in 1987. He was a hot commodity. No, boiling. He could make as much as $20,000 a night for an appearance. He made $75,000 walking off the field in Pasadena for saying, "I'm gonna go to Disney World!" and following that by saying, "I'm going to Disneyland!" (In a prearranged promotion, Disney agreed to pay the winning Super Bowl quarterback $75,000 for answering just those ways to the question, "Phil Simms, you've just won the Super Bowl; what are you going to do now?") So how would he handle sudden megasuccess?

He made $650,000 in salary in 1986, $150,000 of which was deferred until 1990. In the five months after the Super Bowl, he could easily have made $1 million. "Quarterbacks who win the Super Bowl are basically guaranteed a living for the rest of their lives," said Simms's agent, David Fishof.

Simms was not going to take that guarantee, at least not right away. In New York February 9 to accept a $17,000 Subaru as part of his Super Bowl MVP award, Simms said as much in a weird scene where he glad-handed Subaru dealers and their families, talked to reporters over the Bruce Springsteen music piped into a ballroom, and signed footballs. Simms had to talk over the Springsteen din to be heard.

Phil Simms, Born to Run.

Phil Simms, Born to be Marketed.

"I'm going to do the same things I've always done in the off-season," Simms said. "I'm going through the Giants' off-season program. I'm going to make a lot of people mad, especially my agent, because I'm going to say no a lot. That's the way it's got to be . . .

"We've got to do the same things we did last year. We've got to have the same attitude. We've got to be hungry. I've sat around and thought about repeating already. I'm curious. I'm wondering about it . . .

"I think we'll come together quicker as a team in training camp. Remember, we've had five weeks of practice while everyone else was sitting home. We got to work on a lot of things other teams haven't been able to work on . . .

"I think this will be my best year . . ."

In February, everyone thought that.

4

Getting It While It's Hot

February 1987
East Rutherford, New Jersey

The rest of the team, except for the marginal players and the very quiet ones, was fattening up on the off-season money. "There's so much out there to do," said linebacker Carl Banks. "Some of the guys are turning down two-thousand-dollar deals. For me, that's a lot of money. The way I look at it, whatever's left over, I'll be happy to take." In the two weeks after the game, Banks had already spoken in Hartford, several towns in New Jersey, on Long Island, and in his hometown of Flint, Michigan.

The going rate for an average Giant to appear at a dinner or speech was $2,000 or $2,500. Simms would make motivational speeches for ten times that much, plus expenses, in the off-season. Everywhere in the region the Giants went, the message was the same.

"People can't get enough of us," strong safety Kenny Hill said. "Twenty-one-year-old kids come up to you and say, 'I've been a Giants fan for thirty years and . . .' I say, 'Right.' "

Already in the off-season, Hill had made two Los Angeles TV appearances; met with a New York agent who told him he had a future in TV sports commentary; gotten the key to the city of New Haven, Connecticut, where he went to college (Yale); vacationed in the Bahamas; spoken in White Plains, New York; and spoken at two affairs in New Jersey.

At the same time, the Giants were getting their business house in order. The club signed all of its assistant coaches, although there was some grousing among the lower-level coaches that the Giants hadn't been fair enough with raises. Some got substantial raises. Offensive coordinator Erhardt, for instance, made $95,000 in 1985 and $100,000 in 1986; his salary jumped to $125,000 for 1987, an amount that would be fortified on his W-2 form by the $64,000 in playoff bonus money that every player and coach earned. That's $189,000—plus a $3,000 Super Bowl ring, plus whatever he could hustle in speeches and minor off-season endorsements.

Parcells needed some time off. He had worked thirty-three weeks in a row. At one point during the season, he had worked 161 straight days—and looked

19

at game film for two hours on the morning of the 162nd. There would be time to worry about repeating, and to face the pressures of repeating, but it wouldn't be now. Parcells told his players to make as much money as they could in the off-season; they had earned that right. But they would have to return ready to play better in 1987. No one knew if they could.

It was a frigid morning in February, about 7:45, when Parcells walked through the darkened offices at Giants Stadium, musing about the future.

"I've got my guys," Parcells said softly. "I think we'll be okay. I think we'll keep our eye on the eagle."

That, to Parcells, meant keeping an eye on priorities, which had been difficult enough in the month after the game.

5

The Crown Is Heavy: The Thesis

March 1987
Lahaina, Hawaii

George Young did not relax very much. When he did, it was usually with his engaging wife, Lovey, or a book. The night the Giants clinched their first division title since 1963, Young was curled up in his New Jersey den with *The Life and Times of Edward R. Murrow*.

So, when the annual National Football League meetings adjourned at the Hyatt Kaanapali Beach Hotel one gorgeous Friday afternoon six weeks after the Super Bowl, Young ambled to the swimming pool just east of the Pacific. He sat down in a large deck chair. He took out a book. It was about Martin Luther King. The title: *Bearing the Cross*.

Entirely appropriate. A few deck chairs away, Tom Flores, then the coach of the Los Angeles Raiders, sunned himself, and he was reminded that he was not bearing the NFL's heaviest cross in this off-season. Flores's Raiders won the Super Bowl in 1984. The enjoyment was something Flores wouldn't trade for anything. But the burden was like a ball and chain.

"The next season," Flores said, squinting into the sun, "twenty-seven teams look for you. You're everybody's playoff game. In the off-season, you need to get away but you really can't. Your season has lasted so long because the Super Bowl is late, and then there's the draft in April. Before you know it, you're back in training camp."

A year after winning Super Bowl XVIII by 29 points, the Raiders lost in the first round of the NFL playoffs. A year after winning Super Bowl XIX by 22 points, San Francisco was squashed by the Giants in the first round of the playoffs—by a 17–3 score. A year after winning Super Bowl XX by 36 points, the Chicago Bears lost in their first playoff game to Washington. Now it was the Giants' turn to buck the trend, or to be swallowed by it.

The heat was searing in the afternoon sun of Maui. Young, a large man who was always trying to lose weight, sat at a table beneath a large grass umbrella and told the waitress he wanted a strawberry fruit drink with no alcohol. Young didn't drink alcohol. He made small talk for a while, often patting his beady brow with his handkerchief to keep the pellets of sweat at bay, looking kind of like Sidney Greenstreet doing the same thing at his cafe in Casablanca.

Then he began to do something he was very good at. He began to talk, with lots of opinions. (In the Giants' locker room and weight room, some of the players called Young "Mr. Wizard" behind his back, because he always had an answer for everything.)

"What are your theories," he was asked, "on why it's so hard for champions to repeat?"

"Repeating," Young began, with a sour look on his face, "is not a word I ever use. This is a recent phenomenon, all the talk about repeating. When I worked for Baltimore and we won Super Bowl five, there wasn't a word after the game about our chances to repeat. We just talked in the off-season about how much fun it would be to win the next year and go to the Super Bowl again. See, people have become preoccupied with repeating, saying you can't do it again. The fact is, there have been repeaters, four in twenty years.

"One of the reasons it's so tough is that there's been a lot more exchange of information than there's ever been before—among the coaches, among the organizations. People wind up copying what you did to win, then they learn what to do against it so they can stop it, too. From a technique and scheme and strategical point of view, there's so much more scrutiny over the winner than there was before.

"The other thing is the economic climate. There are so many people trying to use your players in business deals, and it's so hard to protect your players against that. And they don't want your protection. You have agents, but when you have a lot of success, you wind up with a new level of agents and financial players and strokers, telling the guy how wonderful he is and how much he means to the team. Every guy on your team is a contributor, but . . ." Young was trying to be nice here, saying that every one of the forty-five guys on the team contributes to winning a Super Bowl, but that the forty-third and forty-fourth and forty-fifth guys in importance are being told, ludicrously, that the Giants couldn't have done it without them. "The atmosphere is so much different today than it was years ago for winners, especially in the media centers. Look at the dynasties we've had in this league—Pittsburgh, Green Bay, Dallas, Miami, Minnesota. Minnesota went to the Super Bowl four times, and that's pretty damn good. None of those places are huge media centers, not an L.A. or New York or Chicago. I think the big city can get to a champion today.

"I'm interested to see how our team reacts. All the appearances they make are fine. If Phil McConkey has the opportunity to make a lot of money, fine. Phil Simms, fine. They've never let the off-season stuff interfere with the season. Right now, for them and for the whole team, winning the Super Bowl is a plus. They have the idea that, with hard work, good things happen. Listen to the coach and good things happen. If the players can maintain near the same mission they had last year, they can win. If they have the same desire, they can win. If they're baskers, they won't."

The Hawaiian waitress came by, interrupting the sermonette. "Excuse me," the waitress said, "but they're phasing out your table now."

"What?" Young said. "What's that mean?"

"Well," she said, somewhat uncomfortably, "you'll have to pay now. They're phasing out your table."

"They're already phasing us out," George Young said, chuckling. "I wonder what that means."

It isn't just football. In all of the major professional sports, no teams win like they used to.

Nobody in baseball wins like the midcentury Yankees, who won twenty-eight American League pennants in forty-four years, from 1921 to 1964.

Nobody in hockey wins like the midcentury Canadiens, who won fifteen Stanley Cups in the twenty-four seasons between 1955 and 1979—although the Edmonton Oilers of the eighties are having a nice little run at prolonged greatness.

Nobody in basketball wins like the baby-boom generation Celtics, who won eleven championships in thirteen years, from 1957 to 1969.

Nobody in football wins like the Chicago Bears of the forties (four National Football League championships in six years), the Cleveland Browns of the fifties (ten consecutive pro football championship game appearances), the Green Bay Packers of the sixties (five NFL titles in seven years) and the Pittsburgh Steelers of the seventies (four NFL titles in six).

At the time Young and Flores lounged at poolside, no pro basketball team had won consecutive championships since the Celtics in 1968 and 1969. No baseball team since the Yankees of 1977 and 1978 had won two titles in a row. And no football team since the Steelers of 1978 and 1979 had won in succession. Only in hockey—where Montreal won four consecutive Stanley Cups from 1976 to 1979, the Islanders followed with four in succession from 1980 to 1983, and Edmonton won four Cups in five late-eighties seasons—was there any hint of a dynasty. But the post-Cup Canadiens and Islanders fell to good. They couldn't stay great.

What is it? What is it that has made sports such a sudden bastion of socialism?

Scores of interviews with people in sports have yielded these reasons:

I
The Get-Rich-Quick Factor

Money, like a drug, can poison athletic hunger and be a divisive wedge to building great teams.

Two parts here. One is what can happen to players who make very big money at a very young age. Two is that money can break up teams and front offices.

Part one:

Let us examine the strange case of William "The Refrigerator" Perry, a cuddly 310-pound defensive tackle who occasionally doubled as a fullback in coach Mike Ditka's offense with the Bears in their Super Bowl season of 1985. When he kept his weight in the 310 range, Perry was a relatively quick and mountainous player. When he tried to play fifty pounds heavier, as he did by 1987, he was sort of an athletic Ralph Kramden, a fat slob with all the moves and football skill of a bus driver. And midway through 1988, he weighed 420 pounds. The quick psychological study of Perry shows an undisciplined kid who grew up poor with the same materialistic dreams as the rest of American youth, a kid who scored a few touchdowns as an effective (but freak-show) fullback in goal-line situations in 1985, a kid who cashed in shamelessly on any lucrative ad deal after the Bears won the Super Bowl that season, a kid from the ruralness of South Carolina who, by age twenty-three, had made an estimated $4 million. It ruined him. He scoffed at $1,000-a-week bonuses in his contract if he stayed at the club's prescribed weight. He had no use for thousands. He had millions—with a wife who was everything he could have dreamed for. She could cook. "How were we to know," Bears vice president Bill Tobin mused, "that all those incentive bonuses we planned so carefully wouldn't mean a damn thing to him?" By 1988, Perry would be a wasted Bear, too big for football in more ways than one.

Not everyone has Perry's fat-slob lack of discipline. But Young was very big on this theory. In fact, that topic came up over lunch between Young and his top assistant, veteran football executive Harry Hulmes, before the Giants even won it once.

Hulmes: "Don't you think there's a deterioration of incentive after you've won it once?"

Young: "If one truism ever existed in sports, it's that hungry players are better players. Sports is socioeconomic."

Edmonton coach Glen Sather agreed. "Money," Sather said, "ruins everything."

Most players disagree. And the Giants had a record thirty-nine players participating in four-times-weekly off-season workouts after the Super Bowl. The desire was there. But was the heart? And the mind? One of the great players of the TV Era, Pittsburgh quarterback Terry Bradshaw, thought unequivocally that big money at a young age ruined many an NFL work ethic.

"You're supposed to have goals to work toward, whatever you do in life," Bradshaw said. "I don't think you have those same goals when all the money you're ever going to need is handed to you. After we won the third Super Bowl, I was making $250,000. After we won the first, I was making $60,000. Now, Vinny Testaverde signs to quarterback Tampa Bay and gets $2 million as a signing bonus and a million to play each season. Where's the incentive today, compared to when I played? You're starting on top now. Before, you made what a working man made and worked your way to the top. If Testaverde loses, the fortune's still there. Where's the incentive? I lose the Super Bowl, it's devastating to me. Teams lose the Super Bowl today, it's like, 'Okay, it was a good year. We made some pretty good money.'

"I'm a firm believer that money spoils the heart. When the heart is satisfied, the body doesn't work as hard."

Jim Mora, the New Orleans Saints coach who won two United States Football League championships with the Philadelphia Stars, agrees. And USFL players, on the average, were making only about half of their NFL counterparts. "It's so hard to monitor as a coach," Mora said, "because it's something you can't see. But it's there. It's definitely there. It's something you notice in players after they've won and made a lot of money. It's natural, but you have to fight it. Businesses have to fight it, too."

Part two:

Money and the lure of security have broken up teams and front offices. In football, nomadic coach Chuck Knox coached the Los Angeles Rams to five straight division titles in the seventies, left for Buffalo when the money was better there, and went to Seattle for bigger money in 1983. The Rams continued to be a playoff team when Knox left, but Buffalo lapsed into being one of the sport's worst teams. Near the end of the eighties, Knox had more than quadrupled his annual salary from a decade earlier; he would earn $750,000 from the Seahawks in 1988.

In baseball, the players were set free by an arbitrator's ruling in 1976, and the dynasty has been dead ever since. It almost has to be. When the Cincinnati Reds won their second consecutive world championship in 1976, everyone knew it was the end of an era, because this would be the last fully grown-on-the-farm baseball franchise. "The Reds had great teams because their players couldn't go anywhere," journeyman first baseman Darrell Evans said in 1988. "Don't tell me none of their players wanted to go elsewhere. With free agency, the talent in that franchise was spread out to the other teams in baseball, and it began the spread of parity throughout baseball. It might have been bad for the Reds, but it's been great for baseball. Look at the attendance. Every year we break records."

In the era of free agency, money has prevented a team trying to run a solvent ship from buying up all the unsigned talent in one sport. In the National Basketball Association, players and owners negotiated a uniform salary cap for each team in the league in 1984. Under the salary cap system, NBA teams were allowed to spend 53 percent of the league's gross revenue on salaries. In the 1987–'88 season, each team was allowed to spend approximately $6,164,000 on salaries for its eleven players—with exceptions. In Los Angeles, for instance, the Lakers spent approximately $9 million on salaries because they had chosen to sign several of their own veteran free agents. When a team signed its own veteran free agents, this money was exempt from the salary cap. But when Magic Johnson signed a deal in 1988 before he became a free agent that would pay him $3.14 million per season, it crippled the Lakers' efforts to sign any other team's veteran free agents after the season. Why was this important? Because Kareem Abdul-Jabbar, the forty-one-year-old center headed for the Hall of Fame, needed a replacement, and the Lakers, who picked too low in the draft to get a competent NBA center, couldn't go after a veteran free-agent center like Moses Malone to shore up a weak position.

The salary cap also eliminated a Steinbrenner-like buying of a championship in the NBA. The Lakers, with Johnson's huge salary, couldn't afford to buy any other team's free agents, so that eliminated the chance for Los Angeles to supplement Johnson and James Worthy with a Michael Jordan or Isiah Thomas or Akeem Olajuwon.

"We don't have a salary cap in hockey," said John Muckler, the co-coach of the Edmonton Oilers, "but our club has had so many superstars we simply can't afford to pay them all. We don't get a huge chunk of money from television to help pay our contracts like the National Football League (whose teams earned $17.1 million per club in 1988 from network contracts). So we lose a great defenseman like Paul Coffey. He cannot be replaced." Coffey, a contract holdout in 1987, forced the Oilers to trade him to Pittsburgh. The trade, luckily for Edmonton, turned out to be a good one for the Oilers. But rarely has a team been forced to trade a player because of economics and come out of it with a good deal.

II
The Expansion Factor

Rampant expansion and rival leagues have, by simple mathematics, made it tougher to repeat.

In a generation, here's what happened to team membership of the major sports leagues:

Sports League	Teams in 1960	Teams in 1989	Increase	Percent Increase
Major League Baseball	16	26	+ 10 teams	62%
National Football League	13	28	+ 15 teams	115%
National Basketball Association	8	27	+ 19 teams	238%
National Hockey league	6	21	+ 15 teams	250%
Total	**43**	**102**	**+59 teams**	**137%**

In a generation, then, there has been an increase of 137 percent in the number of teams playing for major sports championships. NBA and NHL membership has more than tripled. The Celtics, in 1960, had to beat seven opponents to win the NBA championship. Today they'd have to beat twenty-six. In hockey, the World Hockey Association battled the established NHL for players for eight years in the 1970s. At one point, thirty-three professional hockey teams battled to sign players that, a decade earlier, would have been divvied up between six teams. The World Football League and the United States Football League both bought famous football players for a few years before committing economic suicide. Millions of dollars in losses by previous failed leagues didn't make a dent in the sporting romanticism of new entrepreneurs: New football and hockey leagues were on drawing boards as 1989 began.

"Our sport is so diluted now," Detroit Tigers manager Sparky Anderson said in 1988. "Now, if one thing goes wrong—like injuries—you're not going to win. It's just not logical to think that the same team can win year after year when all the talent is so diluted. Too many things can go wrong."

Anderson and others in sports think it might be time to redefine the dynasty—not necessarily because the players are better and the player-acquisition process is more efficient, but because of the sheer number of teams in sports today and because of the longer playoff systems. In the NBA, the team with the best record in eighty-two regular-season games must win a best-of-five playoff series, then a best-of-seven, then another best-of-seven, then a third best-of-seven. A champion might have to play twenty-six games to win the NBA crown.

One of the best living natural resources to talk about this is Sam Pollock, the vice president and general manager of the Montreal Canadiens from 1957 to 1978. The Canadiens won twelve Stanley Cups in Pollock's twenty-one seasons managing the team.

Pollock's theory is that as more teams entered the NHL, and as competition to sign players came from the rival World Hockey Association in the 1970s, the job of building a hockey team got exponentially harder. He estimates that in the fifties, before hockey's big expansion, hockey management was 50 percent hockey knowledge and 50 percent business sense. In the seventies, he said, hockey knowledge was 25 percent. Today, it's 15 percent.

More teams. More competition for players. More playoffs, to make money for all the teams.

"Today, with all the teams and all the complications that creates, every bloody thing is geared against the world champions," he said. "In 1964, my job wasn't that hard. On August first every year, you'd sign your players for the next season. One-year contracts. That's it. Then expansion came, and the new league. The WHA would offer the real old, marginal players three- and four-year contracts, and it would have been ridiculous for us to match them. The last six or seven years I did the job, it was really, really hard. It was impossible to plan anything for the future."

III
The Draft Factor

Allocating players by drafts has fostered a sporting socialism.

In baseball in the early sixties, teams were free to sign any amateur player in the world. Same in hockey, with a few territorial restrictions. Today, the best teams in the four major sports choose last in the draft that disperses new talent to professional teams. And in baseball, if a team chooses to sign a veteran free agent to improve its chances of winning, the signing robs the team of its top draft pick or picks. In 1988, for instance, the Yankees signed three veteran free agents, thus losing their top three draft choices in the June 1988 draft. The Yankees didn't have a choice in the 1988 draft, then, until the 104th overall selection. This was one of the reasons the Yankees didn't promote many of their own players to the major-league level. They didn't have many of their own players, and many of the prospects they did have they traded for proven veterans.

The Canadiens of decades ago used the nondraft perfectly, beginning with a veteran hockey man named Frank Selke in 1946. Selke was a hockey executive by profession, a farmer by hobby. His philosophy was the same for both. From 1946 to 1964, he presided over the Canadiens, the most beloved team in the history of his country. In fact, the tentacles of this dynasty—the Canadiens are the only team ever to win five straight Stanley Cups, from 1956 to 1960—stretched quite literally from British Columbia to Prince Edward Island. The Canadiens funded ten amateur teams in Manitoba. They funded the entire amateur hockey system of Regina, in the province of Saskatchewan. In Edmonton, in the fifties, the Canadiens were spending $300,000 to develop amateur players on autonomous teams there. In the home province, Quebec, the Canadiens funded or contributed to the development of every big amateur league.

The Molson Brewery, owner of the team, paid for all of this. But it was a great investment. The National Hockey League, into the sixties, was a company store. Montreal was the boss man.

Because there was no draft, individual scouts for the six NHL teams had to find players themselves and sign them. Although the other five teams had some of the same amateur leagues and teams set up, the majority of the good players could be found in the Montreal-funded leagues or on the Montreal-funded teams. The Canadiens never interfered with the running of the leagues or the coaching of the teenage players. They asked only one thing: that they have the first right to sign a player to a professional contract.

Naturally, the Canadiens signed most of the players themselves and sold them to the other five clubs in the league. This way, Montreal raised about $250,000 a year in player sales—without once selling a player they considered a budding superstar. Before any other team in the league could figure a way to stop Les Habs, the dynasty was on. Nice racket, if you can get it. So Selke planted this system in the late 1940s, fertilized it through the fifties, and watched as the Canadiens won their five straight Cups to close the decade. They might have won eight in a row, with some luck. Montreal won in 1953. In 1954, the Canadiens lost the championship series to Detroit, four games to three, on an overtime goal by the Red Wings in the seventh game. In 1955, they lost the championship series to Detroit, four games to three, and played without their best player, Maurice Richard, who was injured. Of the next five championship seasons, Montreal won one final series four games to none, three others four games to one, and the last four games to two.

Hockey instituted an amateur draft in 1963, but the Canadiens won ten of the next sixteen Cups anyway. Here's why: Until 1967, the NHL allowed teams to protect from the draft players on any of their club-sponsored teams. And because Montreal had spent such a monumental amount of time and energy on its amateur teams across Canada, the league voted to allow the Canadiens to pick two French-Canadian amateur players instead of their first two draft choices from 1965 to 1969. So the NHL handed the Canadiens the two best amateur players in Canada for five years in a row. Montreal also learned the fine art of fleecing the six 1967 expansion teams with one-sided trades. The new franchises wanted to be good fast, naturally, so they looked to acquire better-than-average established players, offering high draft choices in return. Where better to shop than the old company store? The Canadiens won four straight titles to close the seventies. They did it with a nucleus of their final two French-Canadian picks in 1969 (Rejean Houle, Marc Tardif) and draft choices acquired in trades (Guy Lafleur, Bob Gainey, Steve Shutt) and a goalie acquired from Boston (Ken Dryden).

The Canadiens, in the eighties, fell to earth. Because of their deep roots, the decline wasn't precipitous. But the draft—and expansion, to be fair—evened out the other sports much more noticeably.

Football instituted a draft in 1936, baseball in 1965. Is it a coincidence that, after the draft became law in each sport, only one team in the NFL (Green Bay, 1965, 1966, 1967) and one team in baseball (Oakland 1972, 1973, 1974) won as many as three straight championships?

"There are only so many good players in the world," Montreal defenseman Larry Robinson said. "When you're drafting at the end of the first round every year, you can't draft good players, because there are none left."

Pro football, especially, has become a socialist state, and not just because of the annual twelve-round draft. In 1988, Green Bay, in the nation's sixty-eighth television market, raked in the identical $17.1 million from the NFL's television contract as the Jets and Giants, in the New York market, which is the largest in the country. This stems from the revenue-sharing TV agreement adopted by the league in the sixties. NFL teams split gate revenue, too, with 60 percent allotted to the home team and 40 percent to the visitors. This, too, favors bad and small-market teams. Detroit, with an average 1987 ticket price of $15.46, paid out an average of approximately $285,000 to visiting teams that season. When the Lions played in fan-rich Washington in mid-1987, they earned a 40-percent visitor's share of about $455,000. That's more than their average 60-percent home share of that season—about $430,000. So in some cases, the good teams are subsidizing the poor teams with a fat gate check.

Over the years, teams in Miami and Los Angeles tried to fight the pervasive evenness of money-splitting by installing luxury box seats and sharing only the cost of the ticket, not the thousands for the box. But the small-market franchises were fighting that, too, in league committee meetings each spring.

"How good of a game are we going to have," points out Mike Brown, the assistant general manager of the Cincinnati Bengals, "if the Cincinnatis can't be competitive with the New Yorks? New York and Los Angeles need somebody to play every year. If we can't be competitive, who are they going to play?"

IV
The Impatience Factor

It costs so much money to buy into pro sports today that ownership demands quick results.

This could be the biggest reason of all. The skyrocketing franchise costs of the eighties have eliminated pure sportsman owners from the game, unless they're multimillionaire sportsmen. Peter Pocklington, the Edmonton owner, mirrors this. Pocklington bought 50 percent of the Oilers, then losing $1.5 million a year in the fledgling World Hockey Association, in 1976. "It had nothing to do with business," Pocklington said in 1988. "It was strictly ego. I wanted to own a hockey team. Once that novelty wore off, I knew we had to start making money. And today, to me, it's essential to run a good business. That starts with winning."

The cost of football franchises, late in the eighties, was incredibly high. In 1960, Texas millionaire Clint Murchison bought a franchise and roster of players to put in Dallas at a cost of $600,000. In 1984, Murchison sold the Dallas Cowboys to Texas oilman Bum Bright for $60 million, and Bright bought the lease on ultramodern Texas Stadium for $25 million. In 1988, Bright, in financial trouble, was trying to peddle the team for $100 million and the lease for $50 million. Bright sold the team and stadium to Arkansas businessman Jerry Jones in March 1989 for $140 million.

In the five years Bright owned the team, the Cowboys won 36 and lost 44. They made the playoffs once, losing in the first round in 1984. The attendance at Texas Stadium was declining precipitously; there were 8,000 empty seats for the Cowboys' 1987 game with the defending Super Bowl champion Giants. Yet, after these five inglorious years, Bright was trying to make a $65-million pretax profit on his investment. "The prices people are paying for franchises make absolutely no economic sense, because the teams either are marginally profitable or not profitable," Young of the Giants said. "Why do people keep paying for something they know isn't going to be profitable?" There still is a bit of romance in it, yes. There still are tax breaks, yes. But the only way to make big money in sports, it seems, is to sell an existing franchise. While holding on to such an investment, there is pressure at least not to lose money.

How much pressure? In 1987 alone, owners and general managers in sports fired twenty-nine managers and head coaches. Success without continuity is virtually impossible in the NFL, but that didn't stop know-nothing, meddling owners like Bob Irsay of the Colts from shooting their teams in the feet time and again. Irsay had six head coaches and four separate coaching staffs in the ten seasons from 1979 to 1988. The result: two winning seasons. The owners were taking incredible financial risks to try to push their teams from mediocrity. In 1977, the Cleveland Indians guaranteed a onetime 20-game-winning pitcher, Wayne Garland, $10 million over ten years. He ruined his arm the next season. The Indians, it turned out, paid him $10 million to win 28 games over five years. Tampa Bay of the NFL, desperate for hope after winning 12 games in four years, signed Testaverde in 1987 for $8.2 million before he played a professional down. The Portland Trail Blazers, after being sold for $48 million in 1988, spent $16 million spread over eight years to sign the league's sixth- or seventh-best center, Kevin Duckworth, a one-dimensional offensive player battling a weight problem.

Desperate for fiscal responsibility, baseball was injecting some monetary sanity—but not much—late in the eighties, when it realized the long-term guaranteed contracts were largely stupid. It took collusion among club owners to do it, an arbitrator ruled in 1988. By 1986, one salary survey estimated that the twenty-six major-league teams owed $56 million to players no longer on their roster. Most teams by 1988 were giving a maximum term of three years to the starriest of stars.

In football, the scouting industry was booming, and it was booming because the cost of making a mistake on a young player was so high. In 1955, NFL teams employed a total of five full-time scouts and spent about $10,000 each on scouting. By 1985, the twenty-eight NFL teams employed more than 250 full-time scouts and spent between $300,000 and $1.4 million per team on scouting. "There's pressure on NFL teams not to make mistakes with their top picks, because teams are spending a million dollars or more on their top picks," player agent Peter Johnson said. And veteran scout Bucko Kilroy, now a New England Patriots vice president, said: "What's happened over the years is that people found out they can't make a mistake with their top picks. They've found they not only lose the pick, but lose the tremendous amount of money they've spent to sign the pick. Teams are using scouts as insurance policies."

V
The Death-of-Depth Factor

Injuries, compounded by the lack of depth on great teams and in the minor leagues, hurt teams more today than yesterday.

The Yankees won five World Series in a row, from 1949 to 1953. In the early fifties, they had twenty-three minor-league teams developing talent for the future.

The Yankees won no world titles in the first eight years of the eighties. In 1986, they had five minor-league teams.

Basketball and football use the colleges as their minor leagues. But hockey and baseball still develop most of their own players in the minor leagues; very seldom (Wayne Gretzky, Dave Winfield) will a hockey or baseball player go directly from high school or college to an NHL or major-league baseball team. In the fifties and sixties, most hockey teams had three or four minor-league affiliates. In the eighties, most teams had one. Often, NHL teams of today will pool five or six of their own prospects with prospects from two or three other teams to form a team, sharing the expenses equally. The point is, great players are still being developed, in all sports. They're just not being developed in great quantity by any organization.

Some baseball veterans say that good teams can no longer compete for the pennant if hit by injuries to more than two or three significant players in a season. "Look at us," St. Louis coach Red Schoendienst, a former player and manager for the Cardinals, said in 1988. "We've had four starting pitchers hurt this year. No organization in baseball has the depth to deal with that number of pitching injuries in a season. When I managed, and we had some injuries, we'd have fifteen, twenty minor-league teams developing talent to replace 'em. There used to be less big-league teams and more players to fill the teams. That makes a big difference."

"The reason [baseball] teams don't repeat anymore is injuries," St. Louis shortstop Ozzie Smith said. "The parity in baseball is so great today that usually the team that wins is one that hasn't had many big injuries. The next year, if you have a key injury or two you didn't have the year before—that plus the fact that everybody's gunning for you—you're not going to win."

The Yankees, using the depth of a large minor-league system and huge scouting staff, cultivated depth during their dynasty. "It was an honor if the Dodgers or Yankees came into your house to try to sign you," recalled Sparky Anderson, who signed with the Dodgers in 1953 and played one season of second base in the major leagues. In 1951, the Yankees had a World Series –winning team, and Mickey Mantle, Gil McDougald, Jackie Jensen, and Johnny Mize were not everyday players. Elston Howard couldn't break the everyday lineup of the Yankees for three seasons in the late fifties.

Conversely, teams often win today without depth, simply because it's so rare to find quality depth anymore. In 1987, the Minnesota Twins won 29 and lost 52 on the road; their number three starting pitcher, Les Straker, was 8-10 with a 4.37 earned-run average. They won the World Series because the number of off days during the playoffs and series allowed manager Tom Kelly to use his top two pitchers, Frank Viola and Bert Blyleven, much more than if the schedule made the teams play seven days in a row.

Lack of depth hurts great teams as much, or more, in basketball. As the Lakers tried to become the first team in nineteen years to repeat as NBA champions in 1988, the final four men on their bench—Milt Wagner, Mike Smrek, Wes Matthews, and Tony Campbell—were the most marginal of NBA players. When injuries reduced the effectiveness of James Worthy, Magic Johnson, A.C. Green, and Michael Cooper late in the season, the Lakers struggled to replace stardom with competency. This wasn't the Lakers' fault. Drafting late in the player lottery each year, Los Angeles consistently traded or bartered for help, adding Abdul-Jabbar, Worthy, guard and leading scorer Byron Scott, and reserve forward Mychal Thompson through trades. But the Lakers, still great but graying by 1988, were finding they couldn't trade nothing for something as they tried to keep up with the starry young teams. In 1988, they did repeat, but they could just as easily have lost. The bench strength of Dallas and Detroit forced the final two playoff series that year to seven games; the Lakers, with usually valuable subs Cooper and Thompson playing poorly through the playoffs, were forced to exhaust their already tired starting lineup to eke out a championship.

VI
The Information-Overload Factor

In the Video Age of sports, there are no strategic secrets anymore.

This is especially the case in football. When defensive coordinator Buddy Ryan installed a peculiar defense called the forty-six for the Bears in 1985, it freed the quickest Bear defenders to harass the opposing quarterback into untold mistakes. No longer did defenses have to try to batter huge offensive linemen into submission in order to slow an offense. Quickness, not strength, became the defensive order of the day in the NFL. By the end of the season, several teams were employing versions of the forty-six defense. NFL coaches, you see, are unabashed copycats, and it's so easy today to be a copycat. Neatly organized videotapes showing the varying looks of the forty-six defense were sent by Federal Express nationwide from one Bear opponent to another in 1985.

Computers and video revolutionized scouting and planning, in all sports. The Denver Broncos' scouts all have laptop computers that interface with a huge Colorado computer; now, instead of writing reports and mailing them to Denver for insertion in a huge bound volume of reports, the reports go directly into an information bank and can be called up instantly. In the Dallas

Cowboys' $300-million Cowboys Center complex in Irving, Texas, the former vice president for player development, Gil Brandt, had the world of college scouting at his fingertips, too. "I can ask the computer, 'Who are all of the wide receivers in this year's draft who are five-eleven or above, run a 4.6-second forty-yard dash or less, have good quickness, and a 5.0 [Cowboys'] grade or above?' "

The information difference: In 1958, no NFL scout journeyed to the University of Utah to scout quarterback Lee Grosscup, but he was a first-round draft choice. In 1985, at least one hundred different scouts or NFL coaches saw Western Michigan University linebacker John Offerdahl play or practice, and he was a second-round choice.

Denver's and Cincinnati's census ratings fluctuated between the nation's eighteenth and twenty-second largest metropolitan areas; the Broncos' and the Bengals' resources, theoretically, should have been the same. But the Broncos spend about $2.1 million a year to scout players. The Bengals spend about $300,000. The Broncos were in the Super Bowl in 1987 and 1988. The Bengals finished their fifth consecutive nonplayoff year in 1987, but rebounded to play in the Super Bowl the next season.

The scouting by pro teams of other pro teams is infinitely better, too. Before their Super Bowl season, the Giants felt their detailed knowledge of teams in the opposite conference, the American Football Conference, was weak. Many of these teams the Giants played only once every three years. So coach Bill Parcells approached coaches for Kansas City and Denver in the off-season, and a deal was struck: We'll tell you about the teams you have to play this year in our division, and you tell us about the teams we play in yours. The Kansas City coaches flew to New Jersey in the winter, and the Giants coaches flew to Denver in the spring, all armed with flow charts of tendencies and formations of their opponents. The Giants won three of four tough games against AFC West teams in 1986. They beat San Diego by taking Denver's advice of cutting off the short-passing routes of quarterback Dan Fouts and forcing him to the longer throws; the Giants intercepted Fouts on five long passes and won 20–7. "Everything is fair in love and war," Al Saunders, then the San Diego assistant head coach, conceded at the time.

There are other high-tech ways to get information. Pete Rose, the Cincinnati Reds manager in the late eighties, prided himself on his knowledge of other teams, in the American as well as National League. Rose had a satellite dish at his suburban Cincinnati home. After games in Cincinnati, Rose went home, pulled in a West Coast game or two on his big-screen television, then watched the baseball highlights on ESPN, the cable network, at 2:30 A.M. He always tried to watch games of the Reds' next opponent, so he could scout them personally rather than relying solely on the report from the club's advance scout. "If there's an edge to be gained, I want it," Rose said. "Plus, I just love the game."

Baseball also has entered the video age of scouting in the eighties. The

Major League Scouting Bureau, funded by the sport's twenty-six teams, annually makes videotapes of the top players at every position so every team can have the same view of the players. The teams also send their own scouts to see most of the top players. These tapes are invaluable, especially for judging pitchers; each time a pitcher throws, there is a blip on the tape with the velocity in miles-per-hour of the pitch thrown.

"Everything in sports is keyed to trying to help the bad team and trying to knock down the good team," said Sather of Edmonton.

Including the computers.

One other small factor supporting Sather's contention: When the NFL sat down each February to compose its schedule, one of the things the league considered was how to keep the bad teams from playing meaningless games by November. One solution, the league found, was to schedule the best teams head-to-head in September and October as much as possible, with the bad teams also playing each other early in the season. In 1987, the Giants closed the season against four consecutive losing teams. In 1988, four of their first five games were against teams with winning 1987 records, and the fifth was against Dallas, which won 7 and lost 8 but always plays the Giants very tough.

So the NFL wastes away in Parityville. "Wastes" is the wrong verb, though. There's always a playoff race or two or three on the last weekend of the season because of the enforced evenness. How even is the NFL? On Thanksgiving Day, 1987, all five AFC East teams were 5-5.

VII
The Togetherness Factor

True togetherness died in the fifties, when cross-continent travel forced the demise of chummy train trips.

Montreal's Selke insisted on a family atmosphere around his team that has lasted to today. In fact, several of the current Canadiens credit their 1986 Cup win, in part, to the self-imposed month-long exile at a suburban Montreal hotel during the playoffs; young players who were segregated from the veterans by choice during down time during the season were forced to live with them and get to know them in the playoffs. Why? Because the Canadiens think it helped the fifties teams win. Jean Beliveau of the fifties Canadiens remembers eighteen-hour, nonstop train trips to Chicago that would include informal four-, five- and six-hour middle-of-the-night team meetings.

Fast forward to 1987. A couple of months after the Giants won the Super Bowl, the town of Florence, South Carolina, proclaimed "Harry Carson Day." None of his teammates showed. Young represented the team. Carson wasn't upset about it; he didn't invite any of his teammates. But he did notice a change in his team in the twelve years he had been a Giant. "It's not a family

anymore, let's face it," he said. When Vinnie Swerc, a grizzled and irascible
locker-room aide for fifty-five years, died in 1988, only one player bothered
to attend the funeral.

In football, there is an inherent lack of togetherness because, strangely
enough, of the salary structure. When the bidding war with the rival United
States Football League was at a peak in 1982 and 1983, the NFL decided it
must sign its draft choices instead of losing them to the big-money allure of
the rival league. So the top rookies began making significantly more than
most established veterans. "It's patently unfair," Cincinnati linebacker Reggie
Williams said. "It's the one thing in football that the powers that be really
have to do something about."

The Giants drafted an offensive tackle named William Roberts in the first
round of 1984, when rookie salaries had been pushed to their peak. Roberts
signed a four-year contract worth a total of $1,750,000. Over the four years
of that contract, Roberts started only when teammates on the offensive line
were hurt. Brad Benson, the Giants' starting left tackle for ten years and a
Pro Bowl player in 1986, didn't make $1,750,000 in his entire career. "I've
got nothing against William," said Benson, "but the unfairness of the system
sickens me." How could Benson and Roberts be good friends, even if they
had lots in common, which they didn't? The contract thing would always be
a subtle divider.

"It was much easier to build togetherness in the fifties, because of train
travel," said Beliveau. "You'd get on the train and the veterans would be
discussing the game of the previous night, and you'd learn a lot just by
listening. It built a lot of closeness for us, too."

It is true that there is a sort of forced togetherness with some teams that
have off-season workout programs. But with football teams, it rarely bred
very close friendships. No one on the Giants worked harder than Simms in
the off-season program, but after he got married and had kids and moved to
his rambling home in the suburbs, his best friends were neighbors, not
teammates.

VIII
The No-Time-Off Factor

The off-season isn't the off-season anymore.

When the Lakers and Pistons faced off for the NBA championship series'
seventh game on June 22, 1988, it was the first NBA game ever played in
the summer. Fourteen weeks later, both teams would be back in training
camp. The nonplayoff teams got an extra eight weeks off.

The Edmonton Oilers had thirteen weeks off between Stanley Cup championship and training camp in 1988.

The New York Giants, in 1987, had six weeks off between their Super

Bowl championship and the opening of their four-days-a-week, five-hours-a-day off-season conditioning program, which ran right into training camp in July.

Baseball has it easy. The World Series winner plays about 200 of 220 consecutive days, then has sixteen weeks off.

It used to be that players, coaches, and managers in all sports had to work regular jobs in the off-season. But by the late eighties, it was a novelty if a player worked a blue-collar job in the off-season. Most worked some banquets; David Cone of the New York Mets made $1,000 per appearance in 1987 and Mookie Wilson $2,500, and Giant Brad Benson made $5,000 for a couple of off-season roasts after the Super Bowl. Some of the Giants were even working bar mitzvahs.

The players, then, not only didn't have time to get off-season jobs of any length. They were making more money in token appearances than they could have in some $10-an-hour sales job. Why should they have needed off-season jobs anyway? Here were the 1988 average salaries of players in the four major sports:

Basketball, $510,000
Baseball, $410,500
Football, $212,000
Hockey, $156,000

"It's changed in the time I've been in football," Carson of the Giants said. "You don't use training camp to get in shape anymore. You come to training camp in shape."

The money was too good not to.

IX
The Outside-Forces Factor

Drug abuse, the news-media microscope, and the legion of player agents/financial analysts all shadow athletes on their way to the top, and sometimes overwhelm them once there.

Where does one begin?

Drugs: Giants linebacker Lawrence Taylor, the club's first million-dollar-a-year player, had to be saved from himself in 1986, going into drug rehabilitation after debilitating cocaine binges, and again in 1988, when he tested positive for substance abuse before the season.

Bad agents: Kareem Abdul-Jabbar says he was fleeced out of about $8 million by bad advice from an agent midway through his career, and he had to play well past his prime to become rich again.

Oppressive press: Cincinnati outfielder Eric Davis, a twenty-five-year-old carbon copy of Mantle in the first half of 1987, was declared a Hall of Fame player by *The Sporting News* in midseason; from the middle of 1987 to mid-1988, Davis batted .245. Davis, like so many great talents at a very young age in the eighties, was made a coverboy before he could prove himself over the long haul.

The magnitude of it all.

Who really knows what forces players to ruin themselves, but some of the good ones do. Today, when Boston Celtics architect Red Auerbach is asked why it's been so tough for the Celtics to remain great, he begins by saying: "It starts with the Len Bias thing." Bias, a college star at the University of Maryland, was the second overall pick in the 1986 NBA draft, and the Celtics had the good fortune to pick him. Auerbach hoped he'd be the Celtics' keystone player into the nineties, perhaps allowing them to start another dynasty. A few days later, Bias died of a cocaine overdose. His friends said he had been celebrating his selection by the Celtics by ingesting cocaine.

The night before the 1989 Super Bowl, the Cincinnati Bengals were trying to start a team meeting at their hotel outside of Miami. But one player, running back Stanley Wilson, wasn't there. Wilson had scored two touchdowns in the Bengals' first playoff win a couple of weeks earlier, but this wasn't why he was a noted Bengal. Wilson had been in drug rehabilitation for a cocaine problem five times in the previous five years, so when he was missing, alarms went off. The Bengals sent out a search party. They found him on the floor of his bathroom, incoherent, with drug paraphernalia around him. Twenty hours before the biggest game of his life, Wilson—and his career—were both ruined by a drug. "I don't know," said shaken Bengals coach Sam Wyche. "Maybe our country has gone to hell in a handbasket, and we're powerless to do anything about it."

Maybe it's just the enormity of sports, and how big they've become in our society. How stunningly refreshing it was to hear Oklahoma State University running back Barry Sanders belittle winning the Heisman Trophy in 1988. He was thankful for the award, but he told friends he wished he'd never won it. "Too many people place too much emphasis on this," Sanders said. "Too many people think sports is a god. Not to me it isn't."

Television, too, must take part of the credit/blame for the enthusiasm/mindless-obsession surrounding sports. The amount of money television networks give to college and professional sports intrudes on the form, and in fact, the play of these sports. "I think television has hurt the team play in basketball," former UCLA coach John Wooden told the *New York Times* in 1988. "It has brought on more individual, fancy showmanship. There are greater players today, individual players, than ever. And they're amazing in their individual ability. But I don't think you see nearly as good a team play as you used to have . . . There's so much emphasis placed on the fancy dunk, on the behind-the-back stuff, the dribbling and the showmanship, that you have to lose some team play."

For a firsthand look at how the enormity of it all starts in one sport, take a trip to Mobile, Alabama, in early January. That's when eighty of the best college football prospects for the coming draft work out under pro-coaching supervision for the first time. They practice for a week, then play in a game called the Senior Bowl. The practices are attended by scouts from every NFL team and head coaches from most of them. "If they ever bombed this place," Wyche said, surveying the practice field in 1985, "they'd wipe out the whole NFL." After the practices, writers and TV crews from several NFL cities wait to interview the players they think might be drafted by the teams they cover. Back at the players' headquarters hotel, the Airport Ramada Inn, there are five or six stretch limousines (honestly, some come from 150 miles away in Birmingham, because the market for stretch limos in Mobile is not very great) in the front driveway. The cars are hired at $35 to $50 an hour by agents and gofers for agents, all of whom are dressed either in three-piece suits or silk shirts with the top three buttons unbuttoned so their Italian chains are easily visible. The drivers wait by the cars. Inside several of the cars are lovely young things in night clothing, even during the daytime. While the cars wait, the agents or gofers for agents are inside the Ramada Inn, on the house phones, calling the players' rooms, asking if they'd like to go out for a drive or to dinner with a lovely young thing and hear a sales pitch (low-pressure, of course). Most of the agents will ask the players for 5 percent of their total football earnings as a representation fee. So if a high draft choice signs a contract with a $400,000 signing bonus and salaries of $300,000, $400,000, and $500,000, the agent will get $20,000 from the bonus and annual checks from the player for $15,000, $20,000 and $25,000. The players who have already signed with agents will politely say thanks, I've got an agent. The players who don't have an agent but who don't want to deal with the onslaught will say thanks, I've got an agent. The players who one way or another end up in one of the cars will go out for a nice steak, which ends up on the agent's Gold Card, and most likely get asked if they couldn't use $500 or $1,000 or $1,500—in cash—which they wouldn't have to pay back; it would just be tacked onto the agent's fee when the pro contract is signed in a few months. If things are going well and the agent or gofer thinks the player might sign up with him, this might convince the lovely young thing to stay with the player for a while. As a final bit of persuasion, of course.

"What I see out there, to call it sleazy is an understatement," Mobile-based agent Richard Woods said. "All the caricatures you've heard about are true. The gofers and the runners for the agents all feed these kids a line. The women with the short skirts and the low-cut tops are there. It's a real problem for our business."

In 1988 in the NFL, there were 1,316 jobs for players, forty-seven for each of the twenty-eight teams. At the same time, there were more than 1,500 agents registered with the players union. Absurd, certainly. But the scent of a 5-percent commission on a million-dollar contract makes some people work very, very hard. Which is why the limos and lovely young things show up in Mobile each January for a week.

X
The Emptiness Factor

Part one: It is rare, with the money in sports, for formerly poor kids to retain their love of the sport and consequently their greatness in the sport when they have everything they want in life at age twenty-six.

Part two: Everyone stresses to players, from Little League to the big leagues, the importance of winning the ultimate championship. No one teaches them how to deal with the aftermath.

Listen to Phil McConkey, the Giants receiver and return specialist:

"Everything I ever did as an athlete was tied to one game. Every ounce of energy you have in your playing career is spent trying to win so you can go to the next level—win in high school so you can play in college, win in college so you might be able to play in the NFL, win in the NFL so you can go to the Super Bowl and win the Super Bowl. You're taught and taught and taught how to get there. But when you get to the pinnacle, you say to yourself, 'I've never spent one ounce of thought or energy thinking about what I should do now.'"

6

Rest? On What Laurels?

March 1987
East Rutherford, New Jersey

Two weeks after Super Bowl XXI, the Chicago Bears began their off-season conditioning program. "The off-season," coach Mike Ditka said, "is our season now." The Bears lost on January 3 to Washington, but they still had what many people in pro football considered the premier team. And they had a month's head start on the Super Bowl champion Giants in the weight room.

When the Giants reported for the start of official off-season workouts at Giants Stadium, the Super Bowl championship was only six weeks distant. Many of the players were still tired.

Guard Billy Ard told strength and conditioning coach Johnny Parker: "Johnny, it's too early. I'm not ready for this. My body's not ready for this."

But repeating couldn't wait. The regimen couldn't be broken. Ard went against his body's better judgment. He started working. And the alarm rang in Johnny Parker's bedroom with the pretty wicker furniture in the western New Jersey town of Branchburg each Monday, Tuesday, Thursday, and Friday at 4:45 A.M. Parker was in his Chevy for the fifty-minute commute to Giants Stadium at 4:55 A.M. By 7:30 P.M., after finishing with thirty-nine players, he was back home.

Sometimes Johnny Parker thought about what Billy Ard said, but sometimes, most every day, when he was thinking about the season, he would think: "We've got to be better than we were last year to be as good a team, because everybody else is going to be aiming for us. We can't just be as good. We can't let anybody else outwork us."

Johnny Parker, this conditioning fanatic, hoped the players on the team felt the same way.

Bill Parcells was very big at mind games. He made it his business during the season to be in the locker room by 7:45 or 8:00 in the morning every morning, to start planting his mental seeds with each player he saw. Sometimes he'd ignore a player. That was a message. Sometimes he'd go to a rookie whom he knew to be unhappy with his amount of playing time and tell him:

"Look, I just want to tell you we're real happy with your play on special teams and how hard you're practicing. Keep it up." That was a message. Sometimes he'd go to a player who thought he was playing better than he really was and say something like: "There's more where you came from. You know how easy it'd be to replace you?" That was a message.

Sometimes, around players he wasn't very happy with but didn't have a great relationship with either, he could be a charmer. One day, early in the off-season conditioning program, Parcells walked into the weight room, which was something like the closed city of Gorky. It was the exclusive domain of the players and Johnny Parker, and if any outsider wanted in, he'd better have a personal escort from Parcells or Parker. Spartan place, this weight room. Parker was a fanatic for Soviet and Eastern European training methods (mention "steroids" to him and he gritted his teeth and became visibly angry), and the only things on the walls of the red, white, and blue room were black-and-white eight-by-ten glossies of Soviets and Hungarians and Bulgarians lifting weights and straining to lift weights. The room was spotless. On this morning, Parcells strolled in at 7:15 and quite to his surprise, found offensive tackle William Roberts working out already. The Giants drafted Roberts in the first round in 1983, and he had been a disappointment, failing to wrest a starting job from journeyman Brad Benson and missing one season with a knee injury. Roberts's work habits were, at best, mediocre, and the Giants would have cut him had they not had so much invested in him and had they not seen a glimmer of hope that he could still be a competent NFL player.

So here was Roberts, with a sweaty T-shirt at 7:15 A.M., and here was Parcells, feigning a fainting spell at seeing Roberts lifting so early.

"Help me!" Parcells said, holding his chest. "This is the big one! I'm going!"

"Howyadoin', Coach?" Roberts said, smiling.

"Good to see you," Parcells said back.

Parcells had a slight psychological surprise for his players a few weeks after the Super Bowl. He told them to eat the fruits of their Super Bowl labor. In a letter to each player—some, in anticipation of receiving it, were calling it the fat-cat letter, because they expected Parcells to warn them against off-season excesses—Parcells wrote: "The only thing that will keep you from winning it again is not doing the things you did last year to win it the first time." He told them in the letter of the myth of repeating: that all the outside activities they'd be involved in during the off-season would distract them as they tried to repeat. False, he wrote. That's part of the reward, he wrote. You deserve them, he wrote.

The players were more than happy to oblige Parcells. They loved the outside stuff. "We want to get swept away," said Harry Carson. "We've earned it." Eight or ten players were swept, and they made more than $100,000 in the off-season. In the summer of 1985, Brad Benson would make $500 for shaking hands in a mall for a couple of hours. After the fall of 1986, he was making

$5,000 for sitting on a dais in Atlantic City roasting a famous person. "It boggles my mind what's happening," Benson said.

The Most Valuable Dinner Guest was Simms, the Super Bowl hero; he went to dinner at the White House with President Reagan, the prime minister of France, wives, and others. But there was enough to go around. Phil McConkey's dance card was full, too. McConkey, the five-foot-ten, 161-pound receiver and punt-return specialist, was a hit on the rubber-chicken circuit as much for his past as his present. McConkey and Simms came out of college in 1979, McConkey out of the United States Naval Academy and Simms out of Morehead State in Kentucky. Simms went directly to the Giants. McConkey went directly to Navy helicopter training in Pensacola, Florida. While Simms struggled through injuries for five seasons to establish himself as an NFL quarterback, McConkey struggled through a seasickness-plagued five-year military hitch. In 1984, the undersized and inexperienced McConkey made the Giants on guts and effort and hands, and he retained a quenchless work ethic and his rabid patriotism. He regularly railed against Americans forgetting the POWs and MIAs. He campaigned vigorously for conservative Jack Kemp in the 1988 presidential primaries, and he thought, very seriously, that he'd love to be secretary of the navy someday. He played just as vigorously. When he was knocked woozy by a cheap shot from a Minnesota player in 1986, he scrambled up, swaying, and hollered, "Is that your best shot, you pussy?! C'mon, hit me again!" Most of the skin on his chin flapped off when his chinstrap sliced it off on a violent hit in 1986. When he made a diving touchdown catch in the Super Bowl ("My lifetime dream," he gushed after the game), it was as though everyfan caught the ball with him. "Phil is living the American dream," said Joe Ryan, a fan and a Vietnam vet from McConkey's hometown of Buffalo. "He's the classic overachiever. He has no business being where he is today, which is why people regard him so highly. We're proud as hell of him."

McConkey earned $115,000 with the Giants in salary in 1986. But from January to July 1987, he earned more than $300,000.

He went to southern California to tape an instructional football video with Simms, to Arizona to give a motivational speech to investment bankers, to three fund-raisers for Kemp, to a flea market in New Jersey, to a *Sports Illustrated* luncheon for its swimsuit pinups in Manhattan, to Miami to speak for former Dolphin Nick Buoniconti's spinal-cord injury center, to Buffalo for a Vietnam vets luncheon speech. On Saint Patrick's Day, McConkey had a speaking doubleheader: lunch in Paterson, New Jersey, dinner in Wilkes-Barre, Pennsylvania. He went out with a former *Penthouse* pet and a Miss New York and Miss Michigan. He took an acting class, and he was a consultant to Polygram Records in New York. Most weeks he still worked regularly in the conditioning program—Mondays, Tuesdays, Thursdays, and Fridays, for about three hours a day.

McConkey's work ethic wouldn't change, but mentally, there was no way football could be as important to him as it was the day he was discharged from the Navy. And if it was like this for the steely and dedicated McConkey, what would it be like for the less-devoted Giants?

"I'd love to be a politician, with no strings attached," McConkey said one day, back home in Buffalo. "Whether I play another down in the NFL—and I will—I have so many options with my life."

In books alone, the Giants were getting swept. Simms and McConkey and New York writer Dick Schaap split $225,000 for *From Simms to McConkey*, a story about the two players and the 1986 season. Lawrence Taylor and writer David Falkner split at least $112,000 for *LT: Living on the Edge*, the candid story of Taylor's life. Jim Burt and *New York Post* Giants beat writer Hank Gola split $100,000 for Burt's life story. Leonard Marshall and Dave Klein of the *Star-Ledger* in Newark combined on Marshall's story. Parcells and New York *Daily News* columnist Mike Lupica combined on the Parcells book, sifting out the best deal among seven feelers from publishing companies. In addition, Johnny Parker wrote a strength-and-conditioning book, Carson reissued his 1985 book in paperback, two photo-essay books on the Giants' season came out, a history of the Giants was updated and reissued, and NFL Properties licensed a book chronicling the Giants' season.

Eleven books.

Twelve, if you count former Giants player and director of football operations Andy Robustelli's recollections of his Giants years—eight years after his employment with the club was terminated.

"All those books I simply couldn't believe," said former Pittsburgh quarterback Terry Bradshaw, who was on four Super Bowl–winning teams. "I mean, who's going to read all those books? When we won, none of us rushed out to write books."

The philosophy behind the books was a simple one, for most of the subjects and authors. Take Burt, for instance. He made $50,000 for talking about his life on tape for eighty or ninety hours, and then tediously editing the book with Gola. In all, he spent six or seven weeks, on and off, doing the book. Take away taxes and agent David Fishof's 20-percent cut, and maybe he made $28,000 on the deal. In exchange for sitting still for a few weeks and talking about himself, Burt earned enough money, invested wisely, to send his son to the finest college in America ten years hence. When would Jim Burt ever have the chance to make this kind of money again? The bigger names, Parcells and Simms, spent far less time on their books and made even more.

Young had been felt out about books, but he turned down the chance to do one. Anytime anyone asked Young about all of his team's authors, he got a look on his face as if he had raw lemon wedges between his cheeks and gums. "A book is a vehicle of civilization," he said once. "The use and knowledge of language is an art form. Sport books are . . . I don't know . . . they're just . . ." Then he laughed and shook his head in a disgustedly amused way and said that anyway he never read a book without a bibliography.

And ABC called Simms and McConkey to ask about a made-for-TV "From Simms to McConkey."

Charities were getting a good chunk of the Giants' time, too. In April, in a hotel ballroom in nearby Secaucus, New Jersey, a children's cancer fund roasted Brad Benson. Benson was a likable guy. An unnoticed player in his first five pro seasons, Parcells had given him the crucial responsibility of playing left tackle in 1983. "His job," Parcells said, "is to make sure Simms doesn't get killed." The left tackle in football is important because he usually is blocking the opposition's best pass-rusher trying to get at the blind side of the quarterback. Benson was below the average size for a tackle at six foot three and 270 pounds, and he didn't block very well on rushing plays. But he could pass-block. He will be forever immortalized in the eyes of real Giants fans for his performance in the team's victory at Washington the previous December. Both teams were 11-2 entering the game, and the winner would almost certainly win the division and get a bye in the first round of the playoffs. NFL sack leader Dexter Manley had played Benson well during their careers, and he had two quarterback sacks of Simms when the Giants and Redskins met in their first game of 1986. Benson, blood streaming down his face all game from a season-long cut he'd had on the bridge of his nose, held Manley sackless. The Giants won the game 24–14. "The most satisfying day of my football career. Ever," said the thirty-one-year-old Benson. When the season ended, Richard Nixon wrote Benson a fan letter.

In April, the fans remembered. Benson's game jersey (retail value: $75) was auctioned with several other Giants jerseys. Simms's went for $300, Taylor's and Joe Morris's for $500 each. There was a stalemate at $500 for Benson's jersey until real-estate developer Ken McKenzie yelled, "A thousand!" The crowd gasped. "Fifteen hundred!" yelled another voice. The crowd shrieked. "Two thousand!" McKenzie hollered.

Two thousand dollars for a football jersey of a journeyman player.

Welcome to the land of the Giants, post–Super Bowl edition.

7

They've Got Money,
Lots of Money

April 1987
Manhattan

The office of David Fishof, the agent for six Giants, was in this state all the time: harried, busy, messy, busy, confused. And busy. But it was worth it. Fishof worked for his clients, several of whom weren't household names in their own households. Benson and guard Billy Ard were getting nice cuts of the action, which indirectly bothered some of the bigger names on the team who weren't getting as much hoopla. One player with an agent three states away said, "I wish I had Fishof." He was damn good. When the 49ers won the Super Bowl in 1982, Fishof's client, linebacker Jack Reynolds, made more the following off-season than the star quarterback, Joe Montana.

How good was he? Years earlier, while representing singer Roberta Flack, Fishof got a call from a man in Detroit enamored with Flack's hit song "Killing Me Softly With His Song." This man wanted Roberta Flack to come to Detroit for his son's bar mitzvah and sing "Killing Me Softly With His Song." Bizarre enough, but the guy wanted her to sing it over and over again, on demand. They reached a deal: Roberta Flack would sing "Killing Me Softly With His Song" eight to ten times. For $25,000, plus expenses.

He hadn't lost his touch after the Super Bowl. The deal with the Disney people was that Simms's commercials would air for six weeks after the game. But the spots were so popular that Disney kept them on the air two weeks longer than scheduled. Disney, technically, was in violation of the deal it had struck with Fishof. So Fishof called the Disney people, and they reached a friendly five-figure settlement for the extra airings.

In his corner office at 1775 Broadway, the clutter was mind-boggling. Fishof also represented the Monkees and several other comeback rock/pop groups, New York Yankees manager Lou Piniella, and several other football players. Framed pictures of clients covered the walls with inscriptions like this one on a picture of Simms sticking his tongue out:

To David,
Kiss my white Irish ass.
—Phil

Fishof is twenty-five pounds overweight, in a constant state of motion, with eyes always moving. Can't sit still. Money to be made, you know.

"I could book Simms every day of the year, no problem," Fishof said. "If I don't get a call for Simms every day of the week from Kentucky, it's an upset. They want him at this dinner, or that booster club. And you'd be surprised. They've got money. Lots of money."

His private line rang. Fishof said, "Hello. . . . No, no. . . . Fuck his dinner. Why should I go to his dinner? Give me one good reason why I should go to his dinner. I'm not going. . . . Should I go? You really think I should go? I have no interest in going. . . . Okay. . . . Yeah. Bye." (Length of conversation: fifty seconds.)

Fishof continued, "Phil Simms has had an unbelievable off-season. Phil Simms's goal is not to be a onetime monster. He wants his success to last off the field as well as on. So I've had to turn lots of stuff down. And he's tried to lead a fairly normal life off the field. He's told me, 'David, I don't want to spend a lot of time away from my family. And I don't want to miss the off-season program.' So I'm working around those things. It's good, too, good for his image. The other thing you've got to like about Phil Simms is that he's spreading it around. He gives a lot of the things he can't do to other guys on the team. He's being a regular guy about it. He doesn't want to cause animosity like there was with the Bears."

Then Fishof said, "Winning can be lucrative, and it is for my clients. But none of my clients are changing. None of 'em. Endorsements don't make athletes fat. If anything, they make them hungrier, because they see how lucrative it is, and they want to keep working hard so this stuff keeps coming in."

The market for Simms was exploding, and a selective Simms told Fishof, "I'll load the gun. You shoot it." A pop station in New York, WPLJ-FM, wanted Simms to come on Mondays and Fridays, in the morning, to talk about the games. So Fishof went to work on Simms about it.

"Oh, I don't want to do that," Simms said. "I don't want to talk negative about anybody."

"You won't have to talk negative," Fishof said. "They don't want you to."

"I don't know if I'd be home then," Simms said. "I might be on my way to the stadium."

"We'll put a phone in your car," Fishof said.

"That won't be good quality sound," Simms said.

"We'll put sixteen antennas on the car," Fishof said. "We'll make it work."

"I don't want to do it Mondays," Simms said.

So Fishof went to the station. WPLJ reduced the commitment to Fridays only. A New York radio industry source said Simms made more than $100,000 for sixteen of these ten-minute chats with the DJ.

Farmland Dairies of New Jersey wanted Simms, and he made something near what he made for his radio deal to eat lunch with supermarket-chain presidents. With one big Farmland milk-buyer Simms hit a bucket of golf balls.

Simms was secretive about what this off-season was netting him. The best guess was between his scheduled 1987 salary, $700,000, and $1 million. At least.

8

With This Ring, I Thee Tear Asunder

May 1987
Upper Saddle River, New Jersey

George Young, in a jogging suit although he certainly doesn't jog, greeted a visitor with a grunted hello. This was not a man who spent much time throwing out nice-to-see-yous. He'd much rather spend his time looking at his latest piece of nonfiction, or examining his latest contract figures. On this Saturday afternoon, Young was examining the list of agents he'd inherited from the Giants draft in April. Naturally, this launched him into a sermonette on agents and greed and how they were helping ruin the sport. This was one of Young's favorite subjects, and he was quite good at opining on it.

The New York tabloids were nearby. Young and Parcells told everyone they never read the papers, but they invariably did. Parcells stopped on his way to work at a general store near his house to pick up the *Daily News* and the *Post*. In truth, it was slightly harder to coach and manage a team in New York than in other towns because of the glare of the local press. Teams in Kansas City and Cincinnati and Green Bay had two or three reporters around the team every day, with a TV crew or two swooping in for a half-hour of interviews. The Giants had about eighteen writers around them each workday. And some TV. And some radio. When big stories happened—the Super Bowl getting close, Lawrence Taylor fighting drugs, etc.—eighty to one hundred reporters, photographers, and camera people came out. The headlines of Young's papers on this Saturday:

"Girl Hacked to Death With Sword"

"PTL's 'Lost' $92 M . . . While Tammy Lived in a Palace"

"RITA . . . Death of a Goddess"

Young was asked about how the New Yorkness—the bigness, the sampling of the many off-season fruits—was affecting his team.

"My biggest concern," he said, putting down the sheet of agents, "is how we're going to be able to maintain the team mentality. Are we going to be able to pull the plug on it when it comes time and stop being individuals and take care of the team first? I'm worried about the galaxy-of-stars mentality. Our two greatest enemies are going to be ego and greed, mark my words."

See how the guy would get on a roll?

"We have a good thing going. It's how long they want to keep it going. But we're not exactly living in the era of unselfishness, are we?"

A few weeks later, the agent for third-string quarterback Jeff Hostetler called Young to discuss a new contract for Hostetler, whose deal had expired after the Super Bowl. Hostetler, a career bench warmer, had never thrown a pass in an NFL game. But because quarterback was the key position in the NFL, agents always pushed for the backups to make big money. Never could tell, they'd tell management, when the backup or the number three quarterback would be needed. In three years in the NFL, Hostetler had earned an average of $362,000 per year, including bonuses.

Now, for 1987, he wanted $700,000.

Young laughed for a long time.

But inside he was thinking the same thing he had said on that Saturday in his house: "Our two greatest enemies are going to be ego and greed."

At Giants Stadium, remnants of the Super Bowl were still in the air. Literally. Dampened confetti from the club's victory celebration at the stadium two days after the Super Bowl stuck to the cement under some seats. Shreds of plastic pompoms fluttered in the wind from where they had stuck to the scoreboards. In the windy stadium concourses, papers and streamers blew around freely. The stadium, incredibly, hadn't been sanitized since January. With this as a backdrop, underneath the stands in the Giants locker room, Parcells closed the veterans' minicamp with a ceremony awarding the veterans and coaches their Super Bowl rings.

Lawrence Taylor couldn't make it. He was playing in a charity golf tournament with Michael Jordan that day.

The rings cost $3,000 each. On the face of each were ten diamonds formed in a replica of the Super Bowl trophy, encrusted in a deep-blue synthetic stone. One side of the ring had the last name of the player, coach, or club official atop a Giants helmet and "17-2," the club's record in 1986. The other side had "39–20"—the Super Bowl score—and replicas of the Super Bowl emblem and the NFC Championship Trophy. During the ceremony, in a meeting room adjacent to the locker room, Parcells told the players and assistant coaches, "There's a lot of blood, sweat, and tears in these rings. You should be proud." To each spouse and secretary, the Giants gave a pendant with a face like the top of the ring.

Some of the normally placid Giants were moved. Offensive line coach Fred Hoaglin, one of the most unexcitable people in the organization, walked out of the meeting with a broad grin, showing off the ring. "I'm damn proud, boy," he said. "To me, it didn't feel like we were world champions until now."

But Leonard Marshall wasn't happy. He showed off his ring at his locker, then said he was unhappy about his contract. He wanted more money. He wanted to renegotiate. Ten months earlier, Marshall had renegotiated.

Marshall, a defensive end, was twice a Pro Bowl defensive end. After his first Pro Bowl appearance, in 1986, the Giants renegotiated his contract by extending it into a four-year, $1.425-million deal. The Giants were due to pay him $325,000 in 1987, $375,000 in 1988, and $425,000 in 1989. His 1987 salary was the twenty-seventh best among all NFL defensive linemen. Since only six defensive ends made the Pro Bowl each year and Marshall had made it two years in a row, he figured he should be in the $600,000-a-year range. So now, ten months after signing his name to a renegotiated contract, Marshall said he wanted to renegotiate again. "I don't think what happened last summer was fair," Marshall said.

(At the Pro Bowl in Hawaii four months earlier, Harry Carson had said to Jim Burt, "There's only one guy I'm worried about getting a big head. Leonard.")

In the euphoria of this day, Marshall's comments were relayed to Young. "Wonderful," Young said.

And another player that day was showing friends the pendant the Giants were giving his wife. He said, "Look at this cheap-piece-of-shit necklace they gave the wives and the secretaries."

And Parcells told the writers that day he felt tired and needed a long vacation. "I need to muster up some energy to get going again," he said.

It was around this time that Mike Ditka called Bill Parcells on the phone, and they talked about the prospect of the Bears and the Giants playing in the first game of the season.

"I just hope I have enough guys left to play the second game," Ditka told Parcells.

Parcells laughed a hollow laugh. The Giants, as with most good teams in the NFL, found one more reason why it's so hard for teams in the league to repeat as champions. In Manhattan each winter, the NFL schedule-makers tried to make good teams play good teams and mediocre ones play mediocre ones for as much as possible in the first few weeks of the season. The reason, which they didn't talk much about, was to keep interest in each NFL city (and TV ratings) high for as long as possible. This season, the schedule said the Giants would play five successive playoff contenders to start the season— Chicago, Dallas, Miami, San Francisco, and Washington.

After Parcells first saw the schedule, he turned to the club's director of media services, Ed Croke, and said, "Looks like I'm going to have to get a paper route after five games."

9

Mr. Corporation

June 1987
Manhattan

A man like Phil Simms makes corporate America very comfortable. He is white. He is blond. He has a lovely wife and two darling kids. He is competitive. He talks competitive. He looks good in a suit. He says what people want to hear.

And here Simms was, being Mr. Corporation. In the ballroom of the stately Dorset Hotel on West 54th Street, a man in a very expensive and shiny suit was standing in front of other men and women in other expensive suits— and some reporters, too—explaining the lure of Phil Simms to marketing this new product. The man, named Jeffrey Peisch, worked for a company called Vestron Video of Stamford, Connecticut. He and Simms were in this ballroom to announce to video distributors plans for Simms's two-volume instructional football video. On the video, Simms is the host, and ten other football stars join him to show youngsters how to play football.

"Bluntly," Peisch said, "I think we've got a killer marketing plan. With Wheaties, starting in September and continuing through the end of the football season, we'll have Phil and the video on ten million boxes of cereal."

Peisch soon let Simms speak, and he told a joke and then spoke about how the video was a good teaching tool for kids and how fathers could learn techniques from it, too, and how with the right work ethic and practice habits kids could learn to be good football players.

For taping the video and for being its corporate spokesman, Simms earned something north of $100,000.

That wasn't his only video of the off-season. He also taped "Phil Simms's NFL Workout."

He did commercials or print ads for Continental and Eastern Airlines, the New York *Daily News*, the New Jersey Bell Yellow Pages, the Bell Atlantic Yellow Pages, Disney World, Disneyland, Macy's, Drexel Burnham Lambert (an investment firm), Damart Underwear, Antonovich Furs, York Barbells, and WCBS radio. He consulted with the New York Life Insurance Underwriters, Drexel Burnham Lambert, and Farmland Dairies. He made many motivational speeches and TV and radio sports show appearances.

"The thing I like about my off-season," Simms said when the Vestron Video thing was over, "is I did a lot of things, and they all worked out well, and I never had to leave the area, except for making the football video in California."

Simms's friends couldn't help but get the feeling he wasn't getting fat, mentally or physically, from his off-season. Seven days after the Super Bowl, he had called Johnny Parker on the phone, and Parker was just getting home from church and just starting a short vacation and Simms said, "C'mon, Johnny, let's go! A week off's enough! Let's go work out!" When he went to California to film the video, he sandwiched in the Giants workout each day.

The only time his face turned into a frown on this well-orchestrated day was when one of the beat writers who covered the Giants asked him if all this off-season self-promotion would affect him and the Giants in September.

"Well," Simms said, "if we lose and did nothing, you guys would say, 'The Giants were too tight in the off-season.' If we lose and did everything, you guys would say, 'The Giants did too much in the off-season.' Mike Ditka did some things last year after the Bears won. Did that ruin his coaching?' "

A month later, just before the Giants went to training camp, Simms sat in his home in Franklin Lakes, New Jersey, and babysat and reminisced a little bit. Well, he tried to.

"Daddy!" six-year-old son Christopher yelled in to him. "Deirdre's throwing dirt into the swimming pool! She's getting it in the filter!"

Simms peered out from his kitchen table, through the sliding-glass doors, to the in-ground pool. Yep, sure enough, Deirdre, two and a half, was throwing dirt into the pool.

It wasn't bothering him much.

"Dad!!!" Christopher hollered. "Do something!"

"Deirdre, you stop that," Simms said.

She did it again.

"Deirdre, you stop that, I told you," Simms said.

He didn't yell at her. He spoke calmly. It reminded his visitor about running back Joe Morris's description of Simms in the huddle. "He doesn't panic, and he doesn't yell at anybody, even if he's getting killed. He might say, 'Just give me another second and we can get it done.' "

Simms had gotten the extra second consistently in Super Bowl XXI. He completed a remarkable 22 of 25 passes in the game, 88 percent accuracy in the biggest game of his life. With a minimum of twenty attempts, only twice previously in 7,177 National Football League games had a quarterback had a more accurate day. The other two games were in the regular season. This was in The Big One.

At a banquet in March, Simms had seen former Super Bowl quarterback Len Dawson. Dawson said, "Boy, that was some game you played."

"Yeah," Simms said. "I put some numbers up there they'll have a hard time matching, won't they?"

"Fella," Dawson said, "I don't think they'll ever match those numbers."

"Good," said Simms. "I hope they don't. I hope that's how I'll be remembered."

Deirdre had stopped throwing dirt by now. So Simms, an eye on the pool, got to think back. What a great week it had been for him and his team. It started on the Sunday before the game, when, just before the team left for Pasadena, he had smuggled a bottle of champagne into the locker room. Club president Wellington Mara didn't allow liquor in the locker room. So Simms had to sneak into the bathroom, and he motioned to the two players he wanted to share it with: fullback Maurice Carthon and running back Tony Galbreath. Both were underappreciated players, and Simms wanted to show them his appreciation for their unselfish work. Lawrence Taylor walked by, and the four of them sneaked paper-cupfuls before the team plane left for California. "We were going to the Super Bowl," Simms said, "and I was so thrilled. We all were."

Memories. Simms's were strange. He watched a tape of the game on TV a month after the game and was stunned to hear John Elway's name on the pregame show much more than his. The way Simms figures, it was about nineteen thousand mentions of Elway to two for Simms. But he remembers when his name was mentioned, it was mentioned by commentator Terry Bradshaw, and Bradshaw said, "The guy who's going to play better is Phil. The key to playing this game, to being successful in this league, is you've got to experience it all. Simms has had the bad and the good, and he doesn't worry about playing bad today." Bradshaw was right. Simms knew this was his stage, but he didn't worry about playing good or bad. He didn't let the bigness of everything affect him at all. He vowed to teammates the night before the game he'd complete a pass, a 17- to 20-yard incut to Lionel Manuel, on the first play of the game. In fact, he and Phil McConkey dined with comedian Billy Crystal the night before the game and told Crystal to bet on that's being the first play of the game. First Giants play: Simms to Manuel, incut from the left, plus 17.

The lawn service was gone now from Simms's lush fairway of a lawn, and Simms moved to the patio outside, watching his kids play. Training camp was a week away. Listening to him, one got the feeling it wasn't going to be Phil Simms who would screw up and ruin the Giants' season, if it was to be ruined by anything.

"I can't imagine playing a big game this year, and because we won it once, saying to myself, 'Oh, we already won it. It doesn't matter if we lose this one.' I mean, jeez, here I am, worried about training camp, worried about doing everything right."

This is what he hoped: I hope everyone is still worried about doing everything right.

─── 10 ───

The Reign of Steel

July 1987
Sewickley, Pennsylvania

Jack Ham, of Jack Ham Enterprises, wanted the point to be clearly understood. Ham used to play linebacker for the Pittsburgh Steelers, and he played on four Super Bowl–winning teams in the span of six seasons. Now he was leaning forward in his office in a Ohio River town west of Pittsburgh, and he was trying to explain why the Steelers were so good for so long, why there was such an incredible love affair between a team and a city, why Jack Ham would go out to eat at a nice restaurant in Pittsburgh in the off-season and have people line up at his table after dessert for a word and an autograph.

"Chuck Noll," Ham said. "We all became clones of Chuck Noll."

Noll, the Steelers' coach, managed to lord over his players in an era when agents were starting to get so much control over the players. "Control" might be the wrong word. Put it this way: Players were just starting to see how much more money they could earn by exerting pressure on the club through agents' holding them out of training camp and through other enriching attempts. The Steelers won Super Bowls in 1975, 1976, 1979, and 1980. No other team has won four Super Bowls in the twenty-three-year history of the game, and the Steelers did it in half of a decade.

Chuck Noll preached perspective. Each year, when the Steelers made a contract with a ring company after winning a Super Bowl, they mandated that the rings be finished by June 1. Then the rings were mailed with warm congratulatory letters from the club to the players. "We got into a real discussion with one of the ringmakers one year," said Dan Rooney. "They weren't going to have the things done by June first, and we told them they had to be done and in our hands by June first. We wanted that to be in the past by the time training camp started. Chuck made it very clear to the team each year that last year was over, in the past."

Chuck Noll preached preparation. "A life of frustration is inevitable for any coach whose main enjoyment is winning," he said in 1980. "There simply aren't enough Sundays, not enough games. And you're bound to lose a few of those. The most interesting thing about the sport, at least to me, is the preparation—any aspect of preparing for a game. The thrill isn't winning. It's in the doing. Winning is the test."

Chuck Noll once told a friend, "I've never made one decision in my life based on money."

Chuck Noll consistently refused to do commercials or advertisements. He once consented to have his picture taken for a friend who ran a bank, but there was a misunderstanding about the intent of the picture, and when it ended up on a billboard in the south hills of Pittsburgh, he was quite unhappy. "That stuff," Noll said about the off-field enticements, "is for the players. Let them have it. They've earned it."

Chuck Noll guarded his privacy an inordinate amount. He has a wine cellar in the basement of his suburban Pittsburgh home, but he never wanted the world to know about it. When a reporter tried to make small talk with him during a 1983 interview, the reporter asked him how his wine cellar was coming. "I don't know what you're talking about," Noll said.

"This is what Chuck Noll's training-camp speech to us was like," Ham said. "He'd say, 'Put the season in perspective. Not a damn thing you did last year can help you win this year. Everybody's going to be pointing to you because you won it last year. Every team will play better against you. It's going to be harder than it was last year, and you won't win again unless you realize this.'

"We believed it, because we saw it happen every year."

Think of it: The Pittsburgh Steelers' fourth Super Bowl championship in six years is a decade distant now.

It can't be that long ago.

Then again, doesn't it seem like twenty years ago?

It was a decade ago that Ham was eating in a Pittsburgh restaurant at a table next to noted conductor Andre Previn. A well-dressed man walked up to Previn, excused himself, and said, "Excuse me, Mr. Previn. May I borrow a pen?"

Previn found a pen and gave it to the man.

"Thank you," the fellow said. He turned to Ham. "Jack, can I have your autograph?"

"It was an incredible time for us all," Ham said in his office. "But the thing we all knew, and I think this is important, is that we wouldn't have had the opportunity to be recognized and to make money without football. We had so many guys putting football first."

The Steelers were great in that era for many reasons, and dedication to the sport was a prime one. But they also spent the first half of the seventies drafting better than anyone in football. Noll's single-mindedness was certainly critical to the success of the Steelers, and general manager Dan Rooney's tough stance with agents who refused to see the club's when-we-win-we-all-benefit negotiating mode was important, too. But what drafts they had. Check their drafting record from 1969–'74:

Draft Year	Draft Round	Position, Player	Number of Pro Bowls	Steeler Seasons
1969	1	Defensive tackle Joe Greene	10	13
	10	Defensive end L.C. Greenwood	6	13
1970	1	Quarterback Terry Bradshaw	4	14
	3	Cornerback Mel Blount	5	14
1971	2	Linebacker Jack Ham	8	12
	4	Defensive end Dwight White	1	10
	8	Defensive tackle Ernie Holmes	0	6
1972	1	Fullback Franco Harris	9	12
1974	1	Wide receiver Lynn Swann	3	9
	2	Linebacker Jack Lambert	9	11
	4	Wide receiver John Stallworth	3	14
	4	Center Mike Webster	9	15

Five drafts. Eleven Pro Bowl players. Seven, perhaps, in the Hall of Fame someday.

The key: Greene was twenty-seven years old, with six Pro Bowl seasons left in his career, when the Swann-Lambert-Stallworth-Webster class came to Pittsburgh. This team was wonderfully young together.

The second key: "This is corny," said Greene, "but the word 'fat,' we never heard of it. Winning wasn't something we could get tired of."

Nor did they. Starting in 1972, the NFL took notice of this team. The Steelers played Miami—the only 17-0 team in NFL history—in the American Football Conference championship game, and the Dolphins struggled to win, 21–17. Two seasons later, the Steelers embarked on greatness, losing three times in seventeen games and beating Minnesota in the Super Bowl. The next year, they lost only twice and beat Dallas in the Super Bowl. The next year . . . well, most Steelerphiles will tell you the 1976 Steelers were the best team in Pittsburgh's history. The 1976 Steelers opened the season with 1 win and 4 losses. They won their last nine games by 23–6, 27–0, 23–0, 45–0, 14–3, 32–16, 7–3, 42–0, and 21–0.

"We could have taken everyone on that defense, every starter, to the Pro Bowl, and it would have been very fair," Blount said.

But Harris, the NFL's touchdown leader that season, and two other Pittsburgh running backs were hurt for the AFC championship game that year, and the Steelers were beaten by Oakland for the conference title. The next year, Noll began getting worried about the Steelers' staying power. Pro Bowl players Blount and Lambert were contract holdouts, and Noll said in training camp that distractions would derail the Steelers from future greatness if they let them. Noll called the shot. The Steelers won 9 and lost 6 and lost in the first round of the playoffs. Noll's message came across the next season, 1978, and the Steelers didn't have lingering contract problems. Although the Steel-

ers' management had to deal with "Agent Orange," Howard Slusher—so
nicknamed because he was the toughest player representative in the business
and teams thought he could ruin players by his tactics—they came into the
late seventies free of player enmity. Fifteen Slusher clients were on the Steelers,
and none had nagging holdouts in the next two seasons. "Hey, don't be
naive," Dan Rooney said. "Howard Slusher would have done anything on us.
It was the players who kept things in balance. They had perspective."

By 1978, Bradshaw had smoothed all the rough edges on his game, and
the Steelers were not only a smothering defensive team but also a powerhouse
on offense. Over the next two seasons, the Steelers won 32 and lost 6. They
beat Dallas in an exhilarating Super Bowl in 1979, 35–31. "We haven't
peaked yet," Noll said after the game. The next year, they beat the Rams for
their fourth Super Bowl win.

In 1979, the average salary, including benefits, for a player in the NFL
was $68,900.

By 1988, the average salary, including benefits, was $254,000.

But the league's enforced parity started catching up with the Steelers.
Pittsburgh drafted eleven Pro Bowl players who played in a total of sixty-
seven Pro Bowls in the six drafts from 1969 to 1974. In the next seven drafts,
with the Steelers picking lower each year because the best teams picked last
in each draft round, the Steelers chose one player, linebacker Robin Cole,
who eventually made it to one Pro Bowl game. The bad drafts continued
through the eighties, and Rooney was forced to start a family feud and fire
his brother, Artie, who was in charge of the draft for Pittsburgh. "There's
some luck involved in drafting, too," Rooney said. In 1975, the Steelers were
coming off their first Super Bowl victory, and they picked twenty-sixth and
last in each draft round; yet they came up with Swann, Lambert, Stallworth
and Webster, perhaps their best draft class ever. In 1986, the Steelers came
off a 7-9 year, picked ninth in the draft, and came away with only one player,
quarterback Bubby Brister, who is even a relatively valuable member of the
team today.

Still, it was a marvelous run at greatness.

"I will make this statement," said Bradshaw, now a network football
analyst. "No one will ever win four Super Bowls in six years again. Money
is one reason. Pressure's another. It's even more than since 1979. Look at
Chicago. They won the Super Bowl once, and everybody starts calling them
a dynasty. We didn't have any of that when we won. Plus, there's a little
more individualism today. Look at the clauses these guys have in their contracts. They're clauses for individuals, not for the team.

"What made our teams special is we believed that the Rooney family would
treat us with basic fairness. And I know that's not true with players and
management today. No way. You have as much success as we did, and you'd
figure there'd be twenty or thirty guys every year lining up for more money.
There were a few, but not many. We knew the Rooneys would be broke if

we all demanded to be the highest-paid players in the sport. They did an excellent job of convincing us that by not being selfish, we would all profit. And we did. We profited by winning so much, and we profited by being in good position to do something with our lives after we finished playing because we were Steelers."

Today, Bradshaw lives three miles from Texas Stadium in suburban Dallas. He works mostly at his TV job. But he supplements it by working for a cosmetics company, a chewing-tobacco company, an oil company, and for himself as an after-dinner speaker. When Bradshaw won his first Super Bowl, he was making $60,000 a year. After he won his third one, he was making $250,000. Today, he's making at least twice that. Plus, he doesn't get beat up every Sunday.

Blount thinks much of the Steelers' success can be traced to a work ethic from growing up in rural America without the benefits many other kids had in the fifties and sixties. "So many players we had grew up in small towns and were from small schools. Joe Greene, from Elgin, Texas. Terry Bradshaw, from Louisiana; he's as country as they come. I grew up on a farm in Georgia. We didn't have anything. So we were hungry for success in life," said Blount. "Today, it doesn't seem like the hunger is there as much. My daughter's seventeen. She already has her own car. When I was seventeen, I didn't have a bike."

For whatever reason—small-town upbringings, Noll, maturity—there was perspective in Pittsburgh. Three days after winning the first Super Bowl, Blount was home in Georgia putting up fence for the new farming season. Stallworth's four Super Bowl rings rarely come out, even today, of a safe-deposit box in Huntsville, Alabama. Greene turned down movie roles and two commercial offers because they wouldn't portray him as he wished.

Asked why he didn't agree to have a book done on him, Greene said, "I don't think a whole lot of those sports books. You have to do what you have to do. But there wasn't enough of me to write a book about. I hadn't lived long enough to write anything significant."

That hadn't stopped the Giants.

— 11 —

Raining on the Bears

July 1987
Platteville, Wisconsin

Oh, the Bears. How they won a city. How they dominated a league. In 1985, they won 15 of 16 games in the regular season. In the playoffs, they outscored the opposition 91–10. They were big, they were bad, they were charismatic.

The *Chicago Tribune*, which covered the Vietnam War with two reporters, covered the Super Bowl skirmish with New England with twenty-seven. The *Chicago Sun-Times* published Bears running back Dennis Gentry's favorite banana-bread recipe. Radio station WCKG-FM in Chicago broadcast nothing but crowd noise during the three-and-one-half-hour Super Bowl. The quarterback, Jim McMahon, mooned a helicopter near the team's practice field before the Super Bowl. The short-yardage goal-line back, William Perry, weighed something north of 315 pounds. They were so full of themselves that they went out in midseason 1985, made a music video called "The Super Bowl Shuffle" in which they predicted a Super Bowl victory, and went out that week and beat Dallas, 44–0.

They had it all, these Bears. They played in football's weakest division, the NFC Central, with perenially poor Detroit, Green Bay, and Tampa Bay providing six of the sixteen annual challenges. They had a grinding defense and a great rushing game with the game's all-time leading running back, Walter Payton. They had a good motivator, Coach Mike Ditka.

After the 36-point Super Bowl victory, Ditka said, "I don't think you can disrupt what we put together."

New England quarterback Steve Grogan said, "I'm not sure anyone can beat them on any day."

Defensive end Richard Dent said, "Most of the guys here are twenty-five, twenty-six. We've got a dynasty here."

But their quarterback, McMahon, was hurt the following November. They lost at home in the playoffs in 1986, to Washington. By 14 points.

With that loss as a mental wake-up call, the Bears came to Platteville, a bucolic college town way out near Iowa, and hoped they could return to their regular- and post-season form of 1985. This was a snarling team. First of all, they were annoyed that everyone thought they had a crummy season in 1986. They did win 14 of 16 games in the regular season. Secondly, they were collectively angry with Ditka and the front office for bringing in Doug Flutie to challenge Jim McMahon, Mike Tomczak, and rookie Jim Harbaugh for the starting quarterback job. Thirdly, they couldn't stand the lack of privacy they had in this place. It was normal to have 7,000 or 8,000 people at their practices and on the fringe of their spartan dormitories each day, and everywhere the players went they were hounded for autographs.

They seemed quite intent on being good again.

"I'm glad as hell that repeating stuff is behind us," said defensive lineman Dan Hampton, resting on a weight bench in the Bears lifting area. "I came with my teeth gritted every week. But every game was a playoff game. The Giants will find out that every week is Super Bowl Sunday for the other team. They'll find out that the Philadelphias and the Indianapolises get up so much for them. That's what made me respect the Steelers so much.

"The other stuff that came up last year, about jealousies and everybody hating each other, that was ridiculous. I'm not jealous of anyone. Ask anyone. All the off-field stuff, that's extraneous to me. I didn't give a damn. I think, if you want to point the finger at one thing, it's that a lot of these rookies came in and contributed and right away, boom, they went to the Super Bowl. They never went through the hard times. They didn't understand quite what it took to get there, how you had to play on the edge every week, every play. Fridge comes out of college and right away he's in the Super Bowl; that's a pretty good rookie year for anybody. Nothing against Fridge. But we were here for six, seven years busting our ass every day. For a lot of the younger guys, it came a little too easy. And they didn't understand what it was.

"But it's ridiculous to talk about us negatively. We went fourteen and two, and we went through four quarterbacks. We had a hell of a year. You cannot win for long in the NFL without at least stability at quarterback, and that's what happened to us in the playoffs."

Hampton definitely wanted to sweep aside the personal-differences-as-a-factor factor, and in reality, most players aren't influenced at all by whether they hate some teammate or not. But there was a strain on this team, and it was a strain of enviousness and personal differences between teammates. How much of a factor was it? Mike Singletary, the dominant inside linebacker, thought the personal stuff was a big factor. Many players couldn't stand the fact that Perry, by scoring a few touchdowns and being the biggest running back there ever was, was the most beloved Bear of them all across the country. Just watch a practice and you could see that. On a searing July afternoon on a practice-field oasis among the western Wisconsin cornfields was this sight: William Perry, during calisthenics before a practice, his stomach hanging out grotesquely, waving at the air during jumping jacks, waving at his knees during toe-touching exercises. At the front of the group was Mike Ditka, arms folded, jaws murdering the gum in his mouth, his sunglassed eyes staring ahead impassively. Fridge wasn't exercising? Who's going to make him?

And this is what the players thought: This fat slob unproven Perry has four million bucks in the bank, he isn't even doing his toe-touches right, and everyone treats him like it's all right! How can this stiff get away with it!

At dinner that night in the cafeteria at the University of Wisconsin's branch campus in Platteville, Singletary talked about personal differences.

"Our desire was there last year," said Singletary, munching on an ice-cream sandwich. "The big thing that damaged us was personal jealousies and envies. You think: 'Why didn't I get that commercial?' Or, 'Why didn't I get my share of attention? I was here a long time ago, and I was part of the building of this team.' Think about that. It's crazy, but it happened. We should have thought, 'This has very little to do with football. If they don't want me for this commercial, fine. If I don't fit in, fine.' "

Here we are, back at the M word.

Money.

"If you look at when the Packers and the Steelers and the Yankees and Canadiens won, they won basically when salaries weren't that high," Ditka said. "There was an incentive to win to make a lot more money. I think that's what's happened with the escalation of salaries . . . yeah, it's always great to say, 'We're the world champions,' but I don't know how important it is to go back. The first time you do it, you don't really know what the reward is, and when you do it, it's great. The price was worth it. But once you find out what the reward is, I think a lot of people on the team say, 'Well, you know, there wasn't all that much to it.' I think they're wrong, but I think it's the truth.

"For me, the only reward I've ever looked for is the right to be called the best, the world champion. Yeah, the financial remunerations are great, and the ring is great, and those things are important to me. But I mean, we all do one thing in life, and the greatest thing is when people look at you and say, 'They're the best at what they do,' or, 'He's the best at what he does.' There's very few people who can say that. Hey, the $65,000 [Super Bowl reward] is important, but it comes and goes. What they can never take from you is that you were the best at what you did in the whole world.

"A lot of people have different concepts of success. Some people consider success financial success. All I know is this: Success cannot be static. Success to me is not being successful one time. Success is a continuous thing, I think. It's a progression toward excellence all the time. A lot of people in sports don't understand that. They think once they've reached that pinnacle and start looking down at the rest of us, they have it made. There is one statement I have on my desk. 'Success is not permanent. Failure's not fatal.' We asked our football team one question last year, all year. Were they satisfied? We weren't. Our guys, ninety-five percent of them, worked their butts off. I think it showed. You don't go fourteen and two by not working your butts off. What beat us in the playoffs I don't think was the Redskins so much as our own discipline in doing the little things."

Interesting. The guy in the back of the calisthenics pack wasn't doing the little things, and he was getting bigger. In many ways.

───12───

At Camp With the Boys

July 1987
Pleasantville, New York

Welcome to the victors' training camp.

Four nights before training camp began, *Sport Magazine* leaked to ESPN excerpts from Lawrence Taylor's book, which was to be released in September to coincide with the start of the football season. What *Sport* released to ESPN were harrowing snippets from *LT: Living on the Edge* dealing with his rampant drug use from 1982 to 1985. What *Sport* didn't release was as important: details of the Giants' efforts to wean him off the stuff. So the story that came out in the tabloids the next day was basically LT Says Team Knew, Did Nothing.

When camp began on Sunday, July 26, the rookie first-round draft choice, wide receiver Mark Ingram, was a holdout, unhappy with the contract the Giants were offering.

Veteran linebacker Gary Reasons, a Super Bowl starter, was a holdout once the veterans reported five days later.

Jim Burt and Leonard Marshall continued to truly hate each other. They played next to each other on the defensive line, Burt in the middle and Marshall at right end, and now they were dueling authors. Marshall took a swipe at Burt in his book.

And what would camp be without some financial news about Marshall? Two days before the veterans were to report, a sullen Marshall walked out of George Young's office. The Giants redid his contract. Again. Marshall wasn't happy. Again. Young sighed. Again. "I could see he had second thoughts thirty seconds after he signed," Young said. "It's a shame. I don't think he'll ever be happy."

But there was one thing that set some alarms off, quietly, in the minds of Giants brass.

Brad Benson was the perfect Bill Parcells player. Always a dedicated employee, Benson had always worked as hard as any Giant in the Parcells era in the semimandatory off-season program. Each summer, when players have a club-mandated physical examination, doctors check the body fat of each. This

64

is a sophisticated way of telling the club what kind of condition the players are in by measuring the percentage of fat the bodies have. A wide receiver might be a lean 8 percent fat, a bulkier offensive lineman perhaps 10 or 12 percent.

When the Giants checked dedicated employee Brad Benson's body fat in the training camp physical, the count was 4 percentage points higher than in 1986.

─── 13 ───

Just Another Day in Paradise

August 1987
Pleasantville, New York

And a few other things.

In the Giants training-camp physical examination, Lawrence Taylor, the reigning National Football League most valuable player, urinated into a clear plastic cup, as did all of his teammates as part of the NFL-mandated preseason drug test. When the urine was tested at a lab in suburban Philadelphia, the test came up positive for drugs. When the lab performed a confirmation test on the same urine, the drug trace showed up again. No punishment for drug offenders (his cocaine and crack excesses documented in the book didn't count) happens after a first positive test. The team, luckily, was able to keep it quiet.

Right tackle Karl Nelson, the most important blocker in the Giants' most important strategic facet, the running game, laid all scrunched up on a CAT-scan table in Manhattan. The scan revealed a mass, four centimeters by six centimeters, well-shielded beneath his massive breastbone. Karl Nelson had cancer.

The players felt for Nelson and shivered about the fact that he was the fourth Giants player to have a cancer diagnosis in eight years. Could there be a link, they wondered, between playing in this area of proven high toxin levels and getting cancer?

Left tackle Benson found out he had a degenerative condition due to arthritis in his hips, and he steeled himself to the fact that this would be his last NFL season.

Tight end Mark Bavaro, an important blocker with Nelson in the running game, began to have a lot of pain in his feet.

There were rumblings of a players' strike because the National Football League Players Association, which bargained for the players, and the Management Council, which bargained for the owners, were at an unbridgeable impasse. If there was a strike, players would play two weeks, then go out. If there was a strike, management would hire players off the street and play games as usual, in hopes of forcing the real players back to work. The fraud games would count in the real standings. This would be bad for the game but particularly bad for the Giants, who decided during training camp not to sign these replacement players before a strike was called. Young didn't want to disrupt the mindset of his championship-minded players by letting them know the club was hiring their replacements while they were out working toward a title. So if there were strike games, the Giants would be way behind other teams in forming a scab squad.

Parcells prepared as normal. Bad things happened in every training camp. When a couple of bad things would happen in one day, or when Parcells would have to put out some psychological brushfire, he'd mutter to himself or out loud, "Just another day in paradise." It's a saying he learned at a Jersey shore diner one morning before a day of fishing in the off-season. Seems that two hard hats were leaving their booth in the diner this one morning at dawn, and neither looked particularly happy about the prospect of work in that day's heat. "Just another day in paradise," one said to the other. Parcells liked it.

Through it all, on the surface, it wasn't a disastrous training camp. Parcells held the reins tightly, figuring the heads were big enough already and he didn't have to add to the ego, and figuring the less the press knew the better. He always tried to manage the press, and he convinced the players that the press could be the enemy, although by most accounts the Giants' press corps was a relatively docile group. He knew how the press could affect his team, how it could, by reporting either some damaging truths or some rumors, damage team chemistry. In May 1986, with Taylor coming off his drug rehabilitation in Texas, three reporters from the big New York City papers were dispatched to cover Taylor at a charity golf tournament in Westchester County, north of the city. Taylor wouldn't talk to the writers. A photographer for the *Post* caught Taylor in a backswing with his three iron, and the photo appeared, big, on the back page of the *Post*. The caption said: "Ironing out his problems." The next day, an enraged-looking Parcells ripped the writers and told them he'd ban them from the locker room if they didn't leave Taylor alone.

Parcells and Taylor had an unusual relationship, a relationship most of the rest of team resented. Taylor made no apologies for who he was, and he would accept no one's telling him what to do if he didn't want to do it. At his first training camp with the Giants in 1981, Taylor got sick of the constant coaching/badgering of Parcells, who was then the defensive coordinator and a bit of a taskmaster. With the writers and the fans within earshot, Taylor turned after one of Parcells's tirades against him and yelled, "Get the fuck off my back!" Parcells did. When the Giants advised him to stop associating with the owner of a go-go bar near Giants Stadium, The Bench, Taylor refused. He used to say to Parcells, "Hey, Bill, I'm going to The Bench. Want to come?" This was a man who ran his own life, exactly the way he wanted. His passion was golf—sometimes he hustled through forty-five holes a day —and he played as many pro-ams around the country as he could in the off-season. At one such tournament after his MVP season, before the Manufacturers

Hanover Westchester Classic in New York, his first tee shot sliced far off the fairway and landed against the fence abutting a tennis court.

"Where do I drop my ball?" he asked the gallery following him.

"Anywhere you want to," a man in the crowd said.

Ah, the essence of Taylor. When the Giants sent him to a private drug rehabilitator in New York in 1985, he stopped going after a while because it didn't suit him. Parcells might have waived a lesser player for such insubordination. With Taylor, he continued to try to help him. Parcells, in truth, helped save Taylor from cocaine, and he certainly helped save his football career. The cost: The players resented Parcells's double standard, and it damaged his relationship with them. Running back Joe Morris, for one, was from a strict military family, and he couldn't believe what Parcells let Taylor get away with.

Parcells's response: "It's not my job to be consistent. It's my job to be right."

(Don't ever think, by the way, that Taylor was ever able to wean himself off cocaine by any of those quickie rehabs the Giants of the NFL forced on him. Read his book to discover the severity of his problem. One of his teammates, told a month before training camp started of the upcoming details of Taylor's drug use, said he wasn't surprised at all. "This might shock you," the teammate said, "but I thought he was going to die.")

This summer, Parcells was still in the Taylor defense business. After he found that *Sport* had been remiss in stressing the Giants' attempts to rehab Taylor from cocaine, Parcells went on the attack against the press again. When a respected beat writer, Bob Glauber of the Westchester Rockland Newspapers group, quoted substance-abuse specialists as saying Taylor was endangering his rehabilitation by continuing to drink alcohol, Parcells exploded at him.

"That was a horseshit article," Parcells steamed at Glauber. "And you're horseshit for writing it! It was uncalled for. A guy goes in to have two beers and you've got him drinking all those beers. That's horseshit. Who you been talking to?"

"A guy who's an authority in—" Glauber began.

"I don't want to hear it! You tell that doctor . . . Deliver this message: Parcells says you're an asshole! Call him up and tell him that for me."

Glauber must have been on the right track, seeing that Taylor tested positive for drugs during camp.

But part of this was a deliberate attempt on Parcells's part to align himself with Taylor and detour much negative press about him. Parcells knew that Taylor was a loose cannon, but he also knew Taylor was a very loyal person. So he figured that if he was loyal to Taylor and proved he cared about Taylor by defending him at every turn to what was an objective but ready-to-attack media, Taylor would play hard for him and be loyal right back. Taylor did, and he was.

Parcells bent over backward for no other player. In motivational ways, he challenged even the hardest-working players during camp. At a training-camp scrimmage August 8, a leatherlung screamed from a hillside overlooking the field, "Hey, Bill! Don't even think about cutting McConkey!" That day, McConkey had an excellent scrimmage catching the ball. Parcells said, "He wasn't any good." The offensive linemen, before the loss of Nelson, were the objects of scorn from Parcells. They were called the Suburbanites because they all lived the comfy New Jersey suburban lifestyles with kids and dogs and goldfish and station wagons. Early in camp, Parcells said, "They'd better improve or they'll be in for some urban renewal." He wasn't kidding. On August 14, he had a very loud on-field conversation with Fred Hoaglin about the poor line play, after which he kicked a football halfway across the field and walked away in anger. "You gotta find a way to get it done!" he said in frustration to no one in particular that day. That was a Parcellsism. No one cared how you did it, or how long it took to get done. Just find a way, he'd always say. Find a way to get it done.

Parcells also wasn't being as friendly with many of the players, because he wanted to stress the all-business approach. Guard Billy Ard, a positive-thinking but realistic everyman of a player, smiled at Parcells walking past him one day in camp, and Parcells snapped at him, "Biff [his nickname], don't try to make friends with me. We're not friends."

"We're like trained dogs," center Bart Oates said after lunch one day. "We respond to him yelling at us. Sometimes you think, 'Why does he hate me?' But that's him. That's his New Jersey manner. It works."

None of this was very unusual. Outwardly, the camp was the same as any in the Parcells reign, which began in 1983. In some ways, it was the epitome of normal, and the Giants were striving to keep it that way. When George Young talked to big-money-seeking agents on the phone, he told them, in general, "Look, we've got a good chance to have another great year. Let's do it once more, then let's see about the contract." Most agents respected Young. Jack Mills, who had Pro Bowl tight end Mark Bavaro, knew the player was due for a huge raise over his $160,000 salary in 1987, but Bavaro figured he'd play for it, then go for the big deal in 1988. So the agents cooperated, and only Reasons, who was unsigned, stayed out of camp once the preseason games started in mid-August.

The Giants were disgusted with Reasons, an average inside linebacker who they wanted to pay like an average inside linebacker—at the rate of about $300,000 a year. Reasons pointed to all the guys in the league and on the Giants he was more valuable than, and he brought out all the financial figures of these other guys, and he told his story to the press, and . . .

Parcells called Reasons, home in Houston, on the phone one day.

"If you compare yourself to other people in this world salary-wise, you're never going to be happy," Parcells told Reasons. "If you test the market, and you misjudge your worth, it can cost you a lot of money."

The players didn't sit back and reminisce about the good old days of six

months earlier. This wasn't an emotional team, really. Even when they won
the NFC championship at Giants Stadium the previous January, the Giants
did some high-fiving in the locker room afterward but no screaming or boast-
ing. In many ways, the Giants were still a team with something to prove.
Two seasons ago, they'd lost in the playoffs 21–0 at Chicago. The previous
year, most football people thought the Giants and Bears were the two best
teams in the game, and when the Bears were upset by Washington in the
playoffs, the Chicago–New York game everyone wanted to see didn't happen.
Now it would, though. The Bears and Giants would open the season September
14 in Chicago in what the news media was calling Super Bowl XXI½.

"We feel it," Oates said. "There's probably a lot of people who still think
the Bears are better than we are. We have something legitimate to prove."

They beat the Patriots in the first preseason game, at New England in 115-
degree heat on the AstroTurf. The score was 19–17. Nelson played a few
plays at right tackle, but he had no strength in his left shoulder to speak of.
"I can't push anybody," he told Hoaglin dispiritedly after the game.

Three days later, he checked into New York Hospital–Cornell Medical
Center for exhaustive tests on what the Giants thought was an arthritic
shoulder. The CAT scan showed a quarter-sized lump in the chest. The next
day, doctors did a biopsy of the lump. The next day, Nelson was told the
mass was malignant. Nelson had Hodgkin's disease, a cancer of the lymphatic
system. He would undergo forty-three radiation treatments well into the fall,
and he would miss the season. Doctors were confident he would live.

"Thank God he had the shoulder injury," was George Young's first thought.
"We might never have found it."

The news was devastating to Nelson's family, obviously. But he tried to
deflect the concern. If this ordeal proved one thing, it proved that Karl Nelson
was a brave person. Godfrey, one of his closest friends, said later in the ordeal,
"The amazing thing is, with all he had to lose, Karl never once has said,
'Why me?' " Parcells called Nelson daily during his early hospitalization, and
he once asked Nelson how he expected the Giants to block Cleveland defensive
end Reggie Camp in the next preseason game.

Nelson, laying in his hospital bed, said simply, "Bill, you've got to find
a way to get it done."

In more ways than one. There would be conflicting views of how much
this news and this loss affected the team as the year went on. Young said,
"The Nelson sickness is much more hurtful psychologically to the team than
anything else. It puts the players face-to-face with their own mortality."

"Then," Billy Ard said, "you've got to get prepared to play a game and a
season. It's tough."

It was a huge blow to the running game, and a huge mental blow to
Nelson's friends on the offensive line, and a scary thing for the players, who
had to roll around at the Meadowlands complex where the Giants worked
during the season. "This scares the hell out of me," linebacker Harry Carson
said of the wild rumors about a Meadowlands-cancer link.

The Giants and Meadowlands rushed in to assure players that they'd investigate the area fully for any link, but it seemed highly unlikely. The four cases of cancer, team surgeon Russell Warren said, were not similar. Still, the players thought about it, and you can't stop people from thinking what they're going to think. When the writers were doing their preseason previews on the Giants, most mentioned the Nelson/cancer-scare factor. Or, as defensive coordinator Bill Belichick called it, "the Meadowlands cancer thing."

It was at this placid point that the Giants broke camp. Now the players would live at home and practice at Giants Stadium daily until the start of the season.

On the day they broke camp, Parcells was in a sour mood. They had beaten Cleveland in the second preseason game 24–10 amidst the turmoil, but it hadn't improved his mood much. Writers asked him how he would assess his team after training camp, and he said, "We stink. Have you watched us? We stink."

Really, at this point, with the Taylor thing and the Nelson thing and the Benson thing and the Reasons thing and the strike thing, it didn't matter how many commercials anybody had made in the off-season or how many subtle divisive rips were in the pages of all those books. This was a team in trouble.

An hour after he said his team stunk, Parcells was at the wheel of the black Mercedes sedan he got to drive for free for doing an ad for the Mercedes dealership in Manhattan. He eased the car down the Saw Mill River Parkway south of Pleasantville, then onto I-287 over the Tappan Zee Bridge into New Jersey, then onto the Garden State Parkway toward Giants Stadium. It was a forty-five-minute trip normally, an hour on this day with all the back-to-school shopping traffic.

Parcells listened for a while to the Bee Gees sing about how they could mend a broken heart. Then he assessed his team. He said the Giants were fair.

"Fair?" he was asked.

"Fair," he said. "I don't think we'll probably be as good on the offensive line as we were last year, which is a big item, probably bigger than all the others."

Parcells had decided to put William Roberts in Nelson's spot at right tackle, which was a bit of a problem because Roberts, through college and professional football, had been strictly a left tackle. The solidity of the offensive line, with Benson's legs bothering him more and more and with Bavaro's foot continuing to nag at him, was a very large question mark. Parcells knew that outsiders had no idea about the importance of continuity on the offensive line. But for two years, the lineup, from left to right on the line, of Benson, Ard, Oates, Chris Godfrey, Nelson, and Bavaro had started thirty-five or thirty-seven games together. "You get to know exactly what the guy next to you's going to do," Ard said. "You know what play he might not be as good at, and you know what you might have to do on that play to compensate for him. With a different guy next to you, you lose that. It's a huge factor."

Parcells worried about the defensive backfield, which was the perennial weakness of his team. He had hoped second-year safety Greg Lasker would play well enough to win a starting job, but he played as if he weren't thinking and was occasionally out of position. Free safety Terry Kinard, coming back from knee surgery, wasn't playing well. Parcells had decided to replace the erratic-behaving Elvis Patterson at starting left corner with second-year player Mark Collins, and there was a transition there, and there could be more, because right corner Perry Williams was having neck problems.

By the time Parcells wheeled into the Giants Stadium parking lot, the sun was going down over the west side of the stadium. He started down the ramp into the stadium, where, in the inner concourse of the bowels of the place, he parked his car about three hundred and twenty days a year.

A bright splash of late-afternoon, late-summer sun burst into the car as he turned toward his parking space.

"What is the one thing, above everything else, that concerns you most about this team right now?" he was asked just as the sun hit his face.

"Whether we still want it," Bill Parcells said.

Foresight:
March 1988, Arizona Biltmore Hotel, Phoenix, annual NFL winter meetings.

Parcells is relaxing one morning in the 78-degree sun, eating some breakfast out in the courtyard of this marvelously constructed and laid-out oasis. He is quite brown. His eyes are not bloodshot. He is taking it easy.

His breakfast companion says, "When did you know something was wrong last season?"

He jumps on the question, as though he's rehearsed it, or as though he's been asked it privately by some of the other coaches or owners and reeled off the answer almost without thinking.

"Here's what happened. I'm sitting there at the end of training camp last year, and I know—I know—things are not right. It's a sense a coach has watching his team function. Everyone—press, players, everyone—is talking about, 'Well, if you can just pick up where you left off . . .' First of all, that's impossible. You can't pick up where you left off. It's a new deal. It's new circumstances. It's new players. You know what happens? When you win, like at the end of 'eighty-six, I'm standing around during warmups before the game and I don't care what it is—playoff games, regular-season games—I know that somehow we're going to win. Now, this year, you get the reverse circumstances, the reverse thought. Nobody else knows this, but the coach knows this. You start wondering if you can win a certain game."

──14──

That Toddlin' Town

September 1987
Chicago

In the week before the opening game of the season, a temper or two was frayed. At Pittsburgh in the final preseason game, the Giants barely win 26–20, and the first question to Parcells after the game was, "In light of the Steelers playing you so tough tonight, how tough will it be for you to repeat?"

"I'm tired of answering that question," he snarled. "I'm trying to get this team ready to play next week."

"We'll have to play nine thousand times better than this to beat Chicago," Jim Burt said.

The locker room was businesslike but sullen. It was as though the players knew, finally, that the Super Bowl meant nothing to them now, that the Steelers, getting more and more bravado in them as the game went on, were a mediocre team that got fired up to play the Super Bowl champions and really should have won the game. In a quiet corner of the locker room, with the equipment guys silently loading up the club's gear around him, receivers coach Pat Hodgson marveled at the Steelers' play. "Did you see how hard they kept coming at us? What intensity. We'd better expect that this year. We've got twenty-seven other teams in the league who want to kill us," Hodgson said.

On the plane ride back to New Jersey after the game, Parcells thought of his theme for the week. He decided to sell the players on the Bears game as one-sixteenth of the season. The season is a marathon, not a sprint, he'd tell the players. Don't make this a megagame, he'd tell them. And don't say anything stupid in the papers, he'd tell them.

Parcells also had to cut the roster down to the league-required forty-five players, which he did on Monday without surprises, and he had to look for another cornerback to replace the injured Williams, which he did without success, and he had to deal with the flood of reporters and cameras hyping the nationally televised Bears-Giants game, which he did without blinking. (Example: Fifty-three media folk were at the stadium before Wednesday's practice. One writer asked, "With six running backs and two corners on the

73

roster right now, is it possible that—" Parcells cut him off. "Good question. I don't know," he said.) And after Wednesday's practice, he had to scream at the players, using his best expletives, because he didn't think they were working hard enough. He noticed, as did the writers, that several players were half-jogging through postpractice wind sprints. One of those players was Patterson, the cornerback who would have to play right corner because Perry Williams was out for at least four weeks with the neck injury.

But the players were mouthing Parcells's season-is-a-marathon-and-not-a-sprint theme consistently in the press and believing it, and by the time the plane left for Chicago Sunday, Parcells thought his team had a pretty good chance of beating the big, bad Bears.

He didn't count on one of the most important players in the Giants' game plan drinking himself sick the night before the game.

When the Giants arrived at the downtown Marriott in Chicago on Sunday, September 13, they had about five hours free before a team meeting that evening. Patterson, one of two healthy cornerbacks on the team, went out and got himself roaring drunk. The Giants wouldn't say—they haven't said to this day—but a couple of people in team management said they'd spent quite a lot of club owners Wellington Mara and Tim Mara's money counseling Patterson on past personal problems, and that Parcells had reached very close to the end of his rope with Patterson as this season began.

Well, Patterson missed the team meeting that night. The Giants dispatched his roommate, linebacker Andy Headen, and special-teams coach Romeo Crennel to find Patterson. Headen opened the door with his key. The first thing they noticed was the smell. There was vomit in the room. They found Patterson in the room. They judged him to be bombed out of his skull. Patterson was quite ill.

The Giants checked into it and found that Patterson visited a tavern as soon as the team checked into the hotel. When confronted and asked how he'd gotten himself into this condition, he said, "I must have ate some bad chicken."

Yeah. That's the ticket. Some bad chicken.

Understand the significance of this. Patterson and Collins were the only two cornerbacks the Giants employed. The Giants had one of the two or three best defenses against the run in the National Football League. The Bears, though they would be starting backup quarterback Mike Tomczak because of an injury to Jim McMahon, were certain to try to beat the Giants by throwing the ball on them. So now the Giants were going to war with the Bears with one healthy cornerback and one hungover one.

The Giants knew about the Patterson episode and the cornerback quandary, but the outside world didn't. They kept it that way. The morning of the game, Parcells was particularly quiet as he sat in the hotel lobby, as is his morning-of-the-game custom, smoking his Marlboros and drinking his coffee, as are also his customs. He checked out the back page of the *Sun-Times*, which had Ditka chewing on a Macanudo Vintage cigar, curling a dumbbell in his right hand and winking at the camera. It was 6:15 A.M., and the janitor had just finished vacuuming a corner of the lobby.

Coffee, regular. Cigarette, small talk. Cigarette. Cigarette. Autograph to a New Jerseyan. Another coffee. Cigarette. Cigarette. Parcells wasn't saying much.

In a sweatshirt, khaki pants, sneakers, and his usual worried look, he looked up through the cigarette smoke at one point and said quietly, "This is going to be a tough one, boy."

The game was an unmitigated disaster.

It was 67° and clear at gametime, a lovely late-summer night on the western shore of Lake Michigan. Outside archaic Soldier Field on Chicago's near south side, two tickets together on the 30- or 40-yard line were going for $400 a pair. The crowd was quite loud. And were the Bears ever into it! Mike Singletary, the middle linebacker, pounded his mates into oblivion, swatting them on the helmets, backs, and rumps throughout pregame warm-ups. On their side of the field, the Giants, dressed in their visiting white jerseys, were quiet and businesslike, their usual behavior before a game.

The Giants took the ball first and moved efficiently to the Chicago 10-yard line, where Phil Simms was sacked by Bear Todd Bell and fumbled. Chicago recovered. Three plays later, the Giants blocked a punt and scored the first touchdown of the season, safety Tom Flynn recovering the ball in the Chicago end zone. The game was pretty even for the rest of the first half, but there were two alarming things happening to the Giants: Tomczak was getting plenty of time to throw, and he was challenging the Giants on every series; and the Giants couldn't keep Phil Simms from getting beat up. The retooled offensive line, with Roberts in Nelson's spot, couldn't stop the vaunted Bears pass rush from belting Simms once or twice every series.

"We're going at them deep," Ditka told his staff at halftime.

The Bears broke it open in the third quarter, Tomczak hitting two long touchdown passes on successive Chicago plays. The first one made the score 17–7, and the Giants were still in the game. But the second one ruined the game and one career. Patterson, in heat that was certainly not oppressive, kept coming out of the game complaining of leg cramps. But he went back in midway through the third quarter, lined up at right cornerback across from one of the game's fastest players, Willie Gault. The ball was at Chicago's 44. Gault blew past Patterson five yards beyond the line of scrimmage, and Tomczak rainbowed it down the left sideline. Gault had a five-yard lead on Patterson when he caught the ball, at the Giants' 10-yard line. Touchdown.

In the fourth quarter, with the Giants behind by 11 points, they punted to Bear Dennis McKinnon, who caught the ball at the Giants 6-yard line. He ran to the 25, where Giants Zeke Mowatt, Carl Banks, and Robbie Jones converged on him. They outweighed him 705 pounds to 185. McKinnon slipped through and ran for a touchdown.

Ball game. Chicago had 8 sacks of Simms in the game. The Giants had none of Tomczak. Chicago had 416 yards, the Giants 203. Joe Morris got a concussion. The Bears won 34—19.

Patterson (leg cramps, dehydration . . . hangover?) was busy in the locker room alibiing for the Gault play, but how could there be enough alibis to cover five coverage errors by him on Tomczak's twenty completions that night? The rest of the team was shaking the cobwebs out from what Parcells said was "the worst anyone's beaten in us in a long time." Kenny Hill said he felt as if he'd just been mugged.

No one wanted to say what everyone was thinking, that the Giants, despite the season-long marathon talk, had been harmed greatly by this loss. No one who'd just been through what the Giants had gone through on the plastic grass of Soldier Field could possibly have thought that the Giants were currently the best team in football anymore.

Suddenly, finally, the Super Bowl was a memory.

"That right there," said Johnny Parker, "was the harsh reality of winning it again slapping us in the face. It was like Cinderella going to the ball and having the time of her life, then waking up in rags."

When Elvis Patterson woke up the next day in his condo in Boonton, New Jersey, it was the Giants on the other end of the phone. Patterson, who started in the Super Bowl and even had an interception, was fired.

— 15 —

Strike Three

September 1987
East Rutherford, New Jersey

After the first hill of the marathon, the Giants were winded. But here was an aid station, just ahead. The Dallas Cowboys were coming to town, and the Giants were going to fly the 1986 NFL championship flag up the flagpole before the game, and the Cowboys were coming off a game they'd blown to the St. Louis Cardinals, and the Cowboys had the NFL's longest losing streak (6 games), and the Giants were favored by 12 points.

Yes, the Cowboys were awful. The Giants, stunning themselves into tears, were worse. The makeshift offensive line continued to let Simms get killed; Simms threw a career-high 4 interceptions. Joe Morris, who had averaged almost exactly 100 rushing yards per game in the previous two seasons, kept running into the backs of his linemen because there were no holes; he had 26 rushing yards. And the magic the Giants had in their Super Bowl season was gone, too. Their Mexican kicker, Raul Allegre, lined up to kick what would have been the winning field goal from 46 yards away with eleven seconds left in the game. He was confident, because he had made every one of his previous nine late-game winning field goals in his five-year career, and the conditions were calm enough on this one. He did what he always did, setting the kick up and then quickly saying the Lord's Prayer in Spanish. "Padre nuestro . . . ," he said to himself, beginning the prayer quietly. Then he looked up at somebody screaming. It was no. 50 for the Cowboys, Jeff Rohrer, and Rohrer was jumping up so Allegre would see him and screaming so Allegre would listen to him. "NO WAY NO WAY NEVER MAKE IT YOU'RE GONNA HOOK IT NO WAY NO WAY" is the blather that was coming out of Rohrer's mouth. Then center Bart Oates snapped the ball to holder Jeff Rutledge, a perfect snap and a perfect hold. And Allegre kicked it, and it looked good, looked good, started hooking left, hooked, hooked, hooked, and it passed the left upright in the end zone thirty-six inches to the left. Dallas won 16–14. The Giants were 0-2.

The Dallas locker room looked like a first-grade classroom on Christmas Eve. "This," said cornerback Everson Walls, "was our Super Bowl." Although teams throughout recent sports history had the same intensity against defending champs weekly, the knowledge of this didn't help the Giants now.

In the span of six days, the Giants had lost as many games as they did in all of 1986.

After the game, Carl Banks sat at his locker, in full uniform, quietly crying. Harry Carson and Lawrence Taylor held their heads and stared into their neighboring lockers. Father Moore, the team priest, walked around the room, consoling a few people. And Joe Morris was woozy again, from another concussion.

God, what a wake.

Billy Ard, always one of the realistic Giants, buttoned his flannel shirt, put on his old jeans, and was asked for some kind of explanation why the Giants were playing like . . . well, like nothing resembling a good team.

"Don't know," he said. "I'll tell you this. It doesn't feel like the old Giants to me. The old Giants would have put this game away in the third quarter."

He was asked where the old Giants were.

"Same place the old Packers are," he said.

Privately, what disturbed Simms was the fact that the offensive players seemed tentative, nervous. At the end of 1986, this was a consistently clicking offensive machine, the offensive line blowing defenses off the ball and Morris picking his holes and allowing the Giants to control the clock and win at will. In this game, another line cog, right guard Chris Godfrey, went down with strained knee ligaments, and Benson played with a sore knee. So by week two of the new season, this line that was solid for two solid years had lost Nelson to cancer and Godfrey to a knee injury, and Benson (hips, knee) and Bavaro (foot) were playing hurt. And why did they keep screwing up a play or two a game that cost them? Perfect example: Backup running back George Adams was in his third year but still making rookie mistakes. Against Dallas, on a pass pattern out of the backfield, Adams missed a sight-adjust. This is footballese for a running back not adjusting to the fact that a linebacker is blitzing the quarterback, and also not adjusting his pass pattern to the shorter, quicker route because of the blitz. Simms threw the ball where he was supposed to. Adams didn't sight-adjust. The ball landed eight yards from Adams. Simms stared at Adams. The crowd booed Simms, of course, because it looked as if he threw the pass while taking a nap.

It's debatable how much of football is mental, but the atmosphere around a winning team is so much different than the atmosphere around a losing one. There was a kind of a conservative swagger around the Giants late in 1986 that had vanished now. Late in 1986, before the NFC championship game, Simms sat by his locker late one day and said something flippant but something meaningful. "I don't care what Washington tries to do to us," he said, "because I know what we can do to them." And he knew that, if his passes were falling short or the wind was batting them down, he could count on the line and Morris controlling a game well enough for them to win. Now he knew no such thing. And he knew now that there was blood in the water around the Giants, that they were now thought of as eminently beatable around the NFL.

Some dynasty.

The players of the National Football League went on strike two days later.

This is what happened: The National Football League Players Association for years had pushed for free agency, the same kind of free agency that freed baseball players from their existing teams after six years. This year, when union officials went from club to club throughout football before the season, they asked the players what their number one bargaining priority was. The union came away from the meetings saying the players had told union leaders they wanted free agency foremost. So the union went out and tried to get free agency from the NFL, and the club owners told them to forget it because it would boost salaries so much. There were various unfair-bargaining practices, but the bottom line is that management wasn't going to give the players any major free-agency concessions, and the union was either afraid or unwilling to drop free agency as a major issue. In 1982, when the players struck for fifty-seven days, they asked management for 55 percent of all gross revenues of the game. Management wouldn't give it to them. Now, according to management figures, ownership was giving players 62 percent of the gross. A large amount of resentment and enmity had been built up toward management by the players already, which was natural. Players were, and are, followers. They'd done what coaches had told them to do all their lives, and now they were doing what their union leadership was telling them to do.

The Giants were quite a subservient strike team, at the start anyway. They trusted their player representative to the union, George Martin, who was a confidant of union executive director Gene Upshaw. They were poorly informed about the strike issues, though, and this would eventually embitter several players indelibly.

The football owners were more adamantly opposed to free agency than ever because of something that happened the day the strike was called. Arbitrator Thomas Roberts ruled the major-league baseball owners had acted in concert against the players for not negotiating seriously with free agents after the 1985 season. The fear now was that, if football gave in to free agency and some owners decided not to sign free agents out of principle, the owners could be accused of collusion.

So now, on September 22, when the strike became official, Giants management tried to round up enough semipro and recently out-of-college players to become the new defending Super Bowl champions as long as the strike lasted. The real Giants put on picket signs and did a halfhearted march around the stadium.

Phil Simms pulled up in his Jaguar and emerged wearing a sign reading: "On Strike to Honor a Commitment to NFL Players, Past, Present, and Future." When Minicams stayed with him as he walked, he was supremely embarrassed. He tried to shield his face from the cameras at one point. "Come on, get out of here. Really. Go find somebody else. Come on." The mood of the players was light, but deep down, as Hill said, it was ridiculous to think that the two sides couldn't have solved this thing. Most of the Giants couldn't care less about free agency. What they cared about were health benefits and the football pension plan. But as long as the union was sticking to its free-agency stand, these negotiations were going nowhere.

Giants president Wellington Mara watched his players picketing from his office windows and smiled a wry smile.

"My gut feeling," he said, sitting on a couch a few feet from his big windows, "is that it will be a long strike."

Down the hall, George Young fell into a stuffed chair in his office. He already looked tired of the strike, and this was only day one. "Why is it," Young said, "that the game has been around sixty-eight years and now that it's more lucrative than ever we're talking about freeing the slaves? We're producing good, close games. Are our players mistreated? No. I don't exactly identify professional athletes as Norma Rae. Hey, football is short. Life will be filled with these situations for the players for the rest of their lives. This is the best that life is right now."

Thirty-two of the fifty-two Giants under contract were making $200,000 or more per year.

Starting that week, the players would begin to lose one-sixteenth of their annual salaries. For the highest-paid Giant, Lawrence Taylor, this meant $56,250 in lost wages each week. For the lowest-paid Giant, tackle Doug Riesenberg, it meant a loss of $4,062.50 per week. (While about 85 percent of the team was consistently involved in informal workouts or team meetings during the strike, Taylor never was. Early in the strike, he told Martin he'd give him two weeks to get the thing solved. Then he was probably going to go back in and play with the strikers, so he wouldn't continue losing $56,250 a week.)

"I can't believe it's come to this," said Stacy Robinson, the wide receiver, who would lose $11,562.50 in the coming week.

Nobody could. The real players were trying to get used to the fact that their season could be over. On the first night of the strike, Harry Carson went home to his condo in Washington Township, a nice little New York bedroom community twenty minutes north of Giants Stadium. Carson was a thoughtful man of thirty-four, quite late in his pro football life. He had made the Pro Bowl eight times in his career. Someday he might be in the Hall of Fame. And now, all he could think of was whether his career might have ended in such a depressing way as the one he found himself in now. Which was to say, losing the first two games of a season and then sitting on the sidelines while replacements wearing Giants uniforms masqueraded as Giants.

On this night in Washington Township, New Jersey, Harry Carson ate his dinner and then put a tape into his VCR. It was a tape of the Giants' Super Bowl victory. Carson had never seen it before.

"I may have played my last football game," he thought to himself as the tape rolled.

──16──

At Quarterback for the Giants, Jim Crocicchia

September 1987
East Rutherford, New Jersey

This was a decision George Young would have to live with for the rest of this bastard season.

He, and the rest of the front office, would not pursue replacement players until there actually was a strike called. He figured privately: Why mess with our chemistry in the first couple of weeks of the season and risk alienating the players by showing them the Giants were planning for a strike all along? So after consultation with Parcells, who tacitly agreed, Young instructed that no action be taken until a strike was inevitable.

Meanwhile, around the league, many teams got head starts with the replacement players. By the time the Giants began calling players and asking them if they'd be willing to work for $3,125 a week—the NFL's minimum—four teams had already signed thirty or more players each. By the time assistant general manager Harry Hulmes, director of player personnel Tom Boisture, and director of pro personnel Tim Rooney began calling players, the list was thin. And grim. Plus, the teams in California, Texas, and Florida had a huge advantage over the northern and eastern teams, because there were so many players already in their backyards, naturally, and because players from local areas wouldn't necessarily have to quit full-time jobs the way they might if they were traveling across the country.

"It was almost a matter of necessity," Hulmes said, "to go to the minor leagues."

Yeccch. The minor leagues. Now, the minor leagues in pro football were not like the minor leagues in hockey or baseball or even basketball. The colleges were the minor leagues almost exclusively now for the NFL, and the minor leagues in football were the domain of guys who loved the game and couldn't get it out of their system, and who often played for nothing. Very occasionally an NFL scout would come. But the Giants, finding most of the prospects on any of their lists already signed, had to beat the bushes for bodies. They found some on the (East Haven) Connecticut Giants and the (New Brunswick) New Jersey Panthers. When two Giants assistant coaches, Ray

Handley and Mike Pope, showed up at a Panthers practice, they found a shoe
salesman and a forklift operator with some potential. In East Haven, the
Giants found fourteen Giants and had them bused to a hotel near the stadium
for indoctrination and physicals and team meetings. The Connecticut coach,
Jimmy Jackson, was running off the list of his players in the lobby of the
hotel on that day, a Thursday, and he temporarily forgot one. He thought
for a minute. "Yes! Royce Fontes! Wide receiver! This guy's got hands of
gold!" Jackson said.

At Giants Stadium, receptionist Colleen Radigan was being besieged by
guys off the street trying to be fake Giants. A high school player came with
his mother. A steelworker came from Long Island. Two guys came from south
Jersey, and frustrated because they couldn't talk to somebody who'd give them
a tryout, they went outside and found George Young's high-windowed office.
Young had his back to the window, as he always did when he worked at his
desk. The two guys started banging on the window.

"WE WANT A TRYOUT! HEY, LET US IN! WE WANT A TRYOUT!"
they yelled.

Young tried to wave them off.

"WE WANT A TRYOUT! HEY, LET US IN! WE WANT A TRYOUT!"
they yelled.

Young closed the curtain. He called security.

Back in the lobby, a professional wrestler from Canada, Steve Blackman,
told Radigan he'd driven all night from Canada to get a tryout. That didn't
matter, Radigan said. There wasn't an open tryout camp. Blackman, twenty-
three, weighed 265 pounds and looked as though he'd been lifting weights
since he was a fetus.

"I've come a long way," Blackman said insistently. "I want to see somebody."

"I could have saved you the trip," Radigan said, and refused him entry.

So Blackman went along the outside of the stadium, trying all the locked
gates to see if he could get in. He couldn't. So he got in his car. He said he
was going back to Canada.

They should have let him in, obviously. At least he looked something like
an athlete. What a scurvy-looking group of saps the Giants brought in to
help the Management Council break the strike. On their first day of practice
at Giants Stadium, Parcells stood in the end zone and watched his charges
do their wind sprints. A few fat blobs out there were really struggling, and
Parcells was alternately shaking his head and trying to suppress consistent
chuckles. "I believe there are a few guys out there who the Heisman voters
overlooked," he said.

On the replacement players' second full day of practice, the real Giants
worked out, too, on a grassy elementary school field in Harry Carson's town,
Washington Township. They couldn't work much, though. Somebody forgot
to bring the footballs. Afterward, Carson said solemnly, "The relationship
between players and management, and anyone who's perceived as being man-

agement—trainers, equipment people—is never going to be the same again."

These guys needed a good laugh. They felt powerless over the nonnego-tiations between players and management. They felt thousands of dollars slipping through their hands daily. They should have seen Torin Smith. That would have made them happy for a minute or two.

Torin Smith hadn't played football for over a year when the Giants called. He was working with emotionally disturbed kids in Florida, and his last football was played with the semipro Pensacola Stars the previous year. He was a defensive tackle, but he said he would play anywhere that the team needed him. He weighed 325 pounds. He was pleasant. He was Southern. He didn't move very quickly. So Torin Smith was beat after his first tough day of practice, and he went to the trainers and asked for some Ben-Gay, so his joints could get loose. The trainers had no Ben-Gay. Smith said he'd take anything hot. They gave him Atomic Balm, a superhot salve that loosens up muscles better than anything. He put it on, all over his legs and up into his groin. Nothing. He put on some more and went into a team meeting.

AAAAAAAAHHHHHHHH!

Torin Smith hopped up from his seat all of a sudden and asked if he could cool off in the shower. He was excused. He jogged into the locker room— *"Ooooohhhhahhhhhaaaahhhh"* was something like what was coming out of his mouth—and jumped in the shower. That only opened his pores more. The trainers, laughing, finally filled a bath with rubbing alcohol. Smith got in and got the stuff off.

That afternoon, the fake Giants gathered at midfield after their practice, put their hands in the middle of the group atop each other's, and said in unison, "One, two, three, GIANTS!"

"Golly!" one of the writers gushed in the end zone. "I hear Babs and Mindy are coming over with hot chocolate after practice, and then they're all going to the malt shoppe, and then all the guys are going over to Scooter's house to watch *Leave It to Beaver!*"

"It's like coaching the Bad News Bears," said defensive coordinator Bill Belichick.

The first game was against San Francisco, on Monday night football, on national TV.

Against the Phoney Niners, as the *New York Post* said.

Har har.

While the real Giants picketed outside, the fake Giants lost 41–21, with 16,471 people watching. Most of them were gone with the score 34–7 in the fourth quarter. Kevin Manahan of the *Star-Ledger* in Newark said, "Hey, I gotta leave early. I'm giving the crowd a ride home."

With a couple of minutes left, the ABC camera panned the Giants bench and found 300-pound defensive lineman Reggie "Cadillac" Carr asleep on the bench. Well, his eyes were closed and he wasn't moving. ABC focused on him for twelve seconds. He wasn't moving. Don't you think the nation had a good time with that?

Carr said after the game he hadn't been sleeping. "No, I wasn't dozing," he said seriously. "I was tired. In a way, I was tired of losing. But my coaches in the past have told me I should conserve my energy as much as possible during a game. I was conserving my energy out there on the bench."

Sure looked like he was sleeping.

Now the Giants were 0-3. And Bill Parcells was more fed up than he'd ever been as a coach, stretching way back to 1963 in Wichita, Kansas. He took a slap at George Young after the game, distancing himself from the horror that was his fake team. "I didn't have any control over the situation," he said brusquely. "I'm just playing with the hand that was dealt me."

That week was an interesting week in Parcells's life.

A couple of days after the game, he was lying in bed after the alarm rang, about 5:30 in the morning. Now, Parcells rarely was in bed when the alarm rang. He usually was dressed and ready for work by then, and out of the house by maybe 5:45 heading for his two coffee stops and then work. But this day, he lay awake, not getting up.

"You're not going, are you?" his wife, Judy, said.

"What?"

"You're not going to work," she said.

"Oh, I'm going."

He went, although he truly didn't want to go into this hopeless situation. When he pulled his car into his parking space at the stadium, he sat in the car for several minutes. He just didn't want to get out. Finally, as he knew he would, he got out and trudged up a flight of stairs to his office because the Maras were paying him to be a football coach, and he supposed that's what he should try to do at this point.

Later that week, one night, Judy Parcells said to her husband: Why don't you quit? We could go to Hilton Head and get a condo and live like normal people. Right, Parcells said. I'd enjoy that for about a day.

So he kept going to work.

In the second week of the strike games, the real Giants practicing every day near Carson's house dwindled to fifteen or so. Simms came with interesting news one day. Seems the Disney people liked his first commercial so much that they came to his house, set up a bunch of equipment on the front lawn, and had Simms, with son by his side, answer a question about what he's doing with his time now that he was on strike.

"I'm going to watch the Disney Sunday movie on ABC," he said, smiling into the camera.

Television industry sources say he got $75,000 for that sentence.

The fake Giants lost the next game, 38–12, to Washington. They were 0-4. After the game, Parcells was asked what it would take for the Giants to get back into playoff contention.

"Ha ha ha ha ha," Parcells said.

Guard Joe Dugan told one reporter, "I feel sorry for the coaches. I really do. They don't deserve this shit."

Then another reporter came, and Dugan said, "The guys I'm really sorriest for are the coaches."

Then a couple of other reporters came, and Dugan said, "I feel sorry for everyone involved."

Now the strike was close to being over, mostly because the players were cracking and more and more of them were trickling back to work. After the second replacement game, backup quarterbacks Jeff Hostetler and Jeff Rutledge, safety Adrian White, and Lawrence Taylor returned to the Giants in time to get paid for that week's game in Buffalo. The real Giants were bitter toward Taylor especially for breaking the strike because he didn't take part in any of the team's union activity while they were out. "If you follow Lawrence Taylor," linebacker Robbie Jones said, "you'll burn in hell." You would also have gotten paid that week.

The players agreed late in the week to return to work, but management locked them out of that week's games and mandated they come back the following Monday. So the real Giants watched the fake Giants, plus Taylor and his three real teammates, try to win in Buffalo so they would have some semblance of a chance at the playoffs when they reported back for the final ten weeks of the season.

Taylor, in the days leading up to the Buffalo game, had taken on the role of team player. He'd pull aside starstruck kids and tell them exactly what to do on every play. In the locker room after practice one day, a replacement player came up to him quietly and asked, "Would you mind me getting a picture of you and me together?" Taylor said sure. Several other replacements also had their picture taken with Taylor. And he good-naturedly was elected "scab player rep." President Wellington Mara genuinely appreciated Taylor's returning, and it would erase some of the hard feeling upper management had for Taylor because of his drug history.

Before the game, in the locker room in Buffalo, Taylor told Parcells, "I don't know if one person can win a game or make that big a difference, but I'm going to try to win this game for you today."

When the game was over, some of the Giants' brass, including Wellington Mara, thought it was Taylor's greatest game ever. It was also the strangest. Buffalo designed its offense to have two players blocking Taylor on every play, regardless of where he lined up on the field. The Bills were called for holding Taylor seven times. It was professional wrestling at its finest, with Taylor playing tag teams by himself all day. In the second quarter, Buffalo guard Joe Schulte kneed a stumbling Taylor in the face mask. In the third quarter, Taylor ran over Schulte when the play was on the other side of the field, and certain he was out of the officials' sights, he took his fist and drove it into Schulte's throat. "How do you like that, sucker?" Taylor said vindictively. But he's such a competitor on the field that in a perverse way he enjoyed the game. After the game, he went up to Schulte, who braced for a confrontation with him.

"Hey, you cheap bastard," Taylor said. "Good game."

Schulte was honored. "Thanks," he said. "It was a pleasure to play against you."

The game was scoreless for fifty minutes, a monument to offensive ineptitude. The Bills, in a 3–3 tie late in the fourth quarter, were trying to run out the clock to get the game to overtime. But Taylor, with twenty-four seconds left in the game, forced Buffalo back Carl Byrum to fumble at the Bills' 23-yard line. Parcells wanted desperately to win this game, right now. So for the first time ever, he decided to put Taylor in on offense. To the wonderment of everyone in the stadium, Taylor lined up as a tight end, and Rutledge, the quarterback, sent him deep, toward the end zone, on first down.

He was open, too.

But the player everyone in the Giants locker room had spent a couple of weeks looking at in fascination, Kaulana Park, ran the wrong pattern on the play. Park, a Hawaiian running back, wore a wraparound skirt to the stadium every day, prompting stares and some catcalls. One of Rutledge's favorite stories after the strike was about Park. "I look over in a team meeting one day, and I see this guy in a skirt. I say, 'Hey, we've got a guy on this team who wears a skirt!' "

And now Kaulana Park, out of his skirt for the game, was going to lose a game for the Giants.

Rutledge spied Taylor open near the Buffalo 10-yard line and let fly a pass. It looked as if Taylor were going to be an offensive hero and the lead to an incredible story, and the Giants' traveling party rose as one up in the press box, anticipating this great event, BUT WHAT IN HELL WAS KAULANA PARK DOING COMING INTO THE PICTURE AND GET THAT HAND DOWN KAULANA PARK YOU IDIOT GET IT DOWN, and then the pass bounced off Kaulana Park's fingertips and an agonized Taylor put his hands to his face, the ball bounded away from him, his chance at winning a game on the first offensive play of his life ruined.

"I WAS WIDE OPEN!" Taylor screamed.

The kicker, George Benyola, lined up to kick a 40-yard field goal that would have won the game for the Giants. It looked perfect. Even Parcells, the stone-faced one, raised his arms in anticipatory triumph, grinning a wide grin.

The kick knuckled to the left. It was wide to the left by about eighteen inches.

The Giants lost in overtime 6–3.

The Giants were 0-5.

They were less than two yards left of a goalpost—remember Allegre's miss against Dallas by thirty-six inches—from being 2-3 and having a pretty fair chance at the playoffs with the real players coming back.

Not only were they bad. They were unlucky. Bad and unlucky teams don't have much of a chance to win much of anything in sports these days.

┌─── 17 ───┐

Playing Out the String

October 1987
East Rutherford, New Jersey

It was nearly hopeless. The real Giants had to go 9-1 in the season's last ten weeks. "One bad play," Simms said, "and we're looking at our season going down the toilet."

"We're not in a hole," Harry Carson said. "We're in a canyon. And people are throwing dirt on top of us."

The real Giants faced this message from a grim Parcells when they returned: You guys got us into this hole. You guys went 0-2. You guys get us out of it. Indirectly, he threatened some jobs. He said he was averse to cleaning out his team, the way he did after the 3-12-1 season of 1983, when he changed twenty-three faces on the roster the next season. That was the extent of his message. Other than that, he stayed bitterly quiet with his team, even after the Giants played well in the first poststrike game, a 30–7 win over St. Louis.

Jim Burt, at his locker after the game, marveled in an atypically soft postwin voice at Parcells's behavior. "It's weird, very weird. And I don't think it's a good thing at all, treating us like this after a win. It's like the twilight zone."

"I can see why he's having an anxiety attack," said club vice president Tim Mara, a Parcells confidant. "We're all but dead. It'll take a miracle to keep us alive."

The plug was pulled the next week, at Dallas. The Giants lost 33–24 in what was the strangest, most bitter game of the five-year Parcells era. Dallas scored 19 points in the final ten minutes, helped, incredibly, by four New York turnovers in a nine-minute stretch. And Simms was hurt. He sprained his left knee in the fourth quarter, and he would miss three weeks. Usually after games, the Giants go down to one knee and say the Lord's Prayer, then listen to Parcells address the team. This time, the Giants said the Lord's Prayer. Parcells couldn't bring himself to say anything. And Carl Banks was in such anguish that he'd begin a sentence and end it nonsensically, as if he were in true shock. Like: "This is just utter disbelief GOTTA BE KIDDING ME!"

Here's what happened: The Giants were ahead 24–17, at their own 28, with nine minutes left. Simms dropped back, saw Bavaro wide open 30 yards downfield, and let a pass go for him. Six-nine Ed Jones reached up a big paw and batted the pass away, into the hands of Dallas end Jim Jeffcoat. Jeffcoat scored. "I thought we'd be going up 31–17 right then," Simms said. "Instead it's 24-24."

On the Giants' next series, Joe Morris lost five yards, Brad Benson was called for a false start, Benson was called for another false start, and Simms was sacked back to his own 2-yard line. The Giants punted. Dallas kicked a field goal to go up 27–24.

Giant Lee Rouson fumbled the kickoff. Dallas kicked another field goal to go up 30–24.

The Giants didn't fumble the kickoff. On first down, Simms was sandwiched as he threw, hurting his knee. The ball was deflected—again—by Jones, and landed in the hands of defensive tackle Randy White. But wait. Dallas running back Herschel Walker fumbled on first down, and the Giants recovered. With 2:28 left in the game, they could still win.

On the third play, Jeff Rutledge was sacked by this Jones superman and fumbled. Dallas recovered. Dallas kicked another field goal to go up 33–24. (Jones, thirty-six years old, had five sacks in 1986. He had four in this game.)

Ball game. Season.

Kenny Hill said the Giants "panicked and choked," divisive words in any locker room. Banks said, "I feel like sticking my finger down my throat and throwing up."

One win, six losses.

It was as if the towel was being wadded up, ready to be thrown in the ring. The Giants' charter arrived back in Newark at 5:00 A.M. Invariably after Monday night road games, Parcells and his staff go directly from the plane to their offices, catch an hour or so of sleep, then begin breaking down the films for the next game.

On this night, Parcells told the coaches to go home. He called a meeting for 1:00 P.M. Parcells went home, too. He couldn't bear the thought of going to work right then.

─18─

The End

November 1987
New Orleans, Louisiana

Giants at New Orleans, November 22, playoffs still a mathematical possibility. Giants ball, Saints 21-yard line, fifty-six seconds left in the first half. Saints winning 10–7.

Quarterback Jeff Rutledge, still playing for the injured Simms, went back to throw, and he saw veteran running back Ottis Anderson free at the New Orleans 13-yard line. If he catches the ball, maybe he scores. Maybe he gives the Giants a first down at the 5 or the 3 or the 1. Rutledge throws. Perfect throw. Right in Anderson's hands, in stride, at about the 6.

It bounced off Anderson's hands into New Orleans safety Brett Maxie's. The Saints drove for a late field goal. The Saints won 23–14.

"Freak thing," said Rutledge. "It went right through Ottis's hands."

"I couldn't believe it," Anderson said. "I never drop that ball. Ever. That just doesn't happen."

In Washington the next week, the Giants led by 16 points with seventeen minutes to go. The Redskins won 23–19. After the game, running back Tony Galbreath said, "This is one of those damn years you don't even want to think about."

The Giants finished the season 6-9.

Ice Castles

—19—

The Test

March 1988
Toronto, Ontario

The road trip was not going well for the Edmonton Oilers.

It started in Minnesota, where the Oilers led the North Stars, one of the worst teams in the league, by 5–1 but settled for a 5–5 tie. Then, in Detroit, Edmonton played well and won 3–1. Two nights later, in Madison Square Garden, the Oilers showed up in uniform only, giving up five first-period goals and sleepwalking to a 6–1 loss. Predictably, two nights later on Long Island, Edmonton continued the slide to the strong Islanders, losing 5–3. "They don't look like the same confident team to me," Islanders goaltender Kelly Hrudey had said. Now they came to Toronto, to the venerable Maple Leaf Gardens, to play the worst team in the National Hockey League, and they were in a funk. They were in cruise control, a week before the playoffs were to begin. They were coasting. The Edmonton Oilers, the best collection of skaters and scorers on one team in the world, were, in the eyes of their coach/general manager/president, Glen Sather, a self-satisfied team. Sather honestly didn't know if his guys had it in them to drive for another Stanley Cup.

Understand that Canada, the entire country, did not take well to this. The Oilers had won the Stanley Cup, given to the National Hockey League's annual champion, in three of the previous four seasons, losing only when one of their own defensemen shot the puck mistakenly into his own net in 1986 to lose a playoff series to Calgary. As in other sports and other walks of life, not everyone loved the winners. The Oilers won so much, and people like to see winners fall. The Oilers, in Canada in the late 1980s, were like baseball's Yankees, football's Cowboys, big business's Trump. Love 'em or hate 'em, but feel something.

So when the Oilers came to Toronto on this springlike Monday in late March, in something like disarray, they did not come into a vacuum. The Oilers arrived at Maple Leaf Gardens that morning for their morning skate —an informal thirty-minute loosening-up time on the ice done before every game—and forty visitors waited outside their locker room. Most were TV, radio, and newspaper reporters and cameramen. Some were agents. Some were salesmen for hockey equipment used by the team. "We're never here," one of the TV guys said, "except when Edmonton and Montreal are in town." (The Montreal Canadiens have won twenty-three Stanley Cups.) Toronto is the hub of Canadian journalism, so the scrutiny was expected by the team. The team's—and sport's—biggest star, Wayne Gretzky, did six separate interviews when he came off the ice, all the questioners wondering if the Oilers could rebound and repeat as champions, though they would have to beat the team, Calgary, that passed them in the standings this year. Gretzky said diplomatically each time the question was asked that he didn't know, that the team would have to reach within itself to find the resources to win, and so on. He was quite good at the sporting clichés by now, after nine seasons of being the most interviewed player in the sport.

But the intense man named Sather skipped the ritual of questions. He escaped out a side door.

Sather, though, couldn't escape the nagging doubts he felt about this team, a team he seriously felt was in trouble. He was forty-two, quite handsome, with straight dirty-blond hair parted in the middle, blue eyes, and the same build over the five-foot-ten-inch frame that he had for his years as a journeyman hockey player in the NHL. He had tailors in Edmonton and Toronto, and he put $600 suits over that frame for each game. He had a thing about clothes. He felt the Edmonton Oilers were world champions, and by golly they should look like world champions. The not-so-subtle message to team newcomers was that since sports was a business, they were businessmen and should dress like businessmen. Coats and ties were mandatory on road trips. When they assembled for their Stanley Cup championship team photo the previous season, Sather looked over the team like its den mother. "Marty, get that jersey up. The collar, get it up. Charlie, pull your T-shirt over . . ." He took the same pride in his work that he took in his appearance. Late in his playing career, he went to college during the day while he played hockey at night, majoring in child psychology, figuring he might need to understand the workings of the developing mind when he got into his next profession. He wanted very much to coach. After Sather's last playing stop in hockey, with the Edmonton Oilers of the World Hockey Association in 1977, team owner Peter Pock- lington hired him as the coach.

Sather in 1981 became the president and general manager as well as coach. If there was any decision to be made about the team, Sather wanted to make it. Early in this season, the Oilers had many contract holdouts, the most damaging one by defenseman Paul Coffey, who wanted to make as much money as any defenseman in the game. The Oilers offered him the equivalent of a minimum of $3.44 million over six years, but the deal included a $1.2- million apartment building in Edmonton that, if it appreciated in value as market trends forecast it would, would have made the contract worth more. Coffey could sell the building at any time; Pocklington guaranteed at least a

$1.2-million price if and when he sold. But Coffey kept balking at the deal. Sather very nearly traded him to the Rangers in a package for another offensive defenseman, James Patrick. He almost dealt him to Philadelphia and Detroit. But he made one last effort to try to salvage the contract because he loved Coffey the player so much. He skipped an early-season game to visit Coffey at his parents' home in Toronto. Sather wouldn't sweeten the deal, but he wanted to try to convince Coffey to return. "Paul, do you realize what you're doing?" Sather asked. Coffey said he did. "I don't like real estate," was Coffey's unwavering answer. Flustered and angered, Sather on November 24 traded Coffey to Pittsburgh, where he signed a less-lucrative contract with the Penguins than the one he'd been offered by Sather. Sather couldn't believe it.

"Money," he said after the Coffey affair, "ruins everything."

Sather was a cocky guy, and he was overbearing at times, and he was consumed with the competitiveness that drove him. But he had built one hell of a sports franchise from the ground up, and he was still a young man. What other new team in the recent history of sports won four league championships in its first nine years of existence? The man was a hockey genius.

So Glen Sather had a lot of experience delving into the minds of his veteran players, most of whom had been with the franchise for much of the eighties. Over lunch, he tried to put into words what was troubling him. "This team is acting like a self-satisfied team. When that happens, you're in trouble," Sather said.

Although the Maple Leafs entered the game with 20 wins in 77 games, the game took on a playoff air. Toronto still had a chance to make the NHL's silly playoff system—16 of 21 teams do—and the Gretzky Gang was making its final visit of the year to the Gardens. Interesting place, the Gardens. It looked like a warehouse. It looked nothing like Gardens. If you didn't know hockey, and you were walking down North Church Street north of Toronto's downtown one afternoon, you might think this tan-brick, five-story rectangular building was a huge storehouse for books or fabric or disposable diapers. But walk inside and hockey history came alive, with huge portraits of famous former Maple Leafs lining the walls of the main concourse of the place. The Maple Leafs, you are reminded, used to be good, which is why they still have a cadre of very loyal fans willing to pay $27 for rinkside seats to boo their team.

On this night, the $27 seats were quite marketable for the scalpers outside. The Oilers had lost some of their luster—Calgary had just clinched first place in the Smythe Division, ahead of Edmonton, and it was the first time in seven years the Oilers wouldn't win their division—but they were still the Oilers. A man, fortyish, with a leather jacket and jeans held court near the north side of the Gardens, looking for buyers for his two $27 seats.

Buyer: "How much you want for 'em?"
Scalper: "One-fifty apiece."
One hundred fifty dollars, he meant.

Buyer: "You're crazy. What do you think this is, a circus?"

That's how the night began for Edmonton, like a circus. The Maple Leafs, for two periods, outplayed the listless visitors. With Sather seething behind the bench, he watched the Oilers mount a four-minute spurt of good play in the second period, long enough to take a 3–2 lead. That was all the good he saw. For the rest of the first two periods, he watched an inferior Toronto team beat the Oilers to the puck and pepper young goalie Bill Ranford with 28 shots on their way to what Leafs coach John Brophy afterward would call the team's best game of the season. Edmonton trailed after two periods 4–3.

Sather did something between the second and third period that he knew might be a mistake. It might turn out to be a stupid thing, he knew. But he did it anyway. Sather made a serious threat to his players. He couldn't let what he was seeing—the best team in hockey letting the worst team in hockey control a game, in a shrine of hockey, in front of such serious hockey fans, with the playoffs a week away—go unnoticed.

"Playing like this in fucking Maple Leaf Gardens is a disgrace!" he screamed when the door to the Oilers locker room was closed. "If you don't come back and play good hockey in the third period, we'll practice twice a day, even on game days, until the day before we start the playoffs! I mean it!"

Win, or else.

Maybe fifteen or twenty times a year Sather had to scream at his players like this. But he knew doing it now was a risk. He was coaching a tired team, first of all. As defending champions of the league, the Oilers packed buildings from British Columbia to Boston, from Long Island to Los Angeles. "We never have a regular game. We're always somebody's biggest game of the year," Sather had acknowledged a few days earlier. "That can really wear on a team." The player the Oilers could least afford to lose, all-star goalie Grant Fuhr, was especially taxed. Usually the best goaltenders play in 65 to 80 percent of a team's games. Fuhr had played in 72 of the first 77. Later in this week he would set the all-time NHL standard for games played by a goalie in a season with 75. Fuhr had to play this many because Sather traded his reliable backup goalie, Andy Moog, to Boston after a protracted contract dispute in midseason, and Sather didn't trust Ranford, the new understudy, in important games yet. So here was Sather, threatening to burn out his team with the playoff opening game just days away. The players knew he was serious. They knew they would walk off a four-hour-twenty-minute plane flight the next day from Toronto to Edmonton onto a waiting bus, and they'd go straight from a five-game road trip to a brutal practice.

A couple of the players looked up from the floor at each other as if to say, "Is this guy nuts? We're losing this meaningless game on the road by one goal and he's reading us the riot act." From their perspective, it would be stupid to play with no-tomorrow, playoff-type verve a game in Toronto that meant nothing in the standings. And to make a threat like that . . . To be blunt, several players thought Sather was panicking.

Sather, when he made the threat, wondered to himself if he was doing the right thing. "You can only push the button so many times," he said later, explaining his motivational tactic. "You have to pick your spots. You have to be very careful not to lose guys, but you also have to know how far they can be pushed." This was one of the times he was pushing hard. He was Glen Sather, and he had to.

A couple of days earlier, in New York, he articulated what to him was the essence of this business, the business of trekking across North America winter after winter trying to win silver grail after silver grail. Someone said to him, "I know you're not happy with how your team is playing. But the NHL legislates equality with the draft system. Really, it's a wonder you've been able to be this good this long."

"Yeah," he snapped. "I know our record's great. I know we'll go down in history as a great team. But all of that is so meaningless now. If we just approach each game individually instead of thinking about what a great team we've put together and how much we've accomplished, we should win most of our games. We have better talent. Five, six, seven, eight years from now, our guys are going to wake up and look back on these years and say, 'Damn it, if I'd just done a little bit more. If I'd just played harder . . .' It's within their reach. They can be one of this sport's greatest champions. But they have to want to do it. I don't know if they do."

They did, if the third period of this game was evidence. Again and again they tested Toronto goalie Ken Wregget in the third period, and for sixteen minutes Wregget kept denying the Oilers. Finally, in the last four minutes, Wregget made one last incredible save on Finnish wing Esa Tikkanen, and Tikkanen, fellow Finn Jari Kurri, and the Great Gretzky scored. Edmonton won 6–4.

Saved from practice hell.

The locker room was no different than usual afterward. Players showered, grabbed light beers, and either dressed quickly to watch the Calgary–St. Louis game on the locker room TV or dressed slowly and talked in small groups. All the while, of course, negotiating their way around the media throng of twenty or so around Gretzky. This was a nightly thing in every city. Because Gretzky was so genuinely cooperative and willing to answer the last question every night—and because he quite possibly was the greatest hockey player ever—he got besieged, even after games he didn't influence. In Toronto's small locker room, getting around the Gretzky mob was something like getting around a pregnant lady in a broom closet.

Center Craig MacTavish tied his tie deliberately, surveying the scene. "Games like this in places like this are why it's so tough to repeat," he said. "When you have an offnight, you get your head handed to you. It's been a standing joke around our locker room for a while that we bring more teams out of slumps than any other team in professional sports. Teams can be in big slumps, but they play us, beat us, get some confidence, and sometimes turn their seasons around. That's what happened tonight, almost."

No one knew it that night in the humidity of Maple Leaf Gardens—how could anyone know how to read this team?—but Glen Sather would not scream at his team again all season. Literally. He would not raise his voice in prolonged anger again. He wouldn't have to. The Oilers were on the verge of greatness. Again.

—20—

Roots

The Edmonton Oilers became great for five very good reasons:

1. They had Wayne Gretzky for ten years.
2. They stole a very smart franchise-building plan from their neighbors in Winnipeg, the Jets, who had imitated the Europeans, and stuck to it throughout their first NHL decade.
3. They had three consecutive great drafts in their first three NHL seasons.
4. They had five of the best hockey players on the planet, and they weren't afraid to trade one or two to keep the team at a high level. When sporting economics forced them to trade one of them (defenseman Paul Coffey) in 1987, they acquired the NHL's second-leading goal-scorer in 1987–'88, Craig Simpson, and one of the brightest defense prospects in the sport, nineteen-year-old Chris Joseph.
5. They had Sather. And Sather had a much-needed free hand, because Pocklington left him alone.

The Oilers were members of the barnstorming World Hockey Association until the NHL took in four WHA teams, including Edmonton, in 1979. They were the only original WHA team never to win a league championship. But they were improving as the fledgling league died. Sather saw what Winnipeg coach and general manager Bobby Hull, the former NHL great, was doing with European talent, and he patterned his construction of the Oilers, in part, after Hull's job with the Jets. Winnipeg won three WHA titles under Hull.

"This is what we did in Winnipeg," Hull said over coffee the night the Oilers were in Toronto. He was a fan now, out of the sport, raising cattle in Ontario. Hull loved talking about the fingerprint he has left on hockey, the fingerprint copied in Edmonton.

"I wanted a team that could skate and wheel and pass and shoot like no other team. I wanted exciting hockey. I didn't want the real physical, close-checking two-to-one games. I wanted action.

"One day I got a phone call from our team doctor, Jerry Wilson, who was on sabbatical in Sweden. This was after the '72–'73 season. He calls me and says, 'You ought to see the players over here. There are some great, great skaters, just the kind of guys you want.' So I told Jerry, 'If they can skate at all and are good kids, get 'em over here.' They came over, these Swedes . . . Ulf Nilsson, Anders Hedberg, Lars-Erik Sjoberg. The first day I had them in training camp, I told them, 'Don't you guys change and try to adapt to our style of play. If anyone's going to change, it'll be us, adapting to you. That's how we'll win.'

"When I played in the fifties and sixties, it was a more methodical game. The good Boston teams of the sixties were totally different from today's hockey. They got six great big sons of bitches out there to bomb the puck in there and bang some bodies around and outmuscle people and try to score that way. I think we helped change that in Winnipeg. Our style was to create as many three-on-two and two-on-one situations with the opposition and try to outskate them and outmaneuver them and outscore them. Just throw the puck in there (to the opposing goal), beat people to it, and score. Edmonton is that team now. They've got such great skaters, such speed. You look at teams like the Soviets, like Edmonton, teams with speed that know how to execute their system. That's the key to hockey now. These are the kinds of teams everyone tries to be like now."

This was Sather's blueprint, but he needed financial backing to make it work. He got it from Pocklington, who made his money in meat-packing and real estate in Alberta. The Oilers floundered in the early years of the WHA, and by 1976 they were losing between $1 million and $1.5 million per year. Pocklington was a fan and nothing more until late in 1976, when —he swears this is a true story—he saw Oilers owner Nelson Skalbania dining at a downtown Edmonton steakhouse and on the spur of the moment, bought half the team. Pocklington walked to Skalbania's table, made some small talk, and with the knowledge that Skalbania was losing his shirt running the Oilers, said, "You'd better sell me half [of the team]. This sounds like fun." On a cocktail napkin, Pocklington scribbled a proposal to deal some of his prized private merchandise for a 50-percent share in the club: a 1928 Rolls-Royce touring car, the eight-carat diamond ring on his wife's right hand, and a collection of paintings valued at between $3 million and $4 million. Skalbania accepted. Pocklington emerged from the steak dinner owning half of a sports franchise.

He says his wife understood.

"She knows me, and she made out pretty well in the deal anyway," Pocklington said in his Edmonton office. "She got a better diamond from me, of course."

Pocklington bought Skalbania's half-share in early 1977 (Skalbania bought the Indianapolis Racers of the WHA with Pocklington's proceeds), and he handed all the hockey responsibility to Sather. "He [Sather] had an aggressiveness," Pocklington said. "You become what you think you'll become, and I knew he was bound for greatness." Pocklington's biggest contribution to the team—aside from bankrolling early losses—came in November 1978, when, with Sather trying to gather the European-type players Hull introduced to North America, the owner bought the best one. Skalbania, trying to get out of the doomed WHA with a profit, was having a fire sale on his Indianapolis players, and he had a seventeen-year-old, 160-pound kid named Wayne Gretzky who skated like the wind. Skalbania offered Gretzky to Winnipeg, because he was the Jets' kind of skater. Too slight, the Jets said; not interested. Pocklington was. Without consulting Sather, and not having much of a hockey background except as a leatherlung, Pocklington offered the Racers $250,000 in American money plus the title to a mortgage worth $500,000 on one of his Canadian buildings. Skalbania said yes. Pocklington took back the building and paid Skalbania in cash.

Armed with Gretzky, Sather started to go after the Winnipeg type of players as soon as the Oilers became an NHL expansion franchise in 1979. To understand what the Oilers faced to win, understand that first, as in all sports, champions and expansion teams have the most difficult time in acquiring great players. Champions do because of the draft in all sports, when the worst teams get the highest choices of the best available amateur players. Expansion teams do because they also get low draft picks plus only the leftovers on other teams. But the NHL made it harder on the four new teams (Edmonton, Hartford, Winnipeg, and Quebec) in 1979 by allowing them to protect only four of the players they brought from the WHA. Gretzky was the only one of consequence, as it turned out, that Edmonton protected.

But what a consequential player. The greatest players in the history of the sport played into their late thirties to put records out of reach. Gretzky, it would turn out, would be close to shattering all of their records at age twenty-eight, in 1989. Speed and vision made him so great. At six feet in height and 177 pounds in weight, he was a center who skated low to the ice but had sight lines of an Abdul-Jabbar. "What he sees on the ice when he starts a rush is what I see up in the press box," is how *Edmonton Journal* beat writer Jim Matheson describes the vision of Gretzky. His passing, thus, was pinpoint. He was as fast a young skater as Sather had ever seen. In the beginning, there was nothing else for the Oilers, so they knew they had to draft extraordinarily well to have any chance of being a good team early in their NHL life. To scout, Sather hired another former WHA executive, Barry Fraser. What a catch Fraser was.

Teams in hockey are happy if they can get one good player out of a draft each year. So it is with some amazement that the Oilers look back on their draft in the spring of 1979. Picking twenty-first out of twenty-one teams in the six-round draft, the Oilers picked three players who, over the next decade, made the all-star game a combined fourteen times. Three more mainstays came from the 1980 draft, and two from the draft in 1981.

Three drafts, eight important players. Put this three-year stroke of great fortune in perspective. In the next six drafts, the Oilers got exactly one player—Tikkanen, from Finland, in the fourth round of 1983—who was a valuable contributor to their Stanley Cup teams. Poor drafts? Yes. But hockey experts say that no team in the sport picked young talent as well as Edmonton did in 1979, 1980, and 1981. The odds caught up with them.

Defenseman Kevin Lowe, center Mark Messier, and right wing Glenn Anderson came in 1979. Coffey, Kurri, and Moog (in the seventh round) came in 1980. Fuhr and defenseman Steve Smith (in the sixth round) came in 1981. Sather wanted his scouts to look for very young, very fast skaters, and he didn't care where they looked.

They looked in America and found Messier, floundering in the World Hockey Association. Messier was only the forty-eighth overall pick in 1979 at age eighteen, because in fifty-two games the previous year in Cincinnati and Indianapolis he scored only one goal; Cincinnati left him unprotected, and Edmonton assistant coach Brian Watson told Sather, "The kid hasn't scratched the surface of his potential." Two years later, Messier scored 50 goals.

They looked in Europe and found Kurri, still available on the sixty-ninth pick of 1980. He was a prominent but not starry wing in the Finnish first division, but he had the skating ability the Oilers had to have. And the Oilers found a bonus when Kurri came: He could shoot the puck without controlling it on his stick, even after long passes. This is called one-timing, and what an asset it was. With Gretzky flying through center ice, he knew he could find Kurri even in a crowd and rely on his getting off a quality shot. In 1985, Kurri established the NHL record for goals by a right wing with 71.

They looked in Canada and found some significant free agents, players who had gone undrafted and seemingly unwanted by every team in the NHL. Randy Gregg and Charlie Huddy were the Oilers' No. 2 defense pairing, and both were free agents. Gregg signed while playing in Japan and studying to be a doctor in 1981; everyone was concerned that medicine was very high on his agenda and hockey very low, but he proved he could balance the two well. He became a full-time Oiler in the 1982–'83 season. In 1986, between periods of a game, he stitched up a teammate's wide gash because another physician couldn't be found. Huddy signed in 1979, and it took him four and a half years of seasoning to be of any value to the Oilers. But he was a regular on all four Stanley Cup champion teams of the mid-decade.

There were, of course, bad times with this young team. The Oilers lost eleven more games than they won in the 1979–'80 season, and they earned the sixteenth and final playoff spot; Philadelphia swept them three games to none in the playoffs. In 1980–'81, Edmonton lost six more than it won, qualifying as the fourteenth playoff team. "We were just kids," Gretzky said. "We were just happy to be in the NHL, playing against the best players in the world."

That changed in a remarkable 1981 playoff series. Canadiens and Canadians couldn't believe it, but the team with the league's fourteenth-best record, Edmonton, swept the team with the third-best record, Montreal, three to nothing in the first round of the playoffs. "Imagine the Celtics losing a playoff series to Cleveland, four games to none," said the most analytical of Oilers, Lowe. "That's what winning that series was like. The Canadiens were a national institution, and we were the young upstarts from the WHA. The country was shocked." The Islanders went on to eliminate Edmonton from the playoffs in the next series, but the message was sent: The Oilers were on the verge of greatness.

Fuhr arrived in the following draft, a startlingly high pick at number eight in the first round. Goalies rarely are high first-round picks, but the Oilers had allowed 327 goals the previous year, an average of four a game. No team had ever won a Stanley Cup in league history surrendering four goals a game. The need was dire. Fuhr filled it. He played forty-eight of Edmonton's eighty games in 1981–'82, and he gave up an average of 3.31 goals a game. Offensively, the Oilers scored 89 more goals than in 1980–'81. Gretzky, who turned twenty-one in midseason, scored 92, the most in the history of the league. Messier scored 50, Anderson 38, and Kurri 32. Edmonton finished with the second-best record in the league, but they were stunned in the first round of the playoffs by Los Angeles, one of the worst teams in the league. "Weak-kneed wimps," *Edmonton Sun* columnist Terry Jones called the Oilers, ripping them for not being able to win when they should.

The next regular season was a near-carbon of the previous one: 47 wins and 424 goals. The Oilers had their best postseason, beating Winnipeg in three straight in round one, Calgary in four of five games in round two, and Chicago in four straight in round three. In the Stanley Cup finals, the Islanders won their fourth consecutive Cup, beating the Oilers in four straight games. Sather was furious that the opportunity had slipped away, but now he knew at least the team had been close and knew what it took to win everything.

Now the team was intact. Now the team had the five world-class players —Gretzky, Kurri, Coffey, Messier, and Fuhr—playing together, clearly separating the Oilers from the rest of the league in sheer talent. Now the team needed to go to the next level, the level that separates the good teams from the great ones. Bill Parcells has this theory about team greatness in any sport. It arrives in stages, he thinks. Stage one: Talent is acquired. Stage two: Talent is nurtured, struggles. Stage three: Talent has some success, but when tested, fails. Stage four: Talent matures, fights off the toughest challenges, wins. Parcells used this analogy when speaking about the upstart 1987 New Orleans Saints, who won nine straight games before the playoffs. He didn't think they were ready to win a championship yet. They hadn't played a playoff game in their history. They weren't experienced. They lost their first playoff game, to Minnesota.

"There's a lot to that," Lowe said. He was sitting in an Edmonton restaurant, the 1988 playoffs a few days away. "You work hard for five, six, seven years, and you think you're ready to be a championship team. But there's so much to playoff experience that people don't realize. Very few teams can burst onto the scene and win it all their first year. You have to build to it."

The Oilers had acquired the talent from 1979 to 1981. They had nurtured the talent, losing with it for two seasons before beginning to win big. They had tasted success—beating Montreal in 1981, breezing through three playoff series in 1983—and still lost crushing series to Los Angeles in 1982 and the Islanders in 1983. In the 1983–'84 season, with the great Islanders aging, the Oilers were calendar young but playoff old. Their world-class players were all twenty-three or younger: Gretzky, Kurri, and Messier twenty-three, Coffey twenty-two, and Fuhr twenty-one. "Most of us on this team have been friends since we were teenagers," Gretzky said in retrospect. "We had a bond. I don't care what anyone on any other team says, we're the closest team in sports."

You could see it coming, and it came. The Oilers won 57 games and lost 18 heading into the 1984 playoffs. What an offensive machine, this speed-skating group of selfless players. No team in league history before or since can match its 446 goals scored—5.6 per game. Edmonton played nineteen playoff games that year, scoring 4 or more goals in fifteen of them, and won fifteen. The Oilers broke the Islanders' Stanley Cup streak, winning the championship series four games to one over New York.

"Our team was going to be great. We always knew that," Pocklington said. "We were full of players with a high self-concept, and our organization was, too. We got rid of the players who had a low self-concept or who thought Sather's approach was horseshit. I learned that from the Canadiens, that great self-esteem translates to great play."

Edmonton won just as decisively in 1984–'85, beating Philadelphia four games to one in the finals.

Edmonton lost in the second round of the 1986 playoffs to Calgary, when Smith shot the puck into his own net, off Fuhr's skate.

Edmonton won in 1987, steamrolling Los Angeles, Winnipeg, and Detroit before surviving a physical challenge from Philadelphia and winning the championship series, four games to three.

And none of their important players was anywhere near over the hill.

But some, Sather saw, were changing. Society—and greed, Sather thought—saw to that.

"I knew we were in trouble," Sather said, on the eve of Edmonton's try for its fourth cup in 1988, "the night we won the Cup last year. We come back into the locker room, and in the middle of everybody celebrating such a great moment, Paul Coffey is talking about how underpaid he is."

The nagging things kept nagging. As the playoffs approached, Sather kept getting annoyed by little things. When the Oilers returned home from Toronto and their road trip, he saw Messier that night—out with a stewardess he'd picked up from the Air Canada flight. "This is a night he should be getting some sleep, after such a long trip and with a game the next day," Sather groused. "Late in a season, a player's rest is crucial. That's what bothers me about Messier. A stiff prick has no conscience." He had been annoyed by the recent lackadaisical play of winger Marty McSorley—an important part of the team because he protected the Oilers' flashy players with his physical presence—and decided to bench him for the team's game with Minnesota exactly a week before the playoffs began. This, he knew, would send McSorley into a deep pout. But he had to send a message to the team: Screw up, sit down. Fuhr, the only hope at goalie, was playing poorly, and Sather had no alternative but to play him for all of the playoffs, with Moog gone. Against the Rangers and the Islanders, Fuhr was uncharacteristically beaten by long slap shots. "That never happens," Sather said. "Ever. He looked like a Pee Wee goalie." And Kurri wasn't scoring. His goal production had declined from 71 in 1984–'85 to 68 to 54—and he would finish with 43 this year. The thought of trading Kurri had crossed Sather's mind more than once.

With three games left until the playoffs, Sather was thinking: Maybe it has finally gotten to us. Maybe it's impossible in sports today to win title after title. But if we don't win this year, there will be some changes made. Big changes.

And he was thinking he might not coach anymore, after this season. Maybe he'd let John Muckler, his co-coach, try to motivate the most talented team in the league, because every mental game was gone from his bag of tricks. "After ten years, there are no more tricks. I've used them all."

"The game has changed," Sather said, falling into a cushy chair in a lounge adjacent to the Oilers' locker room. "It's not so much the players. It's the agents pushing the players. They push the price of players up by holding them out and demanding higher salaries. Then the owners' egos push the general managers to win. The general managers' egos push them to win, and to spend. They get hit by the pyramid effect—one guys signs a contract for $1 million, and the next guy wants $1.1 million. Most athletes come into the game with nothing, and they try to handle the big money, learn to adjust to it. They shoot for the championship, so they can make more money. What's left after that? What's the goal after that? None. There is none. So then you look out in the players' parking lot one day and suddenly there are no half-tons and four-wheel drives. There are Porsches, Mercedes, Saabs. You see the players with a higher lifestyle. Their American Express bill triples. It doesn't make 'em bad guys, but a lot of guys after playing for a while want to do other things. We signed Grant Fuhr to a big new contract this year, and what does he have left to play for? He won his Stanley Cup in February."

Actually, this season wore on Sather and his team as had no other in Oilers' history. He would have loved to use the you-can-be-a-part-of-history-by-continuing-to-win-Cups shtick when the players got to training camp, only there would have been very few there to hear it. Seven of their biggest stars cut their off-season by six weeks so they could play in the Canada Cup, a series of all-star games that match Canada's best players against the best from the Soviet Union, the United States, Sweden, Finland, and Czechoslovakia. The Canada Cup ended in a great triumph for the Canadians on September 15. They beat the Soviets, two games to one, in the exhilarating championship round, and all three games were decided by 6–5 scores, two in overtime. "The best hockey ever played," said Muckler, who was an assistant coach on Canada's team. Three nights later, Edmonton's preseason schedule of games began. Incredibly, stupidly, the Oilers played eleven exhibition games in seventeen nights, including what was the worst bit of scheduling anyone around the Oilers could ever remember: In nine nights, they would play seven games in seven different cities (Toronto, day off, Indianapolis, Bloomington, Minn., Chicago, day off, Houston, Dallas, Edmonton). The Oilers flew commercial. If you've never flown it, the Dallas–Edmonton air route isn't the most popular, or the one with the most flights.

The scheduling rankled the players, who thought training camp was a time to train and not a time to barnstorm North America. Repeating was hard enough, but Oilers management, which scheduled the games and profited from them, was making the task a marathon before the real season even started. "In the Canada Cup," Gretzky said, "you've got the best players in the world playing textbook hockey, playing the game the way it was meant to be played. Maybe it was the best hockey ever. I don't ever slack off. I put everything I can into every shift on the ice. But nine, ten, eleven days later, we're in Houston and Dallas playing exhibitions, and they're expecting to see the same hockey we played in the Canada Cup. Emotionally, you can't be at the same high. It's impossible. It was too much."

The schedule wasn't the big reason why the team was unhappy. The team that four months earlier won the Stanley Cup had what Los Angeles Lakers coach Pat Riley liked to call the disease of more. Win a lot, want a lot. Or want to go somewhere where you can make a lot. No position on the team was spared the contract and playing-time problem.

In goal, Moog held out of camp asking for a trade, deciding he didn't want to be Fuhr's backup any longer. To showcase himself to NHL scouts, Moog signed on with the Canadian Olympic team; with a vigorous pre-Olympic schedule, he wouldn't be able to play for the Oilers until at least March. On defense, perennial all-star Coffey was a holdout, stalwart Gregg chose to play for the Canadian Olympic team, and valuable late-season acquisition Reijo Ruotsalainen went home to a big Swedish contract. "I knew he'd be a problem," Sather said of Ruotsalainen. "He's like a prostitute." At forward, the number one line—Tikkanen, Gretzky, and Kurri—was intact, though Kurri was unhappy with his contract. The second line was in tatters. Messier and Anderson were holding out for better contracts, and left wing Kent Nilsson went to Italy for a big contract. Third-line wing Mike Krushelnyski was a holdout.

The real sporting world had found its way to Edmonton, a town of 532,000 four hundred miles north of western Montana. Edmonton was smaller than two cities in Ohio. But the hockey team playing in the modern barn northeast of town was very, very big.

Sather put out the brushfires as best he could. He mollified Messier, Anderson, Kurri, and Krushelnyski, none of whom missed regular-season time.

He renegotiated Fuhr's contract, for the second time in a year. (Fuhr, as happy-go-lucky as they come, had blown most of the money from previous contracts, and Sather tried to take him under his wing and protect him from himself. During the Stanley Cup final series against Philadelphia in 1987, Fuhr spent a free afternoon squeezing in two rounds of golf. Asked why he played thirty-six holes of golf in the middle of the Stanley Cup finals instead of resting, Fuhr said, "Because there wasn't time to play fifty-four.") Sather gave up on trying to satisfy Moog, deciding privately to trade him. He got role players to replace Ruotsalainen and Nilsson. He listened to offers for Coffey, hoping he could find some way to sign him.

Although he treated the players as professionals and was close to several, Sather was a cold and calculating man. This is a business, he figured, and the players treated it as much that way as management did. They withheld their services trying to get more money. They tried to get traded to places where they could make more money. So Sather had zero allegiance to his players, and allegiance only to the standings. A year earlier, he had traded the most loyal of Oilers, Lee Fogolin, to Buffalo, and he sent another team player, Dave Semenko, to Hartford. The moves had sent a chilling message to his players. Lowe said, "If Lee Fogolin can go, any of us could go." Fogolin did anything the organization asked for seven years, and suddenly he was gone. So bitter was Fogolin that he quit hockey before the 1987–'88 season, and though he lived in Edmonton, he didn't go near the Northlands Coliseum once all year. So be it, Sather thought. He didn't want the players to think him cold and unfeeling, but business was business.

This was a big, big reason why the Edmonton Oilers would be a good team for a long time.

"You can't fall in love with anybody," said Pocklington, the owner, in the downtown offices of his mini-empire. "That's something we believe in very strongly. You fall in love with somebody and you end up hanging on to him a year longer than you should have, and he has little trade value. A year earlier, you could have traded him for three players of value. Fans love to see you maintain loyalty to your players, no doubt about it. They want to see Gretzky here forever. People in Boston wanted to see Orr forever. But in order for any body to sustain life, it must renew itself, replenish itself, continuously. It's done in business, in sports, in any field. If you don't keep one eye on the future, eventually you'll fail."

What a chilling, portentious message that was, coming from Pocklington, who in five months would be the most unpopular man in Canada.

Sather's deals for Coffey and Moog showed, as Pocklington said, that he was one of the great trade negotiators in the game. Everyone in the league knew Sather had to deal both players, so he was at a bit of a disadvantage; it's always to a trading team's advantage if it doesn't have a gun to its head. Sather decided to take his time making both deals. This way, he figured, instead of making satisfactory deals at the beginning of the season and having an entire year to mix new players into the lineup, he'd wait as long as it took to get good deals. "In time," Pocklington said, "we had the Rangers, Detroit, Pittsburgh, Philadelphia, and other teams bidding for Coffey." Coffey was the game's premier offensive defenseman, meaning that he was a threat to score (he had 48 goals in the 1985–'86 season) while being a great pure defender as well. Sather liked the package Rangers general manager Phil Esposito put together involving Patrick, one of the four or five best offensive defenseman in the game. He was more tempted by the deal proposed by Philadelphia general manager Bobby Clarke that would have sent a pugnacious high-scorer (and don't underestimate the worth of that kind of player in the rough-and-tumble NHL), Rick Tocchet, to Edmonton. But Pittsburgh seemed the natural team for Sather to deal with. The Penguins had put their general manager, Eddie Johnston, in a win-or-else situation before the season, telling fans the club would refund $80 to each season-ticket holder if the traditionally disappointing Penguins didn't make the playoffs. As Johnston watched the bidding go higher for Coffey, he figured he had to get involved, to give his team a scoring complement to rising star center Mario Lemieux. He did not want to give up his second-best scorer, Simpson, and his best prospect, Joseph. Sather demanded both. The deal: Edmonton sent Coffey, journeyman winger Dave Hunter, and minor-league winger Wayne Van Dorp to Pittsburgh for Simpson, Joseph, and two role players—center Dave Hannan and defenseman Moe Mantha. Two months later he shipped Mantha to Minnesota for forward Keith Acton, who had scored 38 goals for Montreal a few seasons earlier and who would deflect in the winning goal against Boston in game one of the Stanley Cup finals in mid-May.

As the Calgary Winter Olympics neared completion, the Penguins, Los Angeles Kings, and Boston Bruins began bidding for Moog, and Sather had his choice of packages involving three young goalies—Pittsburgh's Steve Guenette, twenty-two, Los Angeles' Roland Melanson, twenty-six, and Boston's Bill Ranford, twenty-one. But Sather had been fishing with Boston general manager Harry Sinden in the summer of 1987, and he remembered Sinden saying how interested he was in Moog. Finally, in February, Sather called Sinden from Winnipeg and said, "The other deals are off. Give me your best offer for Moog." Sinden, most hockey people agree, overpaid for Moog in the end. The deal: Moog, twenty-eight, to Boston for Ranford and twenty-five-year-old winger Geoff Courtnall; Sinden would send another player to Sather after the season.

By the end of this season, Moog would again be a number two goalie, this time behind veteran Reggie Lemelin with Boston. Coffey and Hunter would be on their first team out of the playoffs in seven years, Pittsburgh losing out to New Jersey on the last day of the regular season. Coffey, often injured, scored only 15 goals in forty-six games with the Penguins. Hunter scored 14.

Simpson became the Kurri-type scorer Sather had sought for years as a second-line wing. Sather never worried about his first line of Gretzky, Kurri, and Tikkanen, who he knew would score. The Messier line, with Anderson on right wing, had need a big scorer on left wing, and Simpson provided it. He had thirteen more goals than any other Oiler, with fifty-six. Courtnall, a great open-ice skater who had been stifled by the small ice surface at the Boston Garden, became with the twenty-one-year-old Simpson the organization's best young scorers. Courtnall would finish this season with 36 goals, sixth on the team. Then there was the prospect of Joseph, immediately becoming the best prospect in the Oilers' farm system, a year or two away from being the Oilers' potential defensive anchor.

"Making deals like these," said Sather, in his cushy chair, "is the only way we can stay competitive in this league. The socialistic attitude you have in this sport—in all sports, really—drags down the good teams in an effort to make the poor teams better. After a while, you have to do things you really don't want to do to make sure your team doesn't fall apart. We may have to trade one or two more really good players in the near future, just so we can try to stay on top."

But this time was not a time for Sather to look at the future. Not yet. He was trying to figure a way to drag another Stanley Cup out of them.

"Maybe," he said, "we ask too much of players in all sports. Maybe our guys are burned out. Maybe we burned them out. The Canada Cup series, before the season . . . That's such an intense time, and we had so many of our key players involved in it. Every game we play is such a big game to the team we're playing; for eight years it's been that way. I look at them now, and I try to get them to respond, and they've got that faraway look. They're almost gaunt. Maybe they don't have it to give anymore."

On the same day Sather is sounding so morbidly realistic, Gretzky is upbeat. He was enthusiastic about talking about the dynasty issue, because he wanted to be on the team that left its imprint on sports history. Gretzky would have spent the plane trip from Toronto to Edmonton talking about it, but as is his custom, he turned white as a sheet during takeoff, dug his nails into the seat in front of him, tucked his head between his arms, and bordered on airsickness for four hours. No question, his teammates say. Gretz is the worst flyer in hockey. He'd have to go home to his Edmonton high-rise apartment to sleep off the tension that afternoon. He'd talk the next day, in the players-only lounge and workout room at Northlands Coliseum.

"It can be done," he began. "We can keep winning."

"Why?"

"One big reason," Gretzky said. "Management. We've got really good management. They won't let this team deteriorate. I can't understand why, but some teams in every pro sport seem to hire the wrong people all the time. Bosses are scared of their own jobs, I think, so they hire people who they know won't be good enough to take their job."

"Why, though? Then they'd just get fired."

"I don't know," Gretzky said. "But you see it happening all the time. You see the wrong people getting jobs. Look at the great teams. The Celtics hire the right people because Red Auerbach is smart. The Islanders became so great because Bill Torrey hired the right people. I also think we benefit by being in this market. We don't have all the distractions other teams have because we're so isolated. The negative side on that is the travel. It's unbelievable. After nine or ten years it really gets to you. Because of the geography of the league, if we were in New York, we'd play fifty-two of our [eighty] games within an hour's drive of our homes. Every division game is a bus ride away. Here, we play every other night, and because our division is so spread out, we're flying three, four hours on a lot of off days. You don't drive to Los Angeles."

"How about the fact that every game you play is a big game to the other team?"

"Every game is like a playoff game to the other team," Gretzky said. "We're the same as the Lakers, or the Bears. You think it's tougher for the Lakers to go into Cleveland and win, in front of nineteen thousand five hundred, than it is for Seattle to go in there with ten or twelve thousand? Overall, I think it makes you a better team. Look at the Yankees and Canadiens over the years. When they get into the playoffs, they're used to the pressure. In the end, you're better for it, but it doesn't make any game easy anymore."

"You're engaged now [to actress Janet Jones]. Is that going to change you as a player?"

"Over nine years, you change," Gretzky said, starting his second styrofoam cup of coffee. "I'd be a total degenerate if I didn't. When I came in this league, I was a green kid with a bunch of other green kids, thoroughly happy to be a pro hockey player. We had good times and bad times together. We had the job of beating the Canadiens three straight in 1981, survived the heartache of losing to Los Angeles the next year, and the bad feeling of losing in the finals to the Islanders the next year. Then we won. It's all a progression. Hey, things have changed since I've been a player. In 1978, you saw players who, for them, hockey was everything. It was their whole life. Now in the NHL, you see people planning for their future, taking courses in the off-season or working jobs they hope will turn into careers when they're finished playing. That's a good thing. For me, I'll be a little different now, getting married. I'll probably be in Los Angeles a little bit more. But no matter what happens to me, I'll spend time every year the rest of my life in Edmonton."

"Sather seems to be worried about the team's frame of mine. Are you?"

"Not at all. We want this one more than any other one," Gretzky said. "That's just the way it is. You think it's the greatest feeling in the world when you win it once, but then, the next year, you want it worse. We've talked about it recently, among us. We want to prove how good we are again. It's something we have in us."

That, plus talent.

—21—

The Last Hurrah?

June 1988
Edmonton, Alberta

The Edmonton Oilers finished their season with three wins and a tie in the last week of the regular season.

In a team meeting before the playoffs began, Sather told the team, "This is a once-in-a-lifetime chance. You can be thought of as one of the great teams of all time. Take advantage of it."

They beat Winnipeg, four games to one, in the first playoff series.

Next they played Calgary's Flames, the heirs apparent, apparently, to Edmonton's reign after having the best record in the league this season. "It's the most nervous I've ever been before a playoff series," Gretzky said. In game one in the best-of-seven series, Gretzky assisted on the winning goal and scored an insurance goal. In game two, he slapped the winning goal past Calgary goalie Mike Vernon in overtime. Edmonton swept the series, four games to none. "I don't think we got beat by the Edmonton Oilers," Calgary defenseman Paul Reinhart said. "We got beat by Wayne Gretzky. If we'd put Gretzky on our team, we'd have won it in four straight." Actually, Edmonton won because its four greatest players—Gretzky, Fuhr, Kurri, and Messier—played at their highest levels, and because the Oilers refused to let Calgary make this a boxing match of a series.

"We misjudged how we stood with them," said Calgary's Jim Peplinski. "I think it's because we have four NHL all-star players. They have four world-class players."

Next they beat a bruising and bruised Detroit team, four games to one.

Then they played Boston, which struggled to beat New Jersey in seven games to reach the Cup finals. The Bruins were a physical team, and they would have to beat up Edmonton to have a chance to win the series. League-wide, the Oilers were known as the team that could skate better than anyone, but the team that could be beaten up and taken off their game by lots of well-placed elbows and shoulders.

This would be the Cup the Oilers won defensively. All of Sather's fears were unfounded. This team back-checked and played consistent, unerring hockey. The Oilers were simply much, much better than Boston.

In game one, midseason acquisition Acton broke up a defensive game by beating Moog with the game-winner early in the third period. Oilers, 2–1. In game two, Edmonton's offense dominated, with Gretzky scoring the game-winner midway through the third. Oilers, 4–2. In game three, in Boston, Tikkanen scored three goals. Oilers, 6–3. In game four, a power failure at Boston Garden suspended the game, tied at 3, and forced the teams to play the game over in Edmonton two nights later. In the real game four, Tikkanen scored with the action ten seconds old, and the Gretzkys broke it open with three second-period goals. Oilers, 6–3.

For the first time, the Oilers won a cup with a defense as good as the offense. With Coffey, the offensive defenseman, gone, the Oilers' six regular defensemen became stricter at defense and left most of the offense to the forwards. The result: They surrendered an average of 2.94 goals in their eighteen playoff games, an Edmonton franchise playoff low. In a normal game, a team usually gets 24 to 30 shots in a game. Boston, game by game, had 14, 12, 29, and 19 shots.

"Hockey is like the Super Bowl," Messier said. "The team with the best defense always wins."

"I think we'll be looked at as a complete hockey club now," Muckler said after the series. "I don't think people will doubt we can play defense along with the great offense now."

The D word dominated Edmonton for days after the May 26 Stanley Cup Victory. Dynasty. Sather said he hated the term, because it sounded like bragging. Everybody on the Oilers said they were one. And in late-twentieth-century sports, maybe they were. But Lowe probably put it best. "We're one more Cup from being one of the all-time great teams."

From 1984 to 1989, the Oilers were 17-1 in playoff series.

In 1989, they were 16-2 in playoff games.

In nine NHL seasons, this expansion team had won four Stanley Cups.

But in the back of his mind, Wayne Gretzky had this funny feeling, coming down the stretch of the season. He had this funny feeling that Pocklington was going to trade him.

Gretzky. Trade. In the same sentence.

— 22 —

The King of the Kings

August 1988
Edmonton, Alberta

It wasn't just a feeling.

Gretzky, in the 1987–'88 season, made $1.2 million (Canadian). He had four years left on an extended contract, after which, at age 31, he would have been an unrestricted free agent, able to leave Edmonton without the Oilers' getting any compensation in return. Pocklington, during the season, had asked Gretzky to either extend the contract or remove the free-agency clause. Gretzky, who had been married to long-term deals all his life, wanted the chance at one more contract before his career ended. So he told Pocklington no.

Remember Pocklington's March words: "You can't fall in love with anybody. That's something we believe in very strongly." The Oilers dismissed several attempts in the mideighties to acquire Gretzky—the New York Rangers offered $18 million once, and the Los Angeles Kings' owner, Jerry Buss, called several times but was rebuffed—but the prospect of losing Gretzky four years down the road shook Pocklington. This was not Sather's idea, by the way, to listen to offers for Gretzky. It was Pocklington's, all the way.

Word leaked among some league people, and perennially bad Vancouver offered $22.5 million (Canadian), three No. 1 draft choices, and three players—including anyone on the roster the Oilers wanted. Think of this for a moment. Quebec, a profitable franchise that sold out its building regularly, was sold in 1988 for $14.5 million (Canadian). The six Vancouver entities (three players, three picks) added to the cash probably totaled 27 or 28 million dollars of value.

Gretzky was worth, to some, the price of two NHL franchises.

Enter Bruce McNall, a coin dealer/thoroughbred owner/movie-production-company owner. He had bought the Kings from Buss in February, at age thirty-seven. (At twenty-four, he outbid French finance minister Valery Giscard D'Estaing for a Greek coin made in 460 B.C.) For Gretzky, he offered $18 million (Canadian) plus a couple of players the Oilers loved, plus three top draft choices. Pocklington bit. McNall called Gretzky. Gretzky said he'd go to Los Angeles, where he and his wife, actress Janet Jones, could live happily ever after. Gretzky was fed up with Pocklington's trying to control him forever. A couple of days later, on August 9, Pocklington gave Gretzky a chance to back out of the trade. Gretzky refused. The deal was Gretzky, forward Mike Krushelnyski, and defenseman Marty McSorley to the Kings for center Jimmy Carson, left wing Martin Gelinas, defenseman Craig Redmond, first-round draft choices in 1989, 1991, and 1993, and $18 million (Canadian).

Quite possibly it was the biggest trade in sports history.

Gretzky would go down someday as the best player in history, if he didn't already have the title. Krushelnyski and McSorley were above-average role players, assets to any NHL team. Carson scored 55 goals in 1987–'88. Gelinas was the Kings' best prospect. Redmond was a marginal player.

"Our place in history is shaken," Sather said.

Their place in the league, though, was assured. It was as a playoff contender for years, barring bad drafts. For Paul Coffey and Wayne Gretzky, Edmonton's best two players of the mideighties, the Oilers had gotten a future. This future, at the start of the 1988–'89 season:

Player	Age	Significance	Oilers' first overall pick that year
Simpson	21	Second overall pick, 1985 draft	20
Carson	20	Second overall pick, 1986 draft	21
Joseph	19	Fifth overall pick, 1987 draft	21
Gelinas	18	Seventh overall pick, 1988 draft	19

Plus:
Two first-round draft choices in 1989
One first-round draft choice in 1990
Two first-round draft choices in 1991
One first-round draft choice in 1992
Two first-round draft choices in 1993.

Notes:
Simpson and Carson finished second and third in the league in goals in 1987–'88, with 56 and 55, respectively.

Albertans burned Pocklington in effigy, and the Gretzky deal was certainly a debatable one. "Other teams had fear when Wayne was here," said Ted Green, an assistant coach for Edmonton. "It's like fighters getting into the ring with Mike Tyson." The players were angered by it, thinking Pocklington hadn't done the deal for the future of the franchise as much as he'd done it for the lining of his pockets. The fans were beside themselves. Several Edmonton restaurants canceled their orders with Pocklington-owned meat-packing plants. A sporting-goods store in Edmonton sold sixty-seven Kings jerseys with Gretzky's No. 99 in two days.

Did anybody think trading the King of Canada would be popular?

Maybe Pocklington had acted selfishly. But in purely unemotional terms, no team looked as good as Edmonton did as the nineties approached. "We're not going to be in last place in a couple of years," Pocklington said following the trade. "We're going to be in position to win more Stanley Cups."

This didn't mean they would always be good, of course. The Kings won only thirty of eighty games in 1987–'88, but the infusion of Gretzky helped them to the sixth-best record in the twenty-one-team league midway through the 1988–'89 season. They were ahead of the Oilers for most of the season. Edmonton was getting immediate help from Carson and continued good scoring from Simpson, but—and they knew this would happen—they missed Gretzky terribly. They became a poor power-play team when once they'd been the league's best. They didn't get as many shots on goal. They weren't, as Green said, as feared. But the biggest problem may have been this one: With the Gretzky-Kurri duo followed by the Messier-Simpson scoring punch on Edmonton's first and second lines in Gretzky's last Oiler season, the opposition could never catch a defensive breath. Carson, a great scorer, wasn't the leader or offensive strategist that Gretzky was.

After fifty games in 1987–'88, the Oilers were 27-16-7. After fifty games in 1988–'89, the Oilers were 24-20-6.

But Sather, with the Oilers struggling to avoid third place as 1989 dawned, said he had no regrets.

"It's hard for anyone to trade a Gretzky, and we can't replace him," Sather said. "But the way I look at it is this: In hockey, players start to reach a peak at twenty-six, twenty-seven, and once they get past that, they deteriorate. You're faced with the dilemma of how to avoid getting to that down part of the cycle. This is why, unless you turn them over, four or five years of greatness is about as long as any great team in any sport can have."

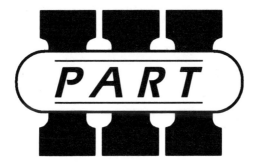

Roundball Redux

23

The Guarantee

April 1988
Inglewood, California

As the eighties prepared to become the nineties, there was great sporting theater being played out just south of Hollywood. There was the kingmaker, Pat Riley (played by Michael Douglas), tugging the strings of costars Magic Johnson (played by Richard Pryor) and Kareem Abdul-Jabbar (played by Jimmy Stewart) in eighty-two annual performances, witnessed nightly by never fewer than fifteen thousand spectators, including Jack Nicholson (played by himself). At intermission, the Laker Girls (played by the Rockettes), the sexiest reason in sports to use the bathroom in the middle of the first half, gave you the left-coast glitz mandatory for L.A. entertainment. The godfather of this group, Chick Hearn (played by Mel Allen), was on headsets theater-wide, just like on Broadway, broadcasting the Lakers the same way he had since 1961.

Heck of a show. The fact that the Lakers were such big stars in the city that fathered glamor was exactly what Riley had to rail against, had to protect against—and why he listened to motivational cassettes in his car day after day, trying to get any edge to make his team better prepared.

"My job," the perfectly coiffed Riley said one morning, leaning back in his Forum office, speaking oh so deliberately, "is to get them to . . . ·

". . . fucking . . . play . . . hard . . .

". . . every . . . night."

This was the life of Riley, a life he'd made especially hard ever since the previous June. Thirty minutes after the Lakers beat Boston to win the 1987 National Basketball Association championship, Riley, wet with champagne, stepped in front of a horde of reporters and pondered this question: Could the Lakers repeat as champions in 1988? No team since 1969 had won titles in succession.

Riley had been lying in wait for the question. In fact, he had written out the answer a week earlier, when he thought he might be confronted with the question any day. This is what he was thinking: Champions in all sports namby-pamby around the repeating question every year, and then, when they

119

lose the next year, they find some reason to explain why they lost. But, Riley thought, this is a team with the talent and the levelheadedness to go into a season with the repeating chip on its shoulder. This is a team that can survive an injury or two, even to the big guys, and win. This is a team that, Larry Bird and Kevin McHale be damned, is simply better than the Celtics. This is a team that wants to go down in history, as does its coach.

So Riley decided to meet the issue head-on. He looked out at all the pens and pads and cameras and faces when someone asked simply, "Can you repeat?" and said, "I guarantee it."

"Guarantee it?" someone asked.

"That's right," Riley said.

His players were stunned at this bit of Ali-like bravado. Abdul-Jabbar, a humorless giant who looks and acts consistently as though sour grapes were his breakfast, said with some annoyance, "He's not the one playing." Several other players thought it was false hubris brought on by the champagne. Truly, none of them liked what Riley did. There was enough pressure in repeating, they thought, without the coach laying some more on top.

When Michael Cooper, the veteran guard, went home the day the Lakers won the championship, he thought of Riley's words.

"Wow," Cooper, a bubbly fellow, said to himself that day. "He's hanging our asses on the line."

He was not very happy about it.

Two or three weeks later, his attitude changed. Good idea, he thought.

"Let's put the practice stuff on," he told a few teammates. They began playing pickup games in June, earlier than Cooper had played after any previous season.

Riley liked that reaction. He was sick of the avoidance of excellence, of the intoxicating satisfaction of winning one championship, of the never-say-repeat attitude he himself had fostered after he coached the Lakers to three previous championships in the eighties. Think only of the task in front of you, he would tell his players year after year, night after night. Think about this one game, then think about the next one. Become experts at the "We take 'em one at a time" quotes. It didn't work. The Lakers were oh-for-three in repeating.

Now it was ten months later, and Riley had no regrets at making this season a kind of personal crusade for greatness. On a beautiful southern California spring day, walking into his tiny Forum office without windows, with a game show droning stupidly from the TV/VCR console in the corner, he began to explain why.

Now, understand something about Pat Riley. He's evangelical. A big fan of motivational author and speaker Wayne Dyer, Riley, forty-three years old, continually searched motivational books and tapes for something, anything, to help his team get an edge. He looked as if he could be a TV preacher— tailored suits, designer ties, perfect black, slicked-back hair, intense but always, always in control—and was big on eye contact. And attitude. Very big on attitude. One of his Dyer tapes told him, "Attitude is an inner concept. It is the most important thing you can develop in your life." He believed that, because he believed that every team in the NBA had enough talent to win some games. It's what teams did with that talent, he thought, and how the talent strove to improve, that decided how good a team was. So when he explained about the greatness, it was a sort of quietly spirited monolog. At the end, you didn't know whether to nod in professional respect or to shout out, "Amen, brother!"

When he walked into the office, his eyes went to the magazine in the middle of his peripherally cluttered desk. This was a Friday, and the magazine was the new issue of *Sports Illustrated*.

"Look at this," he commanded. The cover of the magazine showed the Lakers—players in uniform, coaches, trainer—clustered around a lowered basket. Everyone in the picture smiled. The headline read, "How Good? The Playoffs Will Tell."

"I am so proud of this," he said very sincerely.

"Do you realize this is the first time in the history of *Sports Illustrated* that a team has been on the cover? This is what it's all about. Team greatness. The pursuit of excellence. In ten years, the guys on this team are going to be so proud they were a part of something like this."

Then Riley sat, and preached.

"Did you see *The Color of Money*?" he said. "In *The Color of Money*, Paul Newman is this old pro pool player trying to teach Tom Cruise, the young, talented, and very arrogant pool player, all the tricks. But Cruise is too good for him. In exasperation, Newman finally says to him, 'You don't know the difference between excellent pool and pool excellence.' That's what's happened in this league. Anybody can have one great season. Just because you get your shit together one year doesn't mean you're great.

"What excellence is is sustained excellence. It's natural, after you win, to want to have things, to make the money you've always wanted to make. I call it 'the disease of more.' If you have four or five of those guys who just want to *have*, you'll never win. I try to show my players that if you strive for excellence and achieve excellence continually, money and power will just automatically follow you. The only thing I care about right now is for us to become the greatest basketball team that ever played. To me, that's the only thing left for this team to accomplish.

"By saying what I said last year about repeating, I upped the ante, I took the risk. But I'm glad I did it. I've never felt more alive than I feel right now. We've got the [championship] rings already. We've got the money. Another ring and more money would be nice, but what this is about is leaving footprints. It's about creating legacies. If we win this championship, it would be our fifth in the eighties, and nobody could deny our excellence and will and courage then."

Amen! Hallelujah, brother!

"One question," Riley was asked after the sermonette. "By putting all the emphasis on this year, what's left for next year? How will you motivate your players next year?"

Riley smiled. His eyes twinkled.

"We'll think about that," he said, "next year."

The Lakers spent much of the eighties shedding the shadow of the Boston Celtics, and what a shadow it was. Beginning in 1956, when the Celtics reaped one of the best draft crops in league history, Boston won eleven National Basketball Association championships in thirteen years—eight of them in a row.

What makes the Celtics so remarkable, through a historical view, is that they have had three distinct runs at greatness, all designed and orchestrated by coach-turned-architect Red Auerbach. Check these three separate eras:

• 1956–1969. The Russell Era. Center Bill Russell came in the 1956 draft, joining dominant playmaking guard Bob Cousy, and stayed thirteen seasons. The Celtics went from dominant in this time (they won 75 percent of their games from 1960 to 1965) to survivors; in 1969, with Russell as player-coach, the Celtics finished in fourth place in their division and kept winning playoff games on the road until they won at Los Angeles in the seventh game of the NBA finals.

• 1970–1976. The Unselfish Era. From 1968 to 1970, the Celtics' first-round draft picks were Don Chaney, JoJo White, and Dave Cowens, and Paul Westphal came in the first round of 1972, and John Havlicek was already there, from the first round of 1962. The Celtics won five straight division titles in this time, and NBA championships in 1974 and 1976. How team-oriented was this team? No different than in any Celtic team, which is to say very team-oriented. In the 1972–'73 season, the five starting players averaged 13.1 points, 19.7, 20.5, 23.8, and 13.3 points per game. The Celtics won 83 percent of their games.

• 1979–present. The Bird Era. The year before Larry Bird came to the Celtics in the draft, the Celtics won 29 games. The season he arrived, 1979–'80, the Celtics won 61 games. In 1981, 1984, and 1986, Bird-led teams won championships surrounded by—what else—unselfish players like Robert Parish, Kevin McHale, and Dennis Johnson.

The best thing that ever happened to the formation of the Celtics was the 1956 draft. The Celtics traded two good veterans, center Ed Macauley and forward Cliff Hagan, to St. Louis for the rights to the second pick in the draft, Bill Russell. The Celtics used the sixth overall pick in the draft that year, their own pick, on forward Tom Heinsohn. They used their second-round draft pick, the fourteenth pick overall, on guard K.C. Jones.

Russell went on to be one of the greatest players in league history. In nine seasons, Heinsohn was a great all-around forward ("One of the great underrated players in NBA history," Cousy said), averaging 19 points and 9 rebounds for his career. Jones's forte was defense, and no guard of his era played it better. Russell and Jones ended up in the Hall of Fame.

Contrast this draft to today. There are twenty-seven teams in the NBA today. There were eight teams in 1956. Picking sixth then would be like picking twentieth today. Say the Celtics made a shrewd trade and got the second-best player in the draft today. Then they'd pick twentieth and forty-seventh. Players of the quality of Tom Heinsohn and K.C. Jones would have been gone by the time the Celtics picked in the first round.

"No doubt that set us up," said Cousy, a businessman and Celtics sports-caster today. "Russell and Heinsohn gave us the rebounding presence we didn't have, and they both became incredible players."

Red Auerbach denies it today, but it's certainly harder to build and retool a great team today, with twenty-seven teams, than it was in the era of the eight-team NBA. Most low first-round draft choices today don't play very much; some don't make the team. And second-round picks are strictly desperate darts at a college basketball dartboard.

Actually, Auerbach thinks it's possible to string together a few NBA titles in a row. "It could be done," he said in his office in Washington. He splits his time between Washington, where he first coached an NBA team in 1946, and Boston, the site of his triumphs, the place where there is a statue of him standing downtown. "You get lucky in the draft, and you make a couple of good trades. Cleveland's got a great young team now. Suppose they make a couple of trades and get a couple of good draft picks. They could very well be a power for years."

Many teams could very well have been basketball powers in the last thirty-five years. Only one was.

"Teamwork is the essence of sports," Riley said, "and on no team has that been more apparent than the Celtics."

Riley learned much from the Celtics, much that he applied to his own team. He learned how to have a double standard by not really having a double standard. Riley read in a book that Auerbach and Russell had such mutual trust that Auerbach could go to Russell and tell him: Look, you bust your ass all the time, but it'll look like favoritism if I never yell at you for something; so when I do, just take it. Riley loved that. He had that relationship, in some ways, with Magic Johnson. "I'm telling you, Red had to work his ass off," Riley said. "He had seventies talent in the sixties, and he had to mold it and make it work year in and year out."

Auerbach declined to be interviewed about his motivational tactics ("Read my book," he said), but Cousy did all the talking for him. Cousy believes the Celtics had a mystique unmatched in professional sports. (He actually wrote a book about it, *Cousy on the Celtic Mystique*, in 1988.) He believes Auerbach was the key to it.

"Red was the ringmaster with the whip," Cousy said. "He created this aura around our team, and it affected teams that played us. We were tough and serious, and we wouldn't lose. Teams knew it was going to take an incredible effort to beat us anytime because Red hated to lose so much and we did, too. I just think that made it so much harder on other teams."

By the late eighties, this is the kind of aura the Lakers were starting to throw off. But could it last?

──24──

Beat L.A.! Beat L.A.!

April 1988
Denver, Colorado

There is something that champions say is impossible to truly understand unless you can walk in their sneakers or cleats or skates. It is draining mentally and physically. It is worse when it comes eighteen or twenty hours after finishing a game the night before.

That something is polaying on the road, as a champion.

Picture this scene, then, as an example of what it's like for a premier team in the NBA playing away from home:

After the Lakers beat Portland in California on a Tuesday night, most of the players left the locker room between 10:30 and 11:00 P.M. They were in bed, most of them, by about 12:30. Five hours later, their alarms rang. At 7:20 A.M., their plane left from Los Angeles International Airport for a two-hour flight for Denver, where the Lakers would play that night. Once in Denver, the Lakers went to McNichols Arena, site of the game, for the day-of-the-game shoot-around. At the shoot-around, which lasted for forty-five minutes or so, the team went through a quick scouting report on the Denver Nuggets. Then they bused to the Westin Hotel in downtown Denver, where every player tried to avoid being seen and most went to their rooms for naps. They were back at the arena by 6:00. On their body clocks, with the one-hour time difference, it was 5:00. When the players emerged from the locker room to play the game, at about 7:15 in Denver, most of the 17,022 who would fill the place that night were already in their seats. One guy—about twenty-five, with a Lakers jacket on—leaned out over the tunnel through which the Lakers entered the floor and shouted, "Hey Kareem! Back to back!" But the rest of the crowd booed loudly, and some chanted, "Beat L.A.! Beat L.A.!"

Starting guard Byron Scott, the Lakers' leading scorer, strained some neck muscles the night before and wasn't available to play. He tried to get loose in the locker room before the game, couldn't, and walked to the bench in civilian clothes and watched his teammates during warm-ups.

Cooper, who would take Scott's place, was still gimping around on a sprained ankle that caused him to miss twenty games earlier in the year. He jogged slowly during warm-up drills.

Johnson, the defending NBA most valuable player, couldn't sprint full speed because of a strained right groin muscle that should have sent him to the bench for a couple of weeks. He didn't exert himself during warm-ups.

A.C. Green, one of the first players Riley inserted off the bench during games, had a hip pointer and back spasms, a painful combination that should, too, have idled him for at least two weeks. He ran normally during warm-ups after extensive exercise in the locker room.

James Worthy, a stellar starting forward, would perhaps never again be the showy player he was as a college star at North Carolina in the early eighties because of degenerative tendinitis in his left knee. Worthy could walk fine. It was running that bothered him. That's not good for a basketball player. Before this game, he shuffled some, ran some, walked a lot.

(And Abdul-Jabbar was forty-one. He seemed allergic to running, he did it so infrequently. It was a commentary on the sad state of NBA centers in the late eighties that Abdul-Jabbar was able to play like a mannequin nine out of ten nights and get away with it.)

In basketball, understand, playing hurt isn't unusual. At the end of an 82-game season, every team has one or two important players not playing because of injuries. Five or six more have sprained ankles or sore knees or feet that spend an hour in hot or cold water after every game. But these were the injuries the Lakers didn't have in 1986–'87, when they played 100 games (including playoff games) and won 80. In those 100 games, the Lakers' starting players missed a total of 6. So Riley had his starting lineup intact 94 times. This year, Johnson and Green played the second half of the season never feeling right, Worthy worried constantly about the condition of his knee, and Cooper, the first guard off the bench, had lost his once-respected long-range shooting touch, in part because of his ankle injury. ("He hasn't been able to throw a pea in the ocean, and I mean the Atlantic," Hearn said on the air in Denver.)

The McNichols fans didn't want excuses. They wanted blood. The Nuggets had given out eight-and-a-half-inch by eleven-inch placards to the fans, with "HEY" on one side and "BEAT LA" on the other. Some form of "Hey! Beat L.A.!" was going on all night. The music during time-outs was so loud that Riley and Denver coach Doug Moe both had veins showing in their necks while they screamed to be heard in tight huddles at their benches. It was a close game until midway throuth the third quarter, when Riley inserted four nonstarters (center Mychal Thompson, forwards Green and Tony Campbell, and guard Wes Matthews). The Nuggets led by 4 points then. Eight minutes later they led by 16. The Lakers couldn't keep up with Denver's speed. It was a blowout.

With seven minutes left in the game and Denver leading 105–89, Riley called a time-out, hoping to stop the Nuggets' momentum. A man—about thirty, six foot three, with short blond hair parted in the middle and a sparse blond mustache on his lip, bearing a strong but shorter resemblance to Boston Celtics star Larry Bird—came running out of a tunnel leading to the floor. He was dressed in an authentic Celtics kelly-green road jersey, with Bird's number, 33, on his back. He wore green sweatpants, just like Bird would wear. Problem was, Bird was in Boston, probably showering after a game with Milwaukee this night. The crowd immediately noticed the guy, who was prancing around the arena yelling something about what a great team the Nuggets were. When he got near the Lakers' bench, he started pointing at the players and screaming over the music, "Go back to L.A.! Nuggets number one! Nuggets number one! You guys stink!" With forty seconds left and Denver ahead by 15, fans walking behind the Lakers' bench leaving the arena chanted at them, "Over the hill! Over the hill! Over the hill!"

This is what it is like for a champion on the road.

Denver won 120–106. Laker-bashing, a popular sport in twenty-two NBA venues, was at its best here.

Five Lakers had ice bandaged to some part or parts of their bodies after the game. Johnson had bags of ice on both knees and both ankles—because all four places would swell without the ice—and he said he was able to play at perhaps 80 percent of his normal skill level because his groin still bothered him so much.

"Every team has to get their ass kicked now and then," Riley said later, when all the Minicams had left the locker room. "You've got to realize these teams we play are trying their asses off every night when they play us."

Then he looked a little worried, and he admitted it didn't matter what the Lakers faced every night from Seattle to Boston. Unless a catastrophic injury (Johnson, Worthy) struck, the Lakers were still good enough to win anywhere. When they didn't, Riley seethed. "Until we find our championship heart again, we're going to continue to struggle," he said.

This was another five- or six-hour sleep night. The team bus left the hotel for Denver's airport at 7:00 the next morning. At 6:30, Thompson and Worthy, eyes barely open, ate big breakfasts in the Westin's coffee shop. They talked about how tired they were.

If fatigue—mental and physical—were the only problem.

But age was, and desire was, and the exacerbation of injuries was. Maybe Riley was right. He saw the chance to win one more championship—two, on the outside—before the forces of sporting socialism, money, and physical frailty that rule pro sports today simply caught up to his team.

"Give us credit," Scott said. "We've got three or four guys playing forty minutes a game who are playing with pain, and that doesn't make us any better."

A few lockers away this night in Denver, Mychal Thompson seemed oblivious to the injuries. Thompson, who was Abdul-Jabbar's backup, was being a good company man about the injuries. Thompson's tone: Everyone is playing; ergo, no one is hurt. "As long as we keep our health, there's nobody to dethrone us," Thompson said.

The team's health was, at best, below average. Now the question was, could the Lakers hang on with the hurts they had?

──25──

It Shouldn't Be This Hard, Should It?

April 1988
Inglewood, California

If one game typified this season of challenge to the Los Angeles Lakers, it was the game of April 15, versus the Phoenix Suns. The Lakers had won 57 and lost 19 entering the game. Phoenix was 26 and 50. The Lakers were at home. They should have breezed to a victory. They appeared disinterested instead. Were they falling victim to Riley's "disease of more"? Or were they falling victim to the "disease of disinterest," or the "disease of Ace bandages"?

On the afternoon of the game, Chick Hearn, who would broadcast approximately his 2,300th consecutive Lakers game on this night, relaxed high in the Forum's cheap seats. As he reclined, he worried out loud. "I don't think this team is close to last year's team," he said. "Unless they can make a return to the way they were playing late last year, I don't think they can win it. Cooper, Magic, and Worthy are hurt; the aging of Kareem has had a dramatic effect. Last year they ended the season on such a high. It's just not there this year."

The words of Hearn, over the Lakers radio network, told a fitting story of the team's year-long struggle:

"Now, ladies and gentlemen, live from the fabulous Forum, the world's most beautiful sports theater, it's exciting NBA basketball. Tonight, the world champion—defending Los Angeles Lakers take on the Phoenix Suns. Hi, everyone. Along with Stu Lantz, I'm Chick Hearn . . ."

At the Lakers' morning shoot-around, Riley had gathered his players at midcourt of the Forum and stressed to them they couldn't think of Phoenix, or any team, as an easy win. It was late in the season, he told them. They were logy and felt pain, he told them. "This is still the toughest thing we're ever going to do," he told them. "You can't assume anything. You can't assume you'll beat anybody. Anybody who assumes anything will be on vacation very early this spring." He also told his players, with conviction, "Our total game has to improve."

The Lakers were experts at the total game. Riley's top assistant coach, Bill Bertka, was in charge of compiling tedious statistics on every player in the league. The purpose: to put each Laker in his place against his peers throughout the league. Johnson was compared with starting point guards, Abdul-Jabbar with starting centers, Scott with starting shooting guards, Cooper with sixth men, and so forth. Every ten games, all the Lakers got an updated statistical analysis of their seasons versus the seasons of every other player at their positions in the league. Also, Riley's staff kept separate stats on more vague categories, including offensive rebounding effort, defensive rebounding effort, diving for loose balls. The effort in all of this, for this season, was for every player to have a personal best season when all of these categories were figured. If a player's assists-per-minute figure is down, his offensive rebounding effort had better be up, in other words. "If we can get a one-percent increase from each player in his game, it'll show up," Riley said. "We'll be a better team."

"It's perfect for us," Cooper said of the best-effort thinking. "A lot of people get caught up in wins and losses, and of course that's the most important thing. But with the talent we have, sometimes just winning games can disguise problems we're having. When you chart your numbers, the coaches know what level you can play at. If we hit our all-time best efforts, we'll obviously be a great team. The demands you put on yourself help the team win."

There were two best-effort problems this year. One, obviously, was Abdul-Jabbar, who had gone from consistent stardom in the early eighties to having one impactful game in every ten or twelve this season. Two, Johnson's game was dramatically down from the previous year, when he was the sport's best player. The Lakers' rating on every NBA player was a percentage figure, with 1.000 being a perfect player. Johnson, in 1986–'87, had led the Lakers' ratings of all NBA players with a .765 figure. Late in this season, his average was .680. He was injured, yes. He was helping Scott have his best season, yes. But Riley was disappointed in Johnson's play nonetheless, and in the play of several of his playing-hurt players.

"The question is, are we hurt, or are we protective?" Riley couldn't help wondering to himself quite often.

The fact was, Riley didn't want to hear about injuries. He wanted to hear about greatness. And Worthy and Johnson, the sorest ones, could do nothing to change that.

"The Los Angeles Lakers' magic number to gain home-court advantage throughout the playoffs is two, after Cleveland beat Boston tonight. They'll play without James Worthy tonight. James, with patellar knee tendinitis, finally getting some rest, and boy does he need it, and more than one game . . .

Injured or not, the acquisition of Worthy typified how this team was built. The front-office philosophy was to deal, when possible, with teams of lesser quality, plugging several of their holes in exchange for the best or second-best player on their team. The Lakers also took advantage of stupidity. Cleveland, which in the late seventies was robbed of its top draft picks by terrible trades, tried to recover a bit in the middle of the 1979–'80 season. The Cavaliers traded their first-round pick in 1982 for the Lakers' first-round pick in 1980, and each team threw in a player. The Lakers went on to win the league championship that year, which meant the Cavaliers had the twenty-second pick in the first round. There are eight or ten high-quality players in most NBA drafts, and Cleveland, picking twenty-second, certainly didn't get one of them. The Cavaliers drafted Chad Kinch, who never was a starting NBA player. Two years later, the Lakers, using the first pick in the first round acquired from Cleveland, took the best available college player in America, Worthy.

The Lakers had an incredible roster of players, actually. Four of the eleven players trying to fulfill Riley's quest had been the first player selected in the NBA draft in the year they left college. The Lakers traded for Abdul-Jabbar and Mychal Thompson; they used picks acquired from other teams to pick up Worthy and Johnson. The structure of each deal:

The Kareem Abdul-Jabbar Trade
With Milwaukee
1975

Lakers acquire

Abdul-Jabbar (twenty-eight)
Walt Wesley

Lakers trade

Elmore Smith
Brian Winters
Dave Meyers
Junior Bridgeman

The Magic Johnson Deal
With Utah (née New Orleans)
1976

Lakers acquire

Utah's top draft pick in 1979, as compensation for Jazz's signing a top free agent. Johnson (twenty) is the pick.

Lakers lose

Gail Goodrich

The James Worthy Trade
With Cleveland
1980

Lakers acquire

Butch Lee
Cleveland's top pick in 1982.
Worthy (twenty-one) is the pick.

Lakers trade

Don Ford
Lakers' top pick in 1980 (Chad Kinch)

The Mychal Thompson Trade
With San Antonio
1987

Lakers acquire

Mychal Thompson (thirty-one)

Lakers deal

Frank Brickowski
Petur Gudmundsson
Lakers' top draft pick in 1987 (Ron
Anderson)
Lakers' number two draft pick in
1990

In 1969, Abdul-Jabbar was the first pick in the NBA draft. In successive years, Thompson (1978), Johnson (1979), and Worthy (1982) also were.

"Getting ready to go, Abdul-Jabbar and West waiting for the ball to be tossed by Jess Kersey, the veteran, the redhead. The Lakers will go north on our simulcast. Lakers control the tip, to Rambis. It'll be good to see the Lakers back in a little bit better form tonight . . . Down the middle, underneath, layup, shot, good, basket with the left hand by Tony Campbell, on Magic's perfect bullet pass. Wasn't that a nice cut? Two to nothing."

The results of the Thompson deal and the consistent low-round picks were a poorer pool of talent from which to choose. The Lakers had much in common with other great teams, all of whom had to pick near the end of each round in every draft. Los Angeles' marginal players, then, were quite marginal. Tony Campbell, a starter in this game because of Worthy's injury, had three weeks earlier been in basketball's minor league, the Continental Basketball Association, playing for Albany. The other bench players—Milt Wagner, Wes Matthews, and Mike Smrek—simply filled out the roster and contributed nothing to the team's wins and losses.

So the Lakers played with eight players most often—Abdul-Jabbar, Thompson, Green, Worthy, and Kurt Rambis as forwards and centers, Johnson, Scott, and Cooper as the guards. The do-it-now philosophy of the team was easy to understand once you knew the average age (thirty years, seven months) and average NBA experience (almost nine years) of these eight players as they ended the 1987–'88 season. The Lakers were old, very old by NBA standards.

"Standing ovation for Magic Johnson, as they announce he's the third all-time NBA assist leader . . ."

What a pleasant surprise when the truly great players are truly nice people. The six-foot-nine-inch Johnson, who became the first and greatest of a new era of giant point guard after leaving Michigan State at age twenty, finished his twentieth year by carrying the Lakers to the NBA championship. As a center. What a way to start a career. When Abdul-Jabbar went down with a sprained ankle in the championship series against Philadelphia, Johnson substituted for him at center and scored 42 points with 15 rebounds and 7 assists in the clinching game, becoming the first rookie to win the championship series' most valuable player award.

Understand three things about Magic Johnson, with his mansion in Bel Air and the condo in Palm Springs and the salary of $3.14 million a year owner Jerry Buss gave him in 1987. He loves to compete, loves to play. He loves people. And he changed the Lakers from a playoff team to a championship one, almost by himself.

A snapshot of Johnson the basketball-lover: In March, in New York, Johnson was shopping at Bloomingdale's the afternoon before a night game between the Knicks and the Lakers at Madison Square Garden. The game had been a sellout for weeks; the Knicks, reborn seemingly after four years of bad basketball, had won thirteen straight home games. Shoppers at Bloomingdale's kept telling Johnson, "Thirteen in a row! You better watch out, Magic." Johnson was having severe groin pain from his pulled muscle, and his Achilles tendons seemed constantly sore. Before the game, he lay on the trainer's table, getting treatment for his Achilles tendons, eyes buried in a novel, trying to block out the pain that would one night later sideline him for ten games. Vintage Magic followed. His 14 rebounds and 14-of-14 free-throw shooting helped the Lakers win, 104–99, in front of a kind of nouveau-whacky packed house at the Garden. "I loved it out there," Johnson said later, grinning widely as he sat in his locker stall. "That's what makes this game great, playing on nights like this."

A snapshot, or three, of Johnson the people person: When Magic first came into the league, Hearn and the rest of the organization's longtime employees doubted his Jerry Mathers–like wide-eyed love for life. Hearn remembers thinking, "This guy's got to be a phony." But on every trip to Detroit, Hearn noticed how Magic and his mom, from nearby Lansing, would organize and cook up dinner for thirty—or enough to feed the Lakers and their traveling party—in a room adjacent to the playing floor at the Pontiac Silverdome. Hearn noticed Magic working doggedly for the United Negro College Fund, for which he personally raised more than $1 million between 1986 and 1987 through charity events he organized. Hearn noticed Magic, with a cold one night in Sacramento, dressed in a thousand-dollar suit made by his personal tailor, standing half in and half out of an umbrella, holding up the Lakers' team bus in a steady rain while he signed autographs for every fan who had waited for him. No one on the bus groused. Larry Bird was great and private. Michael Jordan was great and pleasant. Magic Johnson was great and charismatic. He would retire sometime in the 1990s, and basketball without him would be something like Catholicism without John Paul.

A snapshot of Johnson the team-fixer: In the nine seasons before Magic arrived, the Lakers averaged 48.7 wins a year. In his nine years as a Laker, the team averaged 59.3 wins. "Our success," says Cooper, "can all be traced to Magic coming in 1979–'80. He brought this infectious style, this jovial style. Before he came, I thought this team felt basketball was more of a job. When he came, it became play. We've developed a core of players who have fun playing the game."

Johnson, even a sore Johnson, was an infectious guy to be around. After the Lakers' win over Portland earlier in this week, Johnson marveled in Magicspeak about the play of friend and Trail Blazer forward Clyde Drexler, trying to convince a listener that Drexler was one of basketball's underappreciated talents. "Clyde, he fly in there, and he up sooooo high"—smiling, enjoying the visualization of a flying Drexler—"nobody better than Clyde. Nobody get up that high."

In all, this was a dour group of guys—the quiet Worthy was a minister's son, Cooper pleasant and polite but not loud, Green quiet and religious, Rambis a novel-reader, Scott shy, Abdul-Jabbar unwaveringly sour—but a selfless group. One eighty-one-inch ball of friendly fire led them.

"The Lakers, twenty-five percent from the free-throw line, and Riley looking on, obviously not happy. You lose this one, after Boston got beat, and you're in dire trouble. . . . The Lakers are behind thirty-two to twenty-six. The Lakers, with no offense at all right now. Nobody can score. . . . At the end of the quarter, the Suns lead, thirty-two twenty-six, on the world champion Lakers' basketball network."

Riley and Johnson had convinced each new player that leading the league in individual statistics—especially scoring—meant little. Team stuff mattered. So this late in the season, no Laker was in the top ten in the NBA in scoring, rebounding, or any major statistical category except assists.

"When you come to the Lakers," Cooper said, "you leave your ego at the door."

Still, the Lakers had probably the best talent of any team in the league, and they had a great coach and motivator in Riley. But Johnson played down the talent. He legitimately thought other teams had better players than the Lakers. "A lot of teams have more talent than us right now. We're winning in other ways," Johnson said.

A lot of teams have more talent than the Lakers. Hmmm. This just didn't sound right. When the feeling was relayed to Nuggets coach Doug Moe, Moe was aghast.

"You gotta be fuckin' kiddin' me," Moe said with a laugh. "Magic said that? Who's got better talent? Dallas? Seattle? Us? Boston, maybe. Maybe. There's a fine line between some teams, but not between the Lakers and everybody else. You sure he wasn't kiddin'? If he wasn't, he's fuckin' nuts. There's no one on their fuckin' level. They got three of the greatest players ever. In all the years I've been in the NBA, there's not a more dominant team than the one they put out on the floor now—when they're healthy."

Moe was right. Johnson believed, as did several adamant Lakers, that the work ethic and the intelligence of the team was vastly underrated. But to say that Abdul-Jabbar and Johnson, who would both one day be in the Hall of Fame, and Worthy, who might be, and Scott, who was having a season any NBA guard would be proud to have, were surpassed in skill by other teams was just wrong. The Lakers were where they were because of:

1. Talent
2. Work ethic
3. Smart trades
4. Riley.

"Rebound Mychal Thompson, he puts it up underneath, he misses, rebound out to Cooper, in three-point country to Magic, over to Scott in three-point country, he hits! His second three-pointer. Thirty-six thirty-three. Scott's got twelve points. Three guys out there, and none of them wanted to shoot it. Scott said, 'Give it to me. I'll show you.'"

One trade, a very controversial one, seemed to be a bad one for the Lakers for years. It was the Byron Scott deal. In 1983, Scott was the fourth player picked in the draft (the first guard), by San Diego. This disappointed Scott. If there was any way, he thought, any way at all, he could have wound up with the Lakers he would have been thrilled. Even though San Diego was close to his boyhood home—one mile from the Forum, in Inglewood—the Clippers were an awful team and Scott was not happy to be going there. But the Lakers weren't happy either that they had missed out on Scott in the draft. So they put together a package to change shooting guards that most league people thought was excessive. One shooting guard, the well-respected Norm Nixon, went with guard Eddie Jordan (who had been acquired three years earlier for a number one draft pick), and two high draft choices to the

Clippers for Scott and backup center Swen Nater. Nater played one insignificant year with the Lakers. Scott showed flashes of shooting brilliance in his first four Laker seasons, but he disappeared in big games. Nixon had shined in them. Fans wondered why the Lakers had traded a proven 17-point-a-game scorer in Nixon for decidedly not a sure thing. In truth, the Lakers did the deal because they felt Nixon wasn't as team-oriented as most of the other important players.

But the early pressure on Scott hurt him for several years. "It was tough on me," Scott said. "Everybody expected me to come and fit in right away and play up to their level." This season, though, had been a terrific one for him, and the Lakers, who struggled to wins in games that should have been easier, had Scott to thank for much of the season. Riley said they would have been at least ten wins worse without Scott, who had become Los Angeles' most reliable shooter.

At the same time, Nixon was sitting out his second consecutive season with a major knee injury suffered in a softball game in Central Park.

Funny how things worked out for the best so consistently for the Lakers.

"A.C. Green is hurt again. A.C. Green is hurt. I think it's the sacroiliac effect. He got hit in the hip, ran into his own player. Hobbling out is A.C. Green. The Lakers got about three guys who should be put in a van, trucked down to Palm Springs, thrown in the sun for three days, and they'd say, 'We'll pick you up three days from now.' Forty-two thirty-six. Riley, understandably, not happy. There's a twenty-second time-out. You will not beat the Portlands this year, you will not beat the Denvers, you will not beat the Dallases, maybe not the San Antonios and Utahs, with this kind of performance. The Lakers know that better than you and I."

Pat Riley did it. Bill Parcells did it. Glen Sather did it. Rarely if ever were valuable players given adequate time to heal. A.C. Green, a starter for most of the two most recent seasons, got treatment on a painful back injury and a hip pointer for hours every day during the season. On this night, at 5:45, he was out on the floor at the Forum, having a ballboy throw him long passes on an imagined fast break. After half an hour of running through and around the Laker Girls—warming up for their dance routines—he told the kid, "I'm loose. I feel pretty good." Not good enough. The back wouldn't feel right until the off-season.

It didn't much bother coaches, in all sports, to see their players playing with pain. Instead of giving players four or five weeks to get completely over an injury in midseason, coaches were reluctant to break up team chemistry. Even when rest would assure complete health in a player for the playoffs, Riley was much more inclined to continue playing him. Johnson, Cooper, and Worthy could have used more time off than they got, but Riley didn't want his team to get into the habit of losing if these key players were out for very long.

Smart? That's debatable. It's also the way of the world in pro sports. You learn to play with pain.

"Cooper buries another three-pointer. He's two for two. That's got to be a confidence-restorer. Forty-seven forty-five, Lakers. They're four for four in three-pointers in the game."

A problem with many sports teams is that good players who don't start make noise continually about not starting. The reasons are twofold. One, they're competitive people. Having never sat on the bench in their athletic careers, it's hard for them to learn when they've realized their lifetime dream—getting paid to play a game they like. Two, they're greedy people. In very few instances do nonstarters make more money than starters.

Lucky were the Lakers about this. Because the three most valuable players off the bench were three intelligent people who knew the Lakers would be the best team possible if they adjusted to their roles. Rambis, a rebounder and defensive specialist, had to play every minute as if it were his last. He usually did. He annually led the Lakers in what Riley considered an important stat: rebounds per forty-eight minutes, which meant he was making the most of his twelve to twenty-five minutes a game. Cooper was put on the other team's best shooter at one end of the floor and asked to be a crack long-distance shooter on the other end. Thompson, quite self-effacing for being a former top pick, had to spell Abdul-Jabbar and other forwards, a job that could mean thirty-five minutes a night.

"What makes the Lakers great is people blending in," said Cooper, who twice had won the league's best defensive player award despite being a non-starter. "Maybe it's Magic's influence, maybe it's the natural attitude our guys have. We just don't have the ego and money problems a lot of teams have."

"It's not hard for us to fit our roles," Thompson said, "because we've seen how successful it's made us. We're all competitors. We all want to play. I've never been on a team at any level that worked harder to win or was more competitive. It's because we love the game, I think. You look at us off the court. We play cards, golf, softball, anything. To me, there's nothing worse in the world than hitting a bad golf shot. I love to play tennis. I've thrown my share of rackets; I've got John McEnroe syndrome. It's the competition."

Rambis started for great Laker teams for four and a half years being taking his bench role in 1986–'87 with the emergence of Green. He accepted—though without fondness—being a backup, which helped the team remain great. "The important thing about this team is that none of us have settled into comfort zones," Rambis said. "Anytime an athlete settles into a comfort zone, his career takes a downhill turn."

" . . . Under to Kareem, good! Time out Phoenix. Boy, the Lakers are looking so good at this juncture, and Kareem is totally animated tonight. Fifty-one forty-five.

The Lakers are getting some fast breaks, and that's the name of their game, here on the world champion Lakers basketball network . . .

"Back at the Forum, here's the ball out to Alvan Adams, shot is no good. Rebound is out to Magic, Lakers have outscored them ten to nothing over the last three minutes, Magic takes it over to Scott at the baseline, great pass! Scott hits an eighteen-footer. Beautiful pass by Magic. The Lakers look like the Lakers right now. They really look good. They've outscored 'em twelve to nothing in this run. They've taken an eight-point lead."

Riley: "Teamwork to me is the essence of life. Teamwork is why we're great. The beauty of teamwork shows when we're playing well."

"Hornacek, drive, finger-roll, good, he's fouled. Eight-six eighty-one. They're back in this ball game. Hornacek hits the free throw, and the Laker lead is four . . .

"It's ninety eight-six, and if you think these guys aren't keeping the heat on the Lakers, wow. Magic is rushed back to the scene, Matthews out. Boston's a loser tonight. Will the Lakers suffer the same fate? . . . Eddie Johnson hits another one! The Laker lead is one. This all started when Pat Riley decided to give his regulars some rest. You're going nowhere in the playoffs if you don't have a bench. Particularly the Lakers, as badly as they need the rest."

Doug Moe: "I thought this was the year, finally, we'd have a repeat champion in the league. What's it been—eighteen, twenty years? But L.A. was strong or stronger than they'd been last year. Then Magic went down, and they didn't really have the bench to replace him. They got a legitimate shot of repeating. I mean legitimate. It's just that it ain't a lock anymore."

"Cooper and Magic, they're sweating it out. Phoenix was down by twelve at one point. Since that time it's been a roller coaster. Magic missed one free throw, and it was 108–106 Lakers. Then they got tied at 108 at 2:44. Then Magic made a layup to give the Lakers a two-point lead at a minute and a half. Kevin Johnson made two free throws at 1:19 to tie it at 112. Gilliam then made a field goal to give the Suns the lead. Kareem came right back to give the Lakers the lead, and now Magic's two free throws have put the Lakers up by three with twelve seconds to go. The ball goes to midcourt. Alvan Adams, a good passer, will take it out. Also he's six-nine. Inbounds to Kevin Johnson. The clock starts. Kevin Johnson dribbling with eight seconds left. They need three. Over to Hornacek, Hornacek in the air. It counts if it goes! It didn't go, Cooper with the rebound, buzzer goes, the Lakers win, 117–114."

After the game, Riley said the cumulative effect of the injuries was taking a big toll on his team. Repeating was not going to be as possible as it had looked nine months before, when the champagne was cold.

"There may be a little bit of doubt creeping into the backs of our minds now," Riley said, almost alone now, back to the locker-room blackboard a half-hour after the game. He looked tired.

The blackboard read:

> Tomorrow
> Leave: LAX Continental Flight 138 7:25 A.M.
> Arrive: Houston 12:25 P.M.

The Lakers had miles to go before they slept.

—26—

The Hardest Thing
We've Ever Done

June 1988
Inglewood, California

The Los Angeles Lakers finished the regular season with the best record in the National Basketball Association, 62 wins and 20 losses, five games better than the runnerup Boston Celtics. In their first playoff series, the Lakers beat San Antonio, three games to none.

What happened in the next twenty-one basketball games can best be illustrated by the average score of these 1988 Lakers' playoff games, from their three series after the one with San Antonio:

Los Angeles 103, Opponents 102.

When it was over, on the night of the first day of summer, the Lakers had survived surprising Utah, four games to three; they had conquered dogged Dallas, four games to three; and they had brawled past Detroit, four games to three. They bled Laker yellow. They sweated Laker sweat. They won for the fifth time in nine seasons. A dynasty? Well, perhaps not one in the Celtic or Canadien sense. But in the parity-laden sporting world of the late eighties, this was as dynastic a basketball team as one could produce. Consider this when thinking of the accomplishments of this team: Only the Celtics, Canadiens, Yankees, and Packers, in the four major sports, had won championships five times in the same decade.

It took every ounce of motivational effort by Riley, who lost nineteen pounds in the two-month playoff grind and appeared gaunt after the final game. It took the greatest series of games ever by Worthy, who averaged 20 points in the finals with Detroit and earned the playoff most valuable player award. It took the glue of Magic Johnson, who handed out 91 assists in seven games against Detroit. Maybe, most of all, it took the advantage the Lakers gained by having the best regular-season record in the NBA. This advantage allowed the Lakers to play four home games in each of the seven-game series, and it allowed the final two games of each series to be at the Lakers' home, The Forum. They won each game seven.

It took, basically, everything the Lakers had.

"This was the hardest thing we've ever done. Ever," Riley said when it was over.

Looking at the series one by one, it's hard to see how the Lakers survived. They were still hurting after playing San Antonio, so much so that Utah, a miserable road team all year, won at The Forum in game two of their series. In Utah for games three and four, Riley went to see *The Last Emperor*, the movie about a Chinese dynasty, for inspiration. The Lakers weren't prepared for such a challenge from this young team. Was Riley's "disease of more" catching up to this team? Or were the other guys simple as good? Had the world caught up to the Lakers? "This team is mystifying to me. Knowing what's at stake, it seems as if they have to be humbled, really humbled, before they gather strength," Riley told reporters. But the extra home game propelled them past Utah and then past Dallas.

It would be different against Detroit. Almost.

The Pistons actually outscored the Lakers in the series, by 18 points. Detroit was a cocky team with a couple of court personalities. The Pistons could give the ball to their charismatic point guard, Isiah Thomas, the eight-inch-shorter version of best friend Magic Johnson, and let him lead fast breaks all game long, dishing off to speedy streak shooter Vinnie Johnson or to one of several trees growing underneath the basket, pugilistic Bill Laimbeer or beefy Adrian Dantley or sharp-elbowed Rick Mahorn. Or they could play the halfcourt game, with the Pistons clearing out one side of the floor for Thomas to go one-on-one to the basket with a Laker or playing for the best shot underneath from one of the horses. And either way, they could play a stifling team defense.

In game one, the Lakers trailed by 17 at halftime and were routed at the Forum. They looked awful, Abdul-Jabbar missing seven of his famed sky hooks and playing phantom defense. "Kareem should have retired maybe five years ago," Wilt Chamberlain, another basketball giant, said during these playoffs. In game two, the Lakers built a 12-point second-half lead, lost it all, then survived to win by 12. The Pistons, predictably in front of their 40,000 playoff regulars in the Pontiac Silverdome, a converted football stadium, won two of three at home. So the Lakers trailed three games to two, and the series went back to California.

Riley was coming to realize the Lakers were a changed team from the one he had molded into a fast-breaking, excitable, exciting team in mid-decade. In this series, it was the Pistons who were better on the fast break, better at getting a crowd revved up and behind them, better at taking control of a game. The Pistons were coming, damn it, and Riley and the Lakers didn't look as though they'd be able to stop them. "We're not the running team we used to be," Riley conceded after game two. "I don't care what anyone says. We're a little older, both mentally and physically, than we used to be. We used to run like crazy. Now . . ." The sentence went unfinished.

What more did Riley have to say? How many more hurrahs could this team have? The average age of their six most important players as they played Detroit was thirty-one and a half years old. This was, in all likelihood, the last time they'd be able to back up such a guarantee as Riley's year-old one.

It was with these thoughts that the Lakers entered game six on a hot June Sunday in The Forum.

And it was with these thoughts, Cooper said later, that the Lakers played the final minute of game six. The situation: Detroit 102, Lakers 99, Lakers' ball. Byron Scott leaned in over Thomas and made a fifteen-foot jump shot with forty-five seconds left. Laimbeer passed up an open shot to get the ball to Thomas, but Thomas missed a desperate fifteen-footer for Detroit with twenty-seven seconds left. Time out, Lakers. Now the Lakers were down to their most important possession of the season.

"There's no way, and I don't care what's been said, that we don't try to go to Kareem in a case like that," Riley said.

Riley, during the time-out, set two options. The first would be Johnson's getting the ball coming off a pick from Worthy. The second would be to give the ball to Abdul-Jabbar and let him try to win the game himself with his three-inch height advantage over Detroit center Laimbeer.

Detroit cut off the pass to Johnson, eliminating the first option. So the Lakers got the ball to Abdul-Jabbar. With fourteen seconds left, he tried a sky hook over Laimbeer. It failed, but Laimbeer fouled him.

Abdul-Jabbar made both free throws. The Pistons were sunk.

Two nights later, Detroit was playing half a man short. Thomas had sprained an ankle in game six, and though he tossed aside his crutches, he was mostly ineffective in the most important game of his professional life. Detroit still could play defense, however, and led by 5 points at halftime. At halftime, Abdul-Jabbar was his noticeable absent self, with no points, and Johnson and Scott had combined for eight measly shots. At halftime, Riley told them to start running. At the start of the third quarter, the Lakers ran. And scored. Los Angeles scored 20 of the first 25 points of the second half to go ahead by 10. With eleven minutes to go, the Lakers were ahead by 15, and Randy Newman's "I Love L.A." was bellowing from the PA system during a Detroit time-out. Actress Dyan Cannon, a regular in The Forum's courtside seats, danced in the aisle.

But the Pistons scored on ten straight times down the floor, an unheard-of display in such a pressure atmosphere. With a minute to go, the Lakers led 103–100, and Detroit had the ball. Laimbeer missed a three-point shot. The Lakers turned it over. Dennis Rodman missed an awkward shot in the lane. Scott hit two free throws for the Lakers, and it was over.

Exactly fifty-three weeks after guaranteeing a championship, a lighter and more wrinkled Riley went on national TV to accept the NBA championship trophy.

And Abdul-Jabbar stuffed a towel in Riley's mouth when someone asked about repeating.

But the players, in painful hindsight, said they were grateful to Riley for putting the carrot in front of their mouths so early and so adamantly.

"There was a method to his madness," Abdul-Jabbar said. "No one has to tell Riley how to do his job."

"We would not have been as mentally alert or focused throughout the year if he hadn't made his statement," said Worthy.

"I guarantee," Johnson said, "that I will have a great summer."

It had lasted 115 games, this season of promise. After 9 exhibition games, 82 in the regular season, and 24 in the postseason, the Lakers adjourned to a private party at On The Rox on Sunset Strip. Magic Johnson walked in the door, not pausing to get a drink, and danced, nonstop, for three hours. Those who did get drinks got them from bartenders Jack Nicholson and Daryl Hannah. "That's the highlight of my year," said Mychal Thompson, "having Daryl Hannah serve me cranberry juice, on the rocks."

The throne was theirs. For a couple of months, anyway.

Four hours after the party at On The Rox ended, Jerry West, the Lakers' general manager, was in his office. It was 6:30 A.M. on the Pacific coast, 9:30 back East. This was the day before the expansion draft, the day before new teams in Miami and Charlotte would be stocked with a player each from the twenty-three established franchises.

Ten hours after winning, West was working.

Because thirty-six hours after winning, the expansion draft would start.

On the morning after, West had to finalize a trade in order to protect Abdul-Jabbar from being picked by one of the new teams. The Lakers traded a 1991 or 1992 second-round draft choice to Miami in exchange for the Heat's taking forward Billy Thompson, not Abdul-Jabbar, off their roster. The Lakers were allowed to protect eight players in the draft, with Miami or Charlotte picking one from the leftovers; to protect a ninth, Abdul-Jabbar, cost the draft pick.

The regular draft was a week later. The Lakers picked guard David Rivers from Notre Dame. Later in the summer, two Los Angeles veteran free agents, Rambis and guard Milt Wagner, chose to sign with other teams. So the Lakers would begin their 1988–'89 season with a loss of blue-collar significance, Rambis, and an addition of a new man, Rivers.

What hurts the Lakers as the nineties prepare to dawn is what hurts every other champion in every other sport these days: sporting socialism. There would be no more gifts, no more Cleveland Cavaliers and Utah Jazz draft freebies to raise the Lakers above the rest of the National Basketball Association. There would be a drought. Out of the 1983 and 1984 drafts, the Lakers got nothing. Out of the 1985 draft came A.C. Green. Out of the 1986 and 1987 drafts, the Lakers got nothing. Out of the 1988 draft, they got Rivers.

In six years, the Lakers had acquired no starters from the draft, and only two players who even made their 1988–'89 team. As usual, the motivator didn't want to hear about excuses.

"I think we'll be playing championship basketball the next three or four years," Riley said, a week after the season ended. "We've got four or five players still in their primes."

He forgot to mention that they've got a coach still in his. Now, if only he could steal a couple of top draft choices, and Patrick Ewing, and maybe Charles Barkley, the Lakers would be great well into the nineties. But that wouldn't be the even thing to do, would it?

Diamonds
Aren't Forever

──27──

As Terry Leach Goes...

June 1987
Flushing, New York

Mets at Chicago, June 9. In his pregame show from Wrigley Field, Mets play-by-play broadcaster Bob Murphy said, "For the Mets, pitching today, the man they turn to every time they're in trouble . . ."

Dwight Gooden?

Ron Darling?

Bob Ojeda?

Sid Fernandez?

None of the above.

"Terry Leach," Murphy said.

That day, the Mets, with a record of 28 wins and 28 losses, fined and benched right fielder Darryl Strawberry for arriving late to the ballpark. They committed five errors in the first four innings. Leach surrendered eight hits in six innings. The Mets lost 6–5.

It was a couple of weeks before this that gritty second baseman Wally Backman surveyed the locker room after another loss and said, "We're awful."

Baseball, year after year, exhibits so well how fine is the line between great and gruesome. It has been well over a decade since anything remotely resembling a dynasty happened. Even then, in 1976, when the Cincinnati Reds won their second consecutive world championship with the best offensive team of its era, club management knew it wouldn't last. "We're seeing the end of an era," general manager Bob Howsam said the night the Reds finished a four-game World Series sweep of the Yankees. Free agency and desperate trades distributed most of the players on that team across America over the next five years, and the Reds didn't win so much as a pennant in the dozen years after Howsam's statement of doom. And only the Yankees, in 1977 and 1978, could buy enough players and patch enough holes to win successive World Series titles after that.

But the Mets, now here was a team. Around 1983, the seeds of a new dominant team of baseball seemed to be popping up. This was three years after Frank Cashen, a former brewery executive and Baltimore Orioles architect, arrived with one thing in mind. Be good, and be good for a long time.

The Mets are Frank Cashen's child. When he came to the Mets, in 1980, they were moribund, having finished last, last, and last in the previous three seasons. Skip Lockwood and Mark Bomback and Steve Henderson were three of the key players. The farm system was awful, and friends thought that Cashen was loony for taking on such a no-win job. Cashen had been the Orioles' general manager from 1966 to 1975, but there he'd stepped into a great situation. The team was already winning, and Cashen's job would be to keep the team winning, which it did at a handsome clip. The Mets, Cashen knew, had to built so they could be on top someday, and then he would have to figure out a way to keep them there. When club owner Nelson Doubleday interviewed Cashen for the general manager's job in 1980, Cashen had one important question.

"Are you looking for a quick fix?" Cashen said. "If you are, you shouldn't hire me. I'm only interested in building a team that's going to be there year after year, so every year you can go to your season-ticket holders and say, 'We're going to have a good team.' "

Doubleday told him to do whatever he had to do to build the best team in baseball.

That's all Frank Cashen needed to hear.

Then he went and did it.

All the deals weren't great ones. Cashen knew in any business he had to win some today, too, and so he made deals for a fading slugger, Dave Kingman, and a millionaire former slugger, George Foster, neither of whom could slug very well anymore. In Cashen's first four years, the Mets finished fifth, fifth, sixth, and sixth in the six-team National League East.

"But," as Cashen says now, "if you don't have patience when you're building a team and know you're doing things the right way, I don't think over the long haul you'll build a good team."

Here's where the post-Yankees-dynasty rules helped the Mets. Because they were such a bad team, they got to pick high in the draft each year from 1978 to 1984. More than in any sport, the baseball draft is a crapshoot, because it's so difficult to project high school and college players into big-league situations. But the Mets drafted well. They chose infielder Hubie Brooks in the first round of 1978, later using him as the key man in the deal to get all-star catcher Gary Carter in 1984. They chose high school outfielder Darryl Strawberry in the first round of 1980, with the first overall pick. They chose high school pitcher Dwight Gooden in the first round in 1982, with the fifth overall pick. They chose high school outfielder Shawn Abner in the first round of 1984, with the first overall pick.

Cashen picked Davey Johnson, a former major-league infielder, to manage the team after the 1983 season, and there was enough talent in place by then for the Mets to start contending. They finished second to Chicago in 1984, winning 90 games, and second to St. Louis in 1985, winning 98. And Cashen went out and got the final starting pitcher he needed after the 1985 season,

Reconstructive Deal Number One
April 1, 1982

Mets sent Texas:

Outfielder Lee Mazzilli

Mets got:

Pitcher Ron Darling
Pitcher Walt Terrell

Reconstructive Deal Number Two
June 15, 1983

Mets sent St. Louis:

Pitcher Neil Allen
Pitcher Rick Ownbey

Mets got:

First baseman Keith Hernandez

Reconstructive Deal Number Three
December 8, 1983

Mets sent Los Angeles:

Infielder Bob Bailor
Pitcher Carlos Diaz

Mets got:

Pitcher Sid Fernandez

Reconstructive Deal Number Four
December 10, 1984

Mets sent Montreal:

Shortstop Hubie Brooks
Pitcher Floyd Youmans
Outfielder Herm Winningham
Catcher Mike Fitzgerald

Mets got:

Catcher Gary Carter

acquiring Bobby Ojeda from Boston in a deal the team truly agonized over because it had to give up two of the finest pitching prospects in baseball, Calvin Schiraldi and Wes Gardner, to do it. Ojeda had never won more than twelve games for Boston, and he was 9-11 for the Red Sox in 1985. But Cashen had a hunch that Ojeda's biggest problem was pitching in the smallish Fenway Park in Boston, and that coming to New York and pitching in bigger Shea Stadium would be invaluable to Ojeda.

So Johnson went into 1986 with a starting pitching rotation of Dwight Gooden, Ron Darling, Sid Fernandez, and Ojeda. They went into first place in the National League East on April 23 and never came out. The gamble on Ojeda was a good one: he led Mets pitchers with 18 wins and a 2.57 earned-run average. They won 108 games, more than any team since Cashen's 1969 Orioles won 109.

They were the best team in baseball, and no one disputed it. But here came the great equalizer—the playoffs, and the World Series. The Mets struggled to beat Houston, which won 96 games in the regular season, needing a 16-inning game to win the decisive sixth game. Then they played Boston, which won 95 games during the regular season. The Red Sox won the first two games in the best-of-seven Series at Shea Stadium, and they led three games to two entering game six at Shea. Boston took a 5–3 lead in the top of the tenth inning. The Red Sox got two quick outs in the bottom of the tenth inning. Kevin Mitchell of the Mets went into the clubhouse, got on the phone, and called to make a flight reservation home the next day to California. Keith Hernandez went into the clubhouse to smoke a cigarette and to watch the end on television. But the most stunning finish to a World Series game ever produced a Met win. Mookie Wilson's ground ball to Bill Buckner at first base went through Buckner's legs and allowed the winning run to score. Two nights later, the Mets won the Series.

How incredibly tenuous modern baseball greatness is.

"You talk about establishing a dynasty in baseball today," Lee Mazzilli, a Met pinch hitter, says now. "Well, we won a hundred and eight games that year, and we came close to losing in the playoffs against Houston. Then we're down to our last out in our last at-bat in the World Series. Say the ball doesn't go through Buckner's legs. Say we lose that game. Say we lose the Series. We win a hundred and eight games, the most anybody's won in I don't know how long, and then we wouldn't have won the title. You can see how hard it is to win year after year. We had the best team in baseball and it took everything we had to win it once."

After the season, Cashen addressed the final major need: a power-hitting outfielder. He traded the prize of the farm system, Shawn Abner, third baseman Mitchell, and three other prospects to San Diego for Kevin Mc-Reynolds, an unemotional player who the Mets thought could be a consistent 25-homer, 95-RBI force in the middle of the lineup.

They should have won a hundred games and coasted to another division title in 1987.

But as their first manager, Casey Stengel, would say, they should have stood in bed.

"As disasters go," the gray old *New York Times* said in the middle of it all, "the 1987 Mets' starting staff ranks with the major calamities in baseball history."

In 1986, as the Mets cruised to a division title, one starting pitcher missed one start. "I had five starters carved in marble," Davey Johnson said. In 1987, the Mets' pitching staff, collectively, spent 457 days on the disabled list, which veteran baseball people thought was the most disabled days any staff had ever had. That's seven weeks out per pitcher, on the average. The roll call:

March 30—Ace reliever Roger McDowell underwent surgery for a hernia. He missed six weeks.

April 1—Starter Dwight Gooden entered substance-abuse rehabilitation after testing positive on a club drug test. He missed ten weeks.

May 11—Starter Bobby Ojeda was placed on the disabled list with nerve damage in his left elbow. He underwent surgery May 23 and missed the rest of the season.

May 26—Starter Rick Aguilera threw four warm-up pitches before his scheduled start at San Francisco and had to quit because of pain in his elbow. He had a sprained elbow ligament. He missed three months.

May 27—Pressed into emergency duty, David Cone was hit by a pitched ball on the little finger of his pitching hand, shattering the finger. He missed eleven weeks.

August 3—Starter Sid Fernandez, who had missed a start in May when his right knee buckled on him, couldn't warm up before a scheduled start because of shoulder soreness. He missed three weeks.

July 12—Terry Leach, one of the substitute starting pitchers, underwent surgery for a slight knee-ligament tear. He missed a month.

September 13—Starter Ron Darling dove for a bunt by St. Louis outfielder Vince Coleman and his hand bent awkwardly, tearing ligaments in his right thumb. He missed the rest of the season.

Their replacements: Tom Edens, Jeff Innis, John Mitchell, Don Schulze.

That didn't make it any easier for Johnson or the Mets to swallow. In Chicago, in June, the Mets had a little bit of momentum because Gooden had just come back from his drug rehabilitation. In the first game of the series, on June 8, the score was tied at 2 with one out in the top of the ninth inning. The Mets had catcher Barry Lyons on second and third baseman Howard Johnson at third, and pinch hitter Bill Almon at bat. The Mets had the squeeze sign on, meaning that Davey Johnson wanted Almon to bunt on the second pitch, allowing Howard Johnson to score the go-ahead run.

Almon didn't answer the signal from third-base coach Sam Perlozzo, which is a must when any play is on; the player must acknowledge the sign in some small, predetermined gesture (rubbing left hand to right shoulder, for instance) before the play is on. Almon didn't give the acknowledging signal back. Almon took ball one. Almon appeared confused. Perlozzo summoned Almon to him. With the Wrigley Field crowd roaring in their ears, Perlozzo warned Almon a change in plans might be coming.

"Davey might want to change up the signals now," said Perlozzo. "So watch me. I'll let you know."

Perlozzo looked in the dugout and got the new signal from the manager. The squeeze was off now.

Almon never acknowledged the change in signals.

Reliever Lee Smith threw, and Almon bunted. It would have been a perfect squeeze bunt, had the squeeze been on. But Howard Johnson stood there on third base. Almon had blown the play.

Davey Johnson was furious, but he didn't explode. Not yet.

The Cubs ordered Mookie Wilson walked intentionally. The next batter was pitcher Doug Sisk, a career .118 hitter who would have to bat because the Mets had no pinch hitters left.

After intentional ball two to Wilson, Chicago catcher Jody Davis noticed Lyons off second base, staring into the dugout. Davis caught the eye of second baseman Ryne Sandberg, who stealthily crept toward second base. "I can pick this guy off," Davis thought incredulously.

This all happened in the space of about one and a half seconds.

Davis acted as though he was throwing the ball back to Smith on the mound, and Smith, indeed, thought he was. But the ball whizzed three feet over Smith's head and went *whappp!* into the mitt of Sandberg at second base, and Lyons was caught, in horror, staring at the ball and the end of the inning.

Davey Johnson was furious. He swore a little, but he didn't explode. Not yet.

In the bottom of the ninth, with the score still 2–2, Sisk, one of baseball's most erratic pitchers, gave up a leadoff single to Chicago's Dave Martinez. The first pitch to the next batter, Manny Trillo, was blasted over the left-field fence for a home run.

Davey Johnson was furious. Now he exploded.

First he exploded to the team, keeping the door to the locker room closed for an extra ten minutes after the game. He was shaking when the press got in.

"The way we played that last fucking inning, we didn't deserve to win that fucking game!" Johnson hissed. "If we keep our heads up our asses like that, we may not win another fucking game all fucking year. We had a screwup on a squeeze, and then I don't know what Lyons is thinking out there. He's out on a walk in the park. That play works in Little League, not in professional baseball."

Exhausted, spent, Johnson said, "I don't have anything more to say."

"I missed the sign," said Almon.

"I screwed up," said Lyons.

"I've seen it all now," Howard Johnson said.

Not yet. He thought he'd seen it all when, early in the season, an Atlanta Brave named Dion James hit a bird with a routine fly ball and the bird and the ball flopped dead to the ground, feet apart, and James got a double, and the Braves beat last year's ace, Ojeda, 12–4. He thought he'd seen it all in May, when the awful Braves swept the Mets in Atlanta, leaving the Mets below .500 and leaving Davey Johnson to have his third extended clubhouse meeting in twenty days and listening to the manager tell the team he wondered if big money was fucking them up.

He hadn't seen it all. Not yet.

That night, after this bad loss with the missed sign and the pickoff on the intentional walk (is that some sort of bizarre major-league first?) and the home run by Manny Freaking Trillo, Darryl Strawberry went to a downtown Chicago nightclub called Limelight. He drank vodka and cranberry juice quite consistently through the night. At 2:00, some guy with a camera came up to Strawberry and said how much of a pleasure it would be for him to take a picture of Strawberry and the manager of the place together. Sure, Strawberry said. He put his arm around the guy, and the picture was taken. The place closed at 4:00, and Strawberry was there until then, with the vodka and cranberry juice accompanying him.

Now, Darryl Strawberry was a tremendous baseball player. He could hit the ball farther than anyone in the game; that was the common thought in the mideighties in baseball, a thought proven by Strawberry when he hit a ball in 1988 that would have gone an estimated five hundred thirty feet had not the roof of the Olympic Stadium in Montreal interrupted its path. He also took it easy sometimes, which infuriated his teammates and the management of the team. General manager Frank Cashen implied such unfulfilled expectations sometime around this trip to Chicago when he said he thought that someday Darryl Strawberry would be the best player in baseball, someday. The inference was, damn it, Darryl ought to be the best player in baseball right now. Instead, he was in the top seven or eight.

The next day, the photographer took his negative to the *Chicago Tribune*.

The next day, Darryl Strawberry woke up at 11:45 and realized he was late for work.

Strawberry got to the park at 12:12, sixty-eight minutes before the game. The absolute latest he was allowed to arrive was 11:50.

Johnson fined him $250, which Strawberry took out of his wallet and handed to public relations director Jay Horwitz.

"He won't start again until I think it becomes important to him," said Johnson.

"I've played my ass off," Strawberry said, "and now I have to prove to him I want to play?"

Johnson benched him for two days, then made him play an exhibition game between the Mets and their highest-classification farm team, in Norfolk, Virginia, the next day. Strawberry was furious.

Meanwhile, there was a game that day. In the bottom of the fourth inning, the score was tied at 2, just as the previous day. Martinez hit a ground ball toward Keith Hernandez, thought to be the best-fielding first baseman by most baseball people. Hernandez bobbled it, allowing Martinez time to reach first. Then Hernandez, wrongly thinking he had a chance to get Martinez at first, threw wildly to pitcher Terry Leach, covering the base. Martinez went to second.

In the first fifty-two games and three innings of the season, Hernandez had made one error. On this play, he made two.

Chicago second baseman Ryne Sandberg hit a routine ground ball to Tim

Teufel of the Mets at second base. It went through Teufel's legs. Martinez scored, and the Cubs led 3–2.

Sandberg tried to steal second base, and the throw from Barry Lyons sailed into center field. Error number four.

The score was tied at 4 in the eighth inning when Sandberg hit a line drive off reliever Roger McDowell's heel. Two runs scored.

In the top of the ninth, Strawberry pinch-hit with two outs and the game on the line. There were two strikes. Lee Smith threw a fastball to Strawberry at the knees. Strawberry watched. Strike three.

The next day the *Chicago Tribune* ran the picture of Strawberry in the nightclub.

It wasn't a very good day for Strawberry.

The Mets would get back in the race this season, but the 1987 season, for them, was a case of a very good team getting hurt physically and playing stupid mentally. Howard Johnson, in May, tried for a triple play in Houston with Kevin Bass, a fast runner, running to first; it failed, and it cost the Mets a 2–1 loss. In June, Ron Darling had a no-hitter and a 4–0 lead after seven innings, but Philadelphia beat relievers Jesse Orosco and Roger McDowell in ten innings, 5–4. Orosco, in July, had a 5–2 lead over Houston with two out in the ninth inning but Houston proceeded to: single, single, single, homer. Mets lose. In September, against St. Louis, the Mets were one strike away from a 4–1 victory and moving to within one-half game of the National League East lead; they lost, 6–4. A week later, in Pittsburgh, the Mets lost leads of 1–0, 6–2, 7–6, and 8–7, and they lose 9–8.

And one more thing. Davey Johnson wanted a contract extension. For more money, of course. This story broke with a week left in the season, with the Mets still in the pennant race. Cashen was furious. Cashen would give no extension. Cashen once said that he thought Johnson was "obsessed" by money.

Welcome to the eighties.

When the season was over, Davey Johnson leaned back in his swivel chair in the manager's office and said, "We had the usual postchampionship-season overconfidence, the kind of complacency that goes along with winning big."

What a bitter year.

—28—

Ain't Gonna Be No Dynasties

July 1988
Manhattan

Pete Rose was pissed off at his french fries.

This is the man who dislikes mediocrity as much as anyone, and he had expressly told the waiter at the lobby restaurant in the Grand Hyatt Hotel he didn't want his fries sitting around and getting cold and soggy before they were brought out. "Yes, sir," the waiter had said. But sure enough, the damn things came out cold and soggy, and Rose couldn't stand it.

"These fries," he told the waiter, "are horseshit."

"Very sorry, sir," the waiter said. "I can take them back—"

"No, forget it," said Rose, but he and the waiter both knew the damage had been done by then, and Rose left only a six-dollar tip for the twenty-seven-dollar check. Pete Rose is a generous man. That is not a good Pete Rose tip.

Even at a lobby-restaurant table at the Grand Hyatt in Manhattan, Pete Rose was intense.

It was six hours before Rose would manage his Cincinnati Reds against the Mets at Shea Stadium, but it looked as if Rose wanted to be there now, the way he was fiddling with his hands and shifting in his seat and looking around the restaurant constantly. He wanted to be in his office at Shea Stadium making out the lineup card is where he wanted to be, writing in Larkin ss, Sabo 3b, Daniels lf, Davis cf, Esasky 1b, Diaz c, O'Neill rf, Treadway 2b, Jackson p. It's as though he was uncomfortable being out of uniform. Come to think of it, have you ever seen Rose out of uniform? "I don't think Pete Rose would ever be happy," baseball veteran Phil Garner said once, "unless he was putting on a baseball uniform every day."

But Rose warmed to this subject. The subject was dynasties, and why they don't work anymore.

"Number one," he said, "there aren't any real teams anymore. Know what I mean? There aren't teams that grow up and grow old together anymore. Everybody's always changing. Number two, and this goes along with that, everybody's playing out their options all the time. Can't blame 'em, but it's happening. It's hard to remember the last time a guy, a star player, played his whole career for a team. Who was it, Johnny Bench? Carl Yastrzemski? Those are probably the only guys recently to do it.

"Look at the Reds. The Reds were a team built through the organization. They developed me, Bench, [Tony] Perez, [Lee] May, [Dave] Concepcion. They traded for [Joe] Morgan, [George] Foster, [Cesar] Geronimo, using players they raised themselves. It was an organization team. Look at our team now. It's an organization team mostly, but how long can that last?"

He chewed on his straw and sucked down iced tea.

"Dynasties are really a thing of the past," he said. "Another reason is expansion. We get Eric Davis hurt now, and what the fuck are we gonna do? We don't have a fuckin' player worth a shit in Triple-A to replace him. Another thing is the salaries. The players are at an all-time high in bucks, and in general I'd say the game just isn't as fun anymore. It's such a fuckin' business. Everything is money. Every salary's on the cover of *Sports Illustrated*. That's all everybody talks about now, money.

"Another thing is it's hard for a great team to make trades. Too many teams have been burned in the past by the great teams. That's why, with the Mets, who the fuck wants to help them get any better? You know if the Mets want to make a deal, they think it's going to make them better. So teams won't do business with the Mets as easily as they'd do business with another team. You know, certain teams twenty years ago, you knew at the start of the season that they were going to lose and lose big. Nowadays, with all the players changing teams and the unpredictability, any team could almost be good any year. Look at the Dodgers this year. They finish sixteen games under .500 two years in a row, then they go out in the off-season and look what they did—they got Jesse Orosco, Jay Howell, Kirk Gibson, Matt Young, Alfredo Griffin, and Mike Davis—and now they're in contention."

Listening to Rose, it seemed interesting that, here he was, forty-seven years old, only two years removed from being an active player, and already he seemed so distant from being a player. This showed when Rose talked about Chris Sabo, his young third baseman. Sabo, who would play well enough to be named the National League's rookie of the year, was a Pete Rose Junior. Others had better ability, but Sabo competed so hard and got his uniform so dirty and just wanted to play so badly that it was hard to defeat him. His teammates called him Spuds, after the beer dog of the same name. His teammates say Spuds and Spuds looked alike.

"What really pisses me off, and it kind of hurts me, is the way Spuds gets treated, the way he gets talked about," Rose said. "He'll bust his ass running out a double, and he'll slide into second base and just beat the tag, and I'll look down the bench and there'll be guys elbowing each other, laughing at him. They're not as happy for him as they are making fun of him. It's a fuckin' shame."

Rose paused then and chewed harder on the straw. He clearly was troubled by the inference of this, that Sabo played his ass off but that the more graceful players who Rose knew didn't play all-out all the time would make fun of him and ostracize him. Hard work wasn't in.

So Rose added all of this up and pronounced the sport free of dynasties, probably forever. "I like the Mets," he said. "They're one of the best teams. But I don't think there's any superteams today. And I don't see any superteams happening."

Free from talking about the game now, Rose was about to live it. So he excused himself. He had a uniform to put on.

"I thought the Mets should have lost that Series a couple years ago," Detroit manager Sparky Anderson was saying in the visiting manager's office, a borough and a week away at Yankee Stadium long before a game one night. "But I thought after they escaped and got through that one, there was nothing that could beat them the next four or five years. Their pitching was so good. Really, after they won in 'eighty-six, I didn't think anybody would be able to touch them."

And now?

"Now," said this wise old sage of baseball, "I've given up on dynasties. They're obsolete. They're a thing of the past."

Anderson is a marvelous natural resource for the sport of baseball. First of all, he knows everybody in it. Second, he likes everybody in it. Third, there's not a negative bone in his body, and his ego is very well under control. When he was fired—unfairly, most Cincinnatians thought, by Reds president Dick Wagner in 1978—Wagner flew to California and met with Anderson at a hotel near his, Anderson's, home. They had breakfast. They chatted about everything except the team. Wagner asked Anderson up to his room in this Marriott Hotel near the airport. "Right near LAX," Anderson said. "Room eleven eighteen. Ten o'clock in the morning. He fired me. Hey, it hurt bad. But it's a business. And that was the business part. I realize that. Business and pleasure are two totally different things. I respect him for how he did it. And to this day, his wife, me, and him have been the very best of friends."

And he realized the role of a manager. Make some moves, especially late in games. But let the players play, and only get in the way if they prove they don't know what they're doing or don't have the ability to get it done. "You wait for me to win one game for you, your wait an eternity," he said. "Ain't got no tricks in my bag. No, sir."

So that's Sparky. "Dumb like a fox," George Steinbrenner once said of him. He'll never let you think he's got much but pipe smoke and a friendly voice coming out of his head, but he's had five teams in the World Series in nineteen managerial years. So he knows a thing or two about excellence, and why it's so fleeting today.

"It used to be," Anderson said, drawing on his pipe, feet up on his desk, uniform long since donned, "if your scouts were sharper and you had more of 'em and they could make friends with the families the best, my God, you were liable to corral everybody good. Not having the draft was a tremendous factor in why there were dynasties. I signed with the Dodgers because of [scout] Lefty Phillips. My father wouldn't allow me to sign with anybody else. Lefty, since I was thirteen years old, did everything for us. So if somebody'd come along with fifty thousand, it wouldn't have mattered. We were indebted to Lefty, and it didn't matter what I got. I was going with the Dodgers.

"The Dodgers and Yankees had about as sharp as scouts as you could see. California was their number one state, both teams, and so much great baseball was being played there. Finally, other teams started going out there, but the Yankees and Dodgers had such a hold of the thing by then that it was hard for the other teams to sign the guys the Yankees and Dodgers wanted.

"Now, of course, everything's equal. You can't hoard no players. The Reds were the last home-grown dynasty, the last of the true home-grown great franchises. With the free agency the way it is today, you can't blame a guy when somebody throws that kind of money out in front of him. I don't blame a guy. If you're gonna make a guy secure for the rest of his life, you'd have to be crazy not to take the security. I don't believe that I personally need security, but most people do. You can't pass up that kind of security. It relaxes them to know that, 'Boy, I can go out there and play and it doesn't matter how I do. I get my money.' Some guys need that. I think it takes some of the fun and challenge away myself, but . . .

"What's gonna happen now is that it's going to be impossible to win every year. A team wins a couple of times and what happens is you'd have salaries so high no owner could pay 'em. So what's going to happen now is if you win a couple of years in a row, you're going to have to let those guys move along. You're going to have to let them free. Because there's no way you can keep all of 'em. You'll keep a few, but not all, because, my God, it'd eat you alive having ten guys on your roster making two million a year. That's twenty million for your starting lineup. No owner can pay that, I don't care who he is. So what it comes down to is I just think there ain't gonna be no dynasty."

Anderson spoke affectionately of the Reds team that won 108 games in 1975, and in 1976, 102. But in the next room, veteran slugger Darrell Evans said he didn't long for the good old days. He is of the opinion that the big money has made the game much, much better.

"Parity has happened," Evans said, "because teams with gaping weaknesses can fill those by signing the player they need. I hear people say we're not hungry anymore. Well, that's not why teams don't dominate now. Teams don't dominate now because we're so close to each other in ability."

While it's not accurate to call it domination, what happened in baseball from 1969 to 1978 surely differed from what happened from 1979 to 1988. Call it a move from slight dominance to absolute parity. To illustrate:

1969–1978

Year	American League winner	National League winner	World Series winner
1969	Baltimore	New York	New York Mets
1970	Baltimore	Cincinnati	Baltimore
1971	Baltimore	Pittsburgh	Pittsburgh
1972	Oakland	Cincinnati	Oakland
1973	Oakland	New York	Oakland
1974	Oakland	Los Angeles	Oakland
1975	Boston	Cincinnati	Cincinnati
1976	New York	Cincinnati	Cincinnati
1977	New York	Los Angeles	New York Yankees
1978	New York	Los Angeles	New York Yankees

1979–1988

Year	American League winner	National League winner	World Series winner
1979	Baltimore	Pittsburgh	Pittsburgh
1980	Kansas City	Philadelphia	Philadelphia
1981	New York	Los Angeles	Los Angeles
1982	Milwaukee	St. Louis	St. Louis
1983	Baltimore	Philadelphia	Baltimore
1984	Detroit	San Diego	Detroit
1985	Kansas City	St. Louis	Kansas City
1986	Boston	New York	New York Mets
1987	Minnesota	St. Louis	Minnesota
1988	Oakland	Los Angeles	Los Angeles

Summing up two decades of difference:

	1969–1978	1979–1988
Times that American League winner repeated:	6	0
Times that National League winner repeated:	2	0
Times that World Series winner repeated:	4	0

In the eighties, the Dodgers are the only team to have won two World Series. In the eighties, the Islanders and Edmonton have both won four Stanley Cups. In the eighties, San Francisco has won three Super Bowls, the Raiders and Washington two each. In the eighties, the Lakers won five National Basketball Association championships.

What baseball has is the most competitive sport of the day.

29

Winning Isn't Everything

October 1988
Flushing, New York

Keith Hernandez was sitting by his locker, smoking. This time he was smoking a cigarette. Sometimes, he just smoked—about how hard it is to play in New York. "I can't complain, because I had some great seasons in St. Louis in relative obscurity, and when I came here, boom, people knew me all over the country," he said. "But if there's any one thing that can take away from the fun here, it's the media. The big story. The headline mentality. The scoops. They love to put the pressure on you. After a while, it can really wear on you."

The Mets were lucky in this regard in 1988. They didn't give the tabloids much to stir up. There was a brief volcano in March, when Mike Lupica of the *Daily News* and *Esquire* wrote a column in *Esquire* that had Darryl Strawberry ripping everyone in sight. An admirer of St. Louis manager Whitey Herzog, Strawberry said, "I wonder how many games this team would win if Whitey were managing it?" Gary Carter, Strawberry said, "just quit" in 1987. Second baseman Wally Backman, Strawberry said, "spends too much time trying to act like Keith [Hernandez]. But he doesn't have the game to back it up." And on, and on.

Carter said, "Isn't this 1988? We're trying to forget all that happened last year."

Strawberry said he didn't say most of the stuff Lupica said he said.

But it was a mild year, a boring year in comparison to 1987. The Mets went into first place on May 3 and never fell out. The second-place Pirates had the margin down to 2 games after game 100, but a month later the lead was 7½ games, and a month later it was 13. Pittsburgh just didn't have the pitching. Did anyone? The Mets had five starters pitch at least 180 innings each in 1988. The two supposed aces, Gooden and Darling, had the highest earned-run averages, at 3.19 and 3.25 respectively, on the staff.

The club finished 100-60, 15 games ahead of the second-place Pirates. Strawberry and McReynolds combined for 66 homers and 200 runs batted in. In the first game of the year, the Mets hit 6 home runs; they'd never done that in their history. In the last series of the year, the Mets swept St. Louis, getting wins for Darling, Fernandez, and David Cone.

The two new stories of the year were those of Cone and Gregg Jefferies. Cone won 20 games and lost 3, the sixth-best record in the history of baseball pitchers. Jefferies came out of the Mets' farm system in August the best hitting prospect the club had produced since Strawberry, and he hit .321 with 6 homers in 29 games.

Cone was twenty-five. Jefferies was twenty-one. Their best attribute, collectively, might have been perspective. Cone, a Midwestern kid, and Jefferies, from California, realized they wouldn't be helped by getting caught up in the New Yorkness of the Mets. They were good, very good. But they knew they didn't need to be reminded of that every few minutes.

Example: Jefferies and the book.

After seventy-four major-league trips to bat, and one trip to the front page of *Newsday* because of his great hitting, Jefferies was sitting alone at his locker one day before a game at Shea Stadium.

"Excuse me," said a writer who had stopped at Jefferies's locker. He introduced himself and asked, "Would you be interested in writing a book after the season? I've got a publisher who's interested . . ."

Jefferies thought the guy was kidding.

He asked the guy if he was kidding.

The guy said no.

"I appreciate you asking," Jefferies said. "But no thanks."

Later, Jefferies said, "It was like, I'm sure this guy's kidding. Then I found out he wasn't, and I was shocked. What have I done?"

Jefferies, in fact, thought he'd found the key to playing and hitting in New York. "During the season," he said, "I won't read the papers, and I won't listen to what people say about me. It can't help me. None of that stuff can. So I ignore it."

Cone, too. One day in the locker room he was asked about how tough it must be to play in New York. "I don't think it's tough at all," he said, not grasping the meaning of the question. "This is a great pitcher's park."

The Mets lost the National League playoff series to Orel Hershiser and Kirk Gibson, 4–3.

After taking a two games to one lead in the series, the Mets, playing at home, led by two runs with two outs in the ninth inning of game four. Dwight Gooden was pitching. He threw what he would call the following spring "a batting-practice fastball" to Los Angeles catcher Scioscia, who had 3 home runs in 408 at-bats in 1988. Scioscia homered. The game went into extra innings. Gibson, the National League's most valuable player, hit a home run to win the game in the top of the twelfth inning. In the bottom of the inning, Hershiser retired the last batter, Kevin McReynolds, to earn a save.

Half a day later—this was a day game following a night game—Gibson's 3-run homer clinched a 7–4 Los Angeles victory.

In eighteen hours the Dodgers had gone from being down 2–1 in the series to being up 3–2. And they did it on the road.

The Mets won game six, but Hershiser threw a 5-hitter in the seventh game and the Dodgers won 6–0.

Anything goes in these series. "What can you do?" said Hernandez after he had a couple of months to reflect on it. "In baseball, you play one hundred sixty-two games. Then you play seven to win the pennant. Then you play seven to win the World Series. You play by the rules. At least baseball has some integrity. Second place in your division doesn't make the playoffs. Teams under .500 don't make the playoffs. There's no wild card. Winning a division means something."

For the Mets, that wasn't enough in 1988.

30

We Interrupt This Off-season for an Explosion

January 1989
Miami, Florida

Money Note Number One:

Hyatt Regency Hotel, Miami, the day before Super Bowl XXIII. In the Super Bowl press room, a few writers are filing their final pregame stories when Tommy Lasorda, the manager of the world champion Dodgers, walks in. With entourage.

And of course, he's talking about everything.

To be around Lasorda is to be around the neighborhood coffee klatch. Whatever comes up, he'll talk about it, and with joie de vivre. The subject now is money, and baseball spending, and what players are worth.

Lasorda says, "Nobody spent more than Gene Autry spent with the Angels, but what it comes down to is spending the money on the right players. I mean, what have the Yankees always needed? Pitching. And I see they traded Rick Rhoden to Houston."

Sid Hartman of the *Minneapolis Star and Tribune* says, "I'll tell you what though. I'd never pay a million bucks for Rick Rhoden, a thirty-six-year-old pitcher."

Lasorda says, "Christ, a million dollars . . . Hey, let me tell you something. I saw Tom Tresh last week in Nashville. Tom Tresh. Pretty fair shortstop, wasn't he? I said, 'Let me tell you something, Tommy. Alfredo Griffin, our shortstop, hit .199. He made a million bucks. How do you like that?' I mean, compare Tresh with Alfredo Griffin. There's your yardstick. Hey, nothing against Alfredo Griffin. But it's a joke."

Money Note Number Two:

When Cincinnati general manager Murray Cook heard on February 16 that Orel Hershiser had just signed a three-year contract worth $7.9 million with the Dodgers, he told a phone caller, "Excuse me for a minute. I have to scrape myself off the floor."

Not since the days when Oakland A's were getting 400 percent raises to change teams in the midseventies had anything of the magnitude of this off-season hit baseball. Owners who had tried to hold down the skyrocketing free-agent salaries in the mideighties had been found guilty of collusion by arbitrator Thomas Roberts in September 1987, and the effect was finally felt after the 1988 season when some big names had their contract expire.

In 1989, one of every six major-league players made $1 million or more in salary. One of four Mets did. In the space of a month in the off-season, the Mets signed Ron Darling, Kevin McReynolds, and Dwight Gooden to the three biggest contracts in their history. The Mets' 1989 million-dollar club:

Player	Years of Contract	Total Value of Contract	1989 Earnings
Dwight Gooden	3	$6,700,000	$2,250,000
Keith Hernandez	5	$8,400,000	$1,700,000
Kevin McReynolds	3	$5,500,000	$1,600,000
Ron Darling	3	$5,300,000	$1,600,000
Darryl Strawberry	5	$5,400,000	$1,400,000
Mookie Wilson	6	$4,500,000	$1,000,000

In 1987 and 1988: Gooden combined to go 33-16, Darling 29-17; Hernandez batted .285; McReynolds averaged 28 homers and 97 runs batted in; Strawberry averaged 39 homers and 103 runs batted in; and Wilson, a part-time player, batted .298.

And Gary Carter, the aging catcher, was going to make $900,000 from the team and at least $600,000 smiling for different people and corporations in 1989.

(And the nineteen richest Dodgers were signed to play in 1989 for a total of $20,091,962!)

And the Yankees had just signed a $55-million-per-year cable television deal with the Madison Square Garden network, beginning with the 1989 season.

And Strawberry, on the last day of February, was threatening a boycott of spring training because he wanted more money.

Money Note Number Three:
In the Sunday *Star-Ledger* of Newark, New Jersey, on February 19, 1989, here were all the baseball headlines of the day (or rather, the stories having something to do with baseball) as the teams warmed up for spring training:

• Owners Seem to Be Losing Their Control
From Fort Lauderdale, where the Yankees train, writer Moss Klein quotes Whitey Ford saying he made $18 per pitch with his most lucrative contract,

and saying Roger Clemens will make $600 per pitch with his new $2.5-million-a-year contract. "Indeed," writes Klein, "it is hard to believe that club owners have gone so completely out of control again."

• Talented Leiter Ready to Fulfill Potential

From Fort Lauderdale, Klein writes about the brightest Yankee pitching prospect, twenty-three-year-old Al Leiter. "The glory and big money are out there, beckoning to Leiter," writes Klein. "He's star material—rich contracts, spotlights, commercials, endorsements. The works."

• Carter Wins Hearing, Gets $1.63M Contract

From Cleveland, the AP reports that Indians outfielder Joe Carter, who batted .271 with 27 home runs in 1988, has won a salary of $1,630,000, a $790,000 raise over 1988, in salary arbitration. "The Indians had tried to avoid arbitration," the AP writes, "by offering him a five-year deal worth an estimated $9.5 million." Carter refused.

• Not a Word Is Said as Clemens Joins Camp

From Winter Haven, Florida, the AP reports that Boston pitcher Roger Clemens has no comment upon reporting to camp one day late after signing a three-year, $7.5-million contract. "Clemens apparently was irked at criticism for missing the opening practice on Friday," the AP writes.

• Strawberry Wants His Piece of the Pie

From Port St. Lucie, Florida, where the Mets train, outfielder Darryl Strawberry starts campaigning with writer Dan Castellano for more money than Los Angeles pitcher Orel Hershiser just got with his $7.9-million contract over three years. Strawberry says, "If a pitcher, a guy who plays every fifth day, can get $7.9 million, what is a guy who plays every day worth? As good as he is, he plays in, what, 35 games a year? I play in 155 games a year . . . I'm sure somebody will pay me. I'd like it to be the Mets, but we'll have to see how much they want me."

• Myers Won't Report Without Contract

From Port St. Lucie, Castellano writes that Randy Myers, the Mets' ace reliever, will not report to camp without a signed contract. He made $108,000 in his second year, 1988, and his agent, David Fishof, tells Castellano that Myers wants $400,000. Fishof says, "The Mets are showing him some respect this season but not enough yet."

• Teufel Wins Arbitration

From Port St. Lucie, Castellano writes that second baseman Tim Teufel has won his arbitration case with the Mets. Teufel earned $537,500 in 1988 while batting .234 with 4 homers and 31 runs batted in. The arbitrator gave Teufel a $52,500 raise, to $590,000.

• Dodgers Feeling Like a Million

In a baseball-notes column, the AP reports that one-third of the world champion Los Angeles Dodgers will earn more than $1 million in 1989. The AP says the Dodgers' average salary will exceed $850,000 in 1989, and that the combined 1989 salaries of Orel Hershiser, Fernando Valenzuela, and Eddie

Murray will exceed the total payrolls of the White Sox, Mariners, and Rangers. Hershiser and Valenzuela were a combined 28-16 in 1988, while Murray hit .284 with 28 homers.

• Pirates Sign Van Slyke to 3-Year, $5.5M Deal

From Pittsburgh, the AP reports that Pirates outfielder Andy Van Slyke agreed to the richest contract in club history. The breakthrough to the contract came, the AP writes, when Van Slyke dropped a demand that he be paid in the event he doesn't play because of a threatened strike in 1990. The AP says Van Slyke can earn $270,000 per year in incentive bonuses in addition to his base salaries.

Money Note Number Four:

Perhaps one of the reasons the money is so outrageous today is because it was so imbalanced for years. In 1940, a minor-league shortstop for the Yankees, Phil Rizzuto, was named the minor-league player of the year, and his future was exceedingly bright. When he went to spring training the next season, Rizzuto had to go into general manager Ed Barrow's office to sign his contract. The contract was neatly typed, waiting for Rizzuto when he walked in.

The figure on the contract read "Five thousand and no/100 dollars."

"Mr. Barrow," said Rizzuto, surprised at the low figure, "I was the minor-league player of the year last year, and—"

"Listen, Rizzuto," Barrow bellowed, "sign or get out!"

He signed.

Now Rizzuto says, "Negotiations were never really bitter battles. You just accepted that you were beat from the start."

"So," Rizzuto was asked, "wouldn't it have been better if a lot of your teammates could have moved to other teams, so they could start and make more money? Wouldn't it have been better to have free agency back then, for the players?"

"Well," Rizzuto said, "I never knew one Yankee who wanted to go elsewhere. We all wanted that World Series money, and it seemed like we got it most years."

──31──

Cashen's Team

The 1989 season held so much promise for the Mets. Again, they had the best pitching in baseball. Again, it was generally conceded that they had the best team. What they also had, quite possibly, was the brightest director of any baseball team.

There he was, sitting in the Mets' dugout at their lovely spring-training complex, trying to explain how to stay on top of a very dynamic industry—sports—and talking about things like Japanese management techniques, three-year plans, and his ten annual goals. He might have mentioned pitching once or twice in forty minutes. But here was a businessman, talking business.

The reason the New York Mets are good today is that they made some good trades when they were down, they've drafted well (Strawberry, Gooden, Jefferies) for a decade, and they've had foresight. Davey Johnson says, "Part of my job is to be constantly thinking about how every move I make will affect our organization in three years."

Frank Cashen gave this organization foresight. It's very, very important.

Sitting in the dugout on this warm morning, half an eye on outfielders hitting cutoff men on the pristine diamond in front of him, Cashen is clearly proud of all that he sees before him.

"It's my own personal opinion—and people are horrified when I say this —but I think the New York Mets are run more in a businesslike, professional manner than any other club," he said. "People say, 'Business?' Everyone still thinks this is a sport. But to me the teams that survive and thrive today are the teams run like good businesses.

"I'm always thinking, 'Where are we going to be next year? Where are we going to be the year after?' We run our team through management by objectives. That's the theory of management that the Japanese have perfected, where everyone in an organization has a say how the organization's going to be run. Everyone sets goals. What we do is get to July fourth every year— it's an artificial date, but we figure there isn't a hell of a lot the front office can do to affect what goes on on the field after that point—and we start planning for the next year right then. In August, after some planning time, we say to our vice presidents, 'Okay, what are you going to accomplish next year, and what are you going to need to accomplish it?' In September, we start putting things on paper. Everybody lays out objectives for their department, and each year I take ten of the objectives and bring them to our board of directors and say, 'This is what we want to accomplish this year.'

"In 1988, we probably came as close as ever, about ninety-seven, ninety-eight percent, to reaching our objectives. One, we wanted to continue to be the best organization in baseball, to win ninety-plus games, to win the Eastern Division of the National League to put us in the playoffs. Two, we wanted to sell X amount of tickets. We wanted to draw three million fans through the turnstiles. Three, we wanted to improve our ballpark presentation and do some things to improve the scoreboard. Four, we wanted to get new blood in our minor-league system. New staff. I firmly believe that it's just as important to be developing new managers and coaches as it is to be developing new talent. Five, we wanted to computerize our entire operation. Soon, our minor leagues will be on line with us.

"So we did all of this, and we also decided that my job more and more would be to do the planning for the organization for the 1990s. I started to plan for the nineties last year. I'm looking at questions like, where's the talent going to come from? Now that we've had ten years to study player acquisition as an organization, we have to decide how important Latin American talent is, whether we should be looking at colleges more to draft players than we have in the past. I've also looked at what we can do to make young fans Mets fans. A lot of time's been spent on where we're going to be radio-TV-wise in the nineties, and the impact of pay-per-view TV. The study of sports is really a fascinating study. I think there's going to be an explosion in sports in the nineties. Television has really laid out some enormous sums for sports rights recently. We want to be in position to take advantage of that."

But, Cashen was asked, can anyone get into the position of winning World Series year after year today?

He thought for a minute. "I know what it takes to win ninety, a hundred games. I think we can continue to win games. That's not the question. To win world championships in baseball consistently now, I don't think we'll ever see that. You've got the draft distributing talent more evenly. You've got free agency. You've got layers of playoffs. My theory is, the best teams always win the division. You play one hundred sixty-two games, and that's enough to prove who's the best. Then you play four out of seven. Then you play four out of seven again. Maybe the best team doesn't always win. But that's the way it is, and they're the same rules for everyone."

Those rules have been great to the Mets in the regular season but harsh after that. The Mets, entering 1989, were baseball's best recent team. The best regular-season teams from 1984 to 1988:

Team	W-L	Pct.	Games Difference
1. New York Mets	488-320	.604	—
2. Detroit	461-348	.570	27.5
3. Toronto	457-352	.565	31.5
4. New York Yankees	448-360	.554	40
5. St. Louis	435-374	.538	53.5

Davey Johnson said, "Frank Cashen's philosophy has proven to be the most effective in baseball."

And this is not a teetering team now. This is not a team waiting to be taken over. In the last two years, the Mets have acquired enough pitching so that now, in their upper minor-league system, they have the most talented pitching prospects in baseball.

"They didn't want to run into the problem we faced in 'eighty-seven, with all the pitching injuries," Ron Darling said. "So you can see what they've done about that in the last couple of off-seasons. You've got to hand it to them for thinking about that."

In the last two years, the Mets have traded an average-at-best shortstop, Rafael Santana; two fading relief pitchers, Doug Sisk and Jesse Orosco; a marginal outfielder, Terry Blocker; a marginal catcher, Ed Hearn; a marginal starting pitcher, Rick Anderson; a first base prospect, Randy Milligan; and an above-average major-league second baseman, Wally Backman. In return they've gotten eleven minor-league pitching prospects. For Sisk, who won three games with no saves for Baltimore in 1988, they got the Texas League pitcher of the year in 1988, lefty Blaine Beatty, and a lower prospect. For Orosco, the Mets got three pitchers from Oakland who they thought would eventually pitch in the big leagues: starter Wally Whitehurt and relievers Jack Savage and Kevin Tapani.

And everyone in baseball wanted the ace of their minor-league system, left-handed pitcher David West.

The Mets, in 1989, are healthy enough in pitching that they could use some of their prospects to trade for players they'd really need in the future —a first baseman maybe (Hernandez is thirty-five), or a catcher (Carter is thirty-four).

"The Mets are going to be good long after I'm gone," Hernandez said. "They're reaping the harvest now, and they will be for a few years, for making smart decisions in the last few years."

32

The M Word

February 1989
Kissimmee, Florida

One night ten years ago, Phil Garner, then the second baseman for the Pittsburgh Pirates, went to a party in Pittsburgh at the home of former Steelers linebacker Andy Russell. In the living room, Garner struck up a how's-the-weather type of conversation with Russell's wife, and the subject turned to Russell's two children.

He said: "Are your kids going to be good athletes?"

She said: "I'm not sure."

He said: "Why?"

She said: "I think they're too well-adjusted."

Chuckle, chuckle.

Motivation. It's just different now.

"Think about it," said Garner, in the Houston Astros' camp. He is a Houston broadcaster now, after fifteen years as a major-league second and third baseman. "Well-rounded people don't make the best athletes. Well-adjusted people . . . I'm not in any way trying to demean Pete Rose, but I think he's probably so focused on one thing—baseball. I've noticed that about some of the great athletes. Willie Stargell was incredibly focused.

"But I think that's changing some. Kids today don't want to play winter ball as much. They want to spend time home with their families in the winter, which is fine. I think as ballplayers we've changed."

Garner thought for a while. The subject turned to repeating in sports, and the question about how baseball has produced no repeat pennant winners and no repeat World Series winners since 1978. Free agency and the draft distributed players better, he acknowledged. But there was another thing.

The M word.

"I love that song 'Eye of the Tiger,'" he said. "The challenger stalks his prey in the middle of the night. The champion's living the nice life. The challenger is in the gym every weekend, busting his ass. The champion's having weekends at the Hyatt. The motivation changes. All my life my motivation was the World Series. I'd be running in the off-season, and in the

170

last quarter-mile of my running, I'd run harder. I'd say to myself, 'This is for the World Series.' "

In 1979, Garner played in a World Series. He batted .417 in the playoffs as Pittsburgh beat Cincinnati three games to none. He batted .500 in the World Series as Pittsburgh beat Baltimore four games to three.

"Once I got there, and after it was over, I thought, 'Oh, no. Is the thrill of the hunt better than the kill?' That winter, I think I had a letdown. The point is, when all the teams are so close in ability, it's the little things that can be so important in whether you establish yourself over a period of years."

Garner and Hernandez agree that long-term contracts have adversely affected greatness. Their well-thought-out views:

Garner: "Seven or eight years ago, I would have said no, contracts didn't have an effect. But let's look at the cold, hard numbers. The numbers show, as many players have started long-term rich contracts, the couple of years right after he signs aren't as good. I can't argue with that. But the assumption in America is, 'All these players don't care anymore.' Hey, some players come to spring training out of shape, and maybe some of them don't work as hard. Some of them may have relaxed a little bit with their own goals and desires. But I will argue—and I've seen this among some players—that some players will try to overdo when they get the big money. The .290 hitter thinks he has to bat .320, and the twenty-five-homer guy thinks he has to hit thirty-five. [When Joe Carter signed the $1.63 million contract with Cleveland before this season, he said it wasn't going to help him that people thought he had to hit 50 home runs and knock in 150 runs to earn his pay.] Yes, some people did get complacent, but other guys got overconscientious. For some reason, in America, there's a very disturbing trend that almost punishes you for making money. You almost have to apologize for making money. But Carl Icahn and Donald Trump make money and that doesn't bother anyone."

Hernandez: "I've thought about this a lot, and I think now that the five-year contract isn't good for motivation. I have two fives, and the third year, both times . . . you have to find something to keep . . . you have to motivate yourself in the middle of that contract because you're making such good money to keep that mental toughness. You really have to push yourself. When you're out to prove yourself all the time, you've got that incentive to go out there and not give in on a day you might not feel good, or when you're up against a tough pitcher and you're oh and two in the count and no one's on base. It's so easy to give in. A three-year deal, I feel, is better, because it's over before you know it. You've got the incentive all the way through."

33

The Last Words

February 1989
Vero Beach, Florida

It was a lovely Sunday in Dodgertown, and here came perspective. He rode in from the outfield, along the warning track, down the first-base side of the small stadium here, and as he did, the crowd of a hundred or so seniors in the stands applauded. Then they cheered. It got kind of loud, for a hundred people relaxing and watching a baseball team take batting practice. The man in the cart, Tom Lasorda, waved. He took his cap off and waved that, too.

"Look," said Mike Downey, the columnist for the *Los Angeles Times*. "It's the pope."

No. It was perspective. Tom Lasorda walked behind the batting cage to watch John Shelby, Willie Randolph, and Dave Anderson take their cuts, and without missing a swing, he tried to explain why there can't be extended greatness in baseball today.

"Free agency, one," he began. "Two is the fact that, for example, when the Yankees were winning all those pennants, they had the same guys every year. You didn't turn over those teams unless the guys retired. I mean, look at us. Look at our 1981 championship team compared to this team. Who's left? [Two of twenty-five players, catcher Mike Scioscia and pitcher Fernando Valenzuela.] Three, injuries. Before, you used to be able to bring up kids who could really help a big-league club. But teams are so thin now you get one guy hurt and it can kill you. When I played—and this is no knock against the players of today—you never told anybody about an injury unless you absolutely, positively could not play. Why? When I played, the Dodgers had twenty-six farm teams. TWENTY-SIX FARM TEAMS! You'd get replaced pretty easy. Four, you can't hold on to players forever today. When I played, we had three Triple-A teams—Montreal, St. Paul, and Hollywood. Say you were a catcher and you hit forty home runs one year. Where the fuck you think you're gonna go? You ain't gonna beat out Roy Campanella. So you go back to Triple-A. Now, after six years, even a minor-leaguer becomes a free agent. Do you realize I played nine years for the same Triple-A club. You ain't never gonna see that again. NEVER!"

In other words, you ain't never gonna see a baseball dynasty again. Never.

PART

Meanwhile, in the Meadowlands

—34—

All Is Not Forgotten

*R*edskins' interlude:

It is a day after Super Bowl XXII, in San Diego, California, a year after the Giants' Super Bowl victory. The Redskins are adjusting to the shock of their 42–10 victory over Denver the previous day, and Joe Gibbs, their coach, is trying to get away from it all, trying to worm his way free of a few reporters in the lobby of the San Diego Marriott Hotel and Marina. He says four things of note while slipping away:

1. "Perspective is our hope."

2. "I don't think you have to worry about me writing a book."

3. "I thought the Giants had the best chance of repeating of anyone recently, because they were superstrong and physical."

4. "We understand ourselves a little bit better, I think, than other teams have."

February 1988
East Rutherford, New Jersey

Some inglorious and divisive things happened to the Giants as the 1987 season was ending.

The players grew apart from Bill Parcells. When the Giants went to St. Louis to play the final pro football game at Busch Stadium in December, they played a terrible first half and went into the locker trailing 27–10 at halftime. In the locker room, Parcells accused his team of laying down, which brought the fiery Carl Banks off his bench to scream at Parcells, "Nobody here's giving up!" After the game, which the Giants lost 27–24, Banks was seething about Parcells's charge. "I ain't countin' the fuckin' days!" he spit out. "Countin' the days my ass." Several players, after the season, said Parcells alienated the players, perhaps for good, for treating them so poorly after the strike.

They didn't play as hard as they did down the stretch in 1986, when they were Super. "They seem like they're not as hungry as they were last year," said Green Bay receiver Walter Stanley after the two teams met in December.

"They're not the ball hawks they were last year. Last year, they played with so much intensity and confidence."

And their stock in trade, the running game, finished the year in tatters. Mark Bavaro would have corrective foot surgery after the season, the tumor wouldn't die beneath Karl Nelson's breast, Chris Godfrey's seven-week recuperation from arthroscopic surgery soured the coaching staff toward him, and Brad Benson's degenerative hips and slower footwork made him a much less effective player. All of this led Joe Morris into mediocrity. Morris, who had gained 280 yards in the first three games of 1986, gained 280 in the first ten of 1987. Morris averaged exactly one yard less per carry than he averaged in the Super Bowl season (4.4 to 3.4).

When a good team goes bad, as this one did, there is a cadre of reasons. There are some mental reasons, some physical ones. This team was no different. Analyzing what went wrong:

Physical Reasons

1. The offensive line was in disarray, and the backup players—William Roberts, Doug Riesenberg, Damian Johnson—didn't mesh.

2. The front office recruited bad strike replacements. "A lot of people thought I was a dodo for that one," Young said. When the strike was over, Young pulled aside one writer who had remarked with surprise how pained he looked in the moments after the Super Bowl victory. "Now I can tell you why," Young said. "These were my exact thoughts right after we won: 'Thank God we were able to do it this year. We're facing the strike next year.' And I knew something could happen to screw us up."

3. The running game, sixth in the league in yardage in 1986, was twenty-fourth in 1987. Joe Morris took the brunt of the blame for this, and he did get banged up more than ever. But the reason the Giants didn't run well is because their fine-tuned line had only two of six constants all year—guard Billy Ard and center Bart Oates. Injuries ravaged the rest.

4. Time of possession. "Football should be renamed," said Bud Goode, a stat freak who analyzes statistical trends for nine NFL teams, including the Giants. "It should be called clockball. The teams who have the ball longest every year invariably win the most." From 1986 to 1987, the Giants had the ball exactly three and one-half minutes less per game. What that is, on the average, is one less long drive per game than the opposition. So naturally the Giants' offensive efficiency was down. The Giants scored on 33 percent of their possessions in 1986. They scored on 26 percent of their possessions in the twelve nonstrike games of 1987.

5. The defense just wasn't as good. The coaches spent lots of film time analyzing this one. It was explainable because the defense had to be on the field more than it was in 1986, and the unit had the emotional drag of being

all but eliminated from the playoff race in October. Football is always, in part, a game of enthusiasm, and this wasn't an enthusiastic team after the strike.

6. They blew so many big plays. They lost twice when their kickers missed potential winning field goals on decisive plays of games. They had four fourth-quarter turnovers, all in the last ten minutes, at Dallas. With a 3-point lead at Washington with five minutes left, cornerback Perry Williams fell down in pass coverage and the Redskins threw the winning touchdown pass to the man Williams was supposed to be covering. And Ottis Anderson dropped the pass at New Orleans. "That play with Ottis, to me, was the season in a nutshell," said Phil McConkey. "One of the greatest football players of our lifetime has an easy pass bounce off him, and instead of us getting a commanding lead, they score and win."

Mental Reasons

1. Readiness. Parcells, throughout training camp, had stressed to his team and to the press that the team wouldn't get off to the slow start it had encountered the previous year. "We weren't ready for the first game last year. I guarantee you we'll be ready this year," Parcells said during the summer. The Giants, opening this season, were badly outclassed at Chicago and embarrassed by Dallas. They'd worked hard in training camp. They seemed in fine physical condition. But one thing wrong with this team was their over-confidence. They thought, coming into the season, that they could turn it on and turn it off when they wanted to. It showed through the preseason and it showed when the real games started. Maybe that's a part of . . .

2. Fatness. Deep in the hearts of each coach and player, they know if their effort was the same or better in 1987 compared to 1986. It was such a bastard season that judging this definitively can't be done, but one club employee said in retrospect, "If you look at the problems we had, keep looking at mental things. It's such a mental game."

3. Poststrike fatalism. This was the attitude of the team, players and coaches, when the Giants returned from the players' strike an 0-5 team: It's over. It was, probably, but there was so much realism around the team that a 9-1 finish—possible the way the '86 Giants had played—was impossible.

4. Parcells's poststrike cold shoulder. After the season, Parcells said he was trying to get his players' anger focused on him and away from the unfulfilling strike they'd just endured; most players had blown one-quarter of their annual salaries over a strike that had gotten them absolutely nowhere, and Parcells didn't want the locker room filled with a bunch of vindictive "fuck management" types. So he used a different motivational technique. Formally cold at their first poststrike team meeting, he then barely spoke to them for two weeks. He pissed the players off, hoping they'd ignore the negative outcome

of the strike and band together against him. At least that's what he said. Some players are immune to the mental games coaches play. Many are not. Phil Simms and Phil McConkey and Lawrence Taylor and Harry Carson and Lionel Manuel were unaffected enough by Parcells's mind games. Kenny Hill, Tony Galbreath, Jim Burt, and Joe Morris were not. "I don't care what your profession is," Hill said. "When a situation exists that isn't conducive to achieving the goal you've set for yourself, you're not going to function at peak levels. I don't care how many penny-ante psychological ploys are used. Football players are dumb, but they're not stupid."

5. A lack of emotion. Losing bothered this team, but it wasn't devastating to most of the players. And when things got bad, the Giants had no one who could stand up and effectively mentally motivate the team. It was nice to call veteran defensive end George Martin a team leader, but he couldn't snap the team out of lethargy. This lack of emotion was effective when the Giants were winning so regularly in 1986, because they didn't rejoice too much after clinching the division or winning a playoff game. "People say we're un-emotional," said Phil Simms. "But it's funny how making big plays can make up for emotion." The Giants had too little of each in 1987. One of the most emotional times of the year—and this is only part facetious—came when Parcells told the team at a team meeting after the Chicago debacle that he'd waived Elvis Patterson, he of drinking fame. The players clapped.

With the benefit of retrospect, there were plenty of theories. Karl Nelson even had one. While undergoing his radiation treatments in Manhattan three times a week, Nelson had lots of time to think. And while being the third man on WNEW radio's Giants' broadcast team, he had plenty of time to see what was wrong.

"The disturbing thing," Nelson said in his quiet way one postseason day, "is it took us three years to learn how to win. And we lost that totally in two weeks."

What this said: Football can be a humbling sport, but the Giants fell to earth so quickly, and with such a thud, that it was certain to have an impact on the team's future.

Hill's negative voice about Parcells wasn't the only one in the wilderness. When the Giants informed Tony Galbreath, their third-down running back, that he'd have to take approximately a 30-percent pay cut in 1988 to stay on the team, Galbreath balked. Galbreath was thirty-four, but he still did the same thing the same way he'd always done it, which is to say take swing passes from Phil Simms and run them ten yards or take handoffs on draws and run six or seven. But the Giants had two young running backs they thought highly of, and Galbreath was a luxury now. He was also the team's seventh-highest-paid player, and he handled the ball only thirty-six times in 1987. So they wanted to cut his salary from $324,000 a year to about $230,000, invite him to camp, and if he won a job, great.

Galbreath lashed out when the Giants informed him of the pay-cut proposal. "I'm hurt," he said from his home in Jefferson City, Missouri. "I did the job they asked of me every Sunday, and my performance gave them no reason to cut my salary like this."

He measured his words carefully about Parcells, because he and Parcells were quite close. Parcells probably kept Galbreath in the game longer than most coaches would, allowing him to earn a few extra years of the big check. The week before the Super Bowl, CBS approached Parcells and asked if he'd allow a player to bring a home video camera into team functions in the days before the game, and CBS would take the home movies and make a football-players-as-human-beings feature for the Super Bowl pregame show. The player would get to keep the camera and make a few thousand bucks besides. Parcells picked Galbreath. "I love Tony," Parcells said once.

"I love Bill," Galbreath said, sitting back there in Jefferson City. "But I think Bill changed last year. He wasn't the same Bill. He just didn't treat us right after the strike."

35

The News Doesn't Get Better

March 1988
Phoenix, Arizona

There started to be this feeling around the Giants right around this time, the kind of feeling that Charlie Brown and Linus have when Pig Pen walks in the room. Can't anything just go right for us?

It's like you're the owner of a small chain of mom-and-pop grocery stores, and a huge A & P moves into town and swallows you. The Giants had gotten away with scant few contract problems in 1987, but the debts were coming due in 1988, and these debts were different. The Giants had three Pro Bowl players who were free agents—linebacker Carl Banks, tight end Mark Bavaro, punter Sean Landeta—and the definition of unsigned "free" agent in football was changing. Three premier linebackers were free agents in this off-season. One was Banks. The other two were Wilber Marshall of Chicago and Andre Tippett of New England. The Patriots signed Tippett. The Washington Redskins wanted a premier outside linebacker in the worst way, even if—in the NFL's definition of "free" agency—it was going to cost them more than a million dollars a year in salary and two first-round draft choices as compensation if the Giants or Bears chose not to match the Redskins' offer within one week of its being tendered.

So the Redskins had to make a choice. Their scouting reports told them Marshall and Banks were close to being equal in talent, both adept at rushing the passer and stopping the rushing game. Either one would improve an aging defense significantly. The stage for their choice would be the annual winter football meetings at the plush and architecturally wondrous Arizona Biltmore Hotel northwest of downtown Phoenix. Not a blade of grass or a brick out of place here.

Someone in the Redskins' hierarchy explained their thought process on whether to bid on Banks or Marshall like this: "Chicago was having financial problems, and we were pretty sure they weren't in a position to totally upset their salary structure and keep Marshall. But the Giants probably would have done just about anything to keep Banks."

The Redskins bid $6 million spread over five years for Marshall. A week later, the Bears chose not to match the contract, and Marshall was a Redskin, the richest defensive player in the history of the National Football League. "If we're starting to pay football players $1.2 million a year, this game is dead," Chicago coach Mike Ditka said. This wasn't the worst salary news for NFL owners, who were already moaning about the stagnation in network television revenues; each team was to receive $17.1 million in 1987, 1988, and 1989, and the spiraling of salaries ignored the leveling off of TV money. There were two other developments this week that bothered the owners, and in addition, George Young:

• The Cardinals, emboldened by league approval of their move to the lucrative new market of Phoenix, signed an above-average quarterback, Neil Lomax, to the fourth-richest contract in NFL history. At an average of $1,425,000 per year over four years, the contract was worth twice the one Phil Simms was playing under. The enormity of these numbers, among owners, couldn't be underestimated. They were surprised by the Marshall contract, stunned by the Lomax numbers. "Holy shit!" was the conservative reaction in the lobby of the Biltmore when the contract figures were leaked to other NFL owners. The owners knew there were better quarterbacks and more valuable players who would piggyback on the Marshall and Lomax contracts to make their own salary cases.

The impact on the Giants worried Young. The Cards were 11-19-1 in the previous two seasons, the Giants 23-11. Simms led Lomax in quarterback ratings in each of those years. Privately, when he heard about the numbers, Simms, a loyal dog, hoped the Giants would come to him and renegotiate his contract. They didn't, and he didn't press the issue—for now. But Young fretted, pointing out that the players had struck in 1982 in an effort to get 55 percent of the gross revenue in the game. "And now we're giving them sixty-three percent, and we're raising the salaries even more," he said with disgust.

• The multimillionaire owners of Denver and San Francisco, Pat Bowlen and Eddie DeBartolo, both told their advisers how nice it would be to have Banks on their team. DeBartolo wanted Bavaro, too.

The impact on the Giants would be felt here, too. Bowlen made much of his money in oil in Canada and wasn't on the wealth stratum of DeBartolo, the mall developer from Ohio. The Broncos eventually decided they'd upset their salary structure too much by even offering Banks a contract, so they dropped out of the Bankstakes. But the Giants were scared of DeBartolo, who wasn't ruled by the bottom line of his football budget. He was consumed by winning. To mollify and unite his players after the four-week NFL strike, DeBartolo had a $10,000 playoff bonus written into every player's contract. When his 49ers lost to the Giants 49-3 in the 1986 playoffs, DeBartolo was so distraught he threw a tantrum in the back of his limo after the game, breaking glass and scratching the interior. Another time in New Jersey,

DeBartolo rented ten limos for his traveling party. During the game, nine limo drivers stayed neutral. One rooted for the Giants. Nine limo drivers got $100 tips. The Giants fan got $50.

So here was DeBartolo relaxing with some of his cronies at poolside of the meetings, just outside his cabana. He saw Parcells, also at poolside, talking with San Diego general manager Steve Ortmayer about a deal involving the exchange of their first-round picks in the April college draft.

"They," DeBartolo said, meaning the Giants, "have a couple of guys at positions we need."

He smiled. "Hey," he said to an aide, "go over there and ask Parcells how big Carl Banks is."

DeBartolo was a sporting fellow, but he came to the same conclusion that the other owners who coveted Bavaro and Banks did. The Giants would match whatever offer they made, within the bounds of the new reason. And by DeBartolo's making an offer, he'd just be pushing up salaries on his team anyway, because the other star 49ers would have seen what DeBartolo would have paid for another team's players. Then they'd ask to be paid in that class. Smart businessman that he was, DeBartolo could see that was senseless.

But the Lomax/Marshall scenario still left Banks and Bavaro wanting very big money, in excess of $800,000 a year. Young thought: This could be trouble. Big trouble.

He was right. Even if Banks and Bavaro weren't going to be bought by another owner, they were attractive enough players to demand huge money from the Giants—and hold out until they got somewhere close to their figure.

And what was bad about this, for the Giants' owners, was that they were already coming off a crushing year financially. Wellington Mara and his godson, Tim Mara, each owned 50 percent of the team. This was the way they made their living, through the Giants. In 1987, it wasn't much of a living. Because at the bottom of a balance sheet somewhere in the red, white, and blue and conservative offices of the New York Giants was this accountant's figure, in red pen presumably, for the football year 1987:

−$2,500,000.

Family businesses, even those with $30 million or so in gross receipts annually, didn't take kindly to $2.5 million losses. So when Banks, Bavaro, and Landeta came calling for their piece of the dough that summer, George Young, who negotiated the player contracts, was not going to be very chummy.

Redskins' interlude:
At the meetings, Washington coach Joe Gibbs is talking about how great it will be to have Wilber Marshall on his team, even if it means totally upsetting the club's salary structure and costing the team its top draft picks in 1988 and 1989. The general feeling about the move in the league was that it was a good move, a bold move—but a risky move. "It's an aggressive move to get me the best players possible,"

Gibbs said. "By making this move, we're saying there's things we need. Our players will understand."

Parcells, for his part, looked as relaxed as he had since the morning after the Super Bowl. He was having fun, too, because he had officially become a millionaire in February. He finally signed a contract that would pay him, on the average, about $825,000 per year through the 1991 season. In other words, Parcells was now about the fourth-highest-paid coach in the National Football League—ahead of Tom Landry, who had coached in five Super Bowls, and ahead of Chuck Noll, who had won four. He was feeling so good about life that he actually took some time off. This was the guy, remember, who once worked 161 days in a row. During the day in Phoenix, he talked trade with several fellow coaches and front-office people he knew, getting as much sun around the Biltmore pool as he could. And he spent time with the man who had the biggest influence on his career, Al Davis. Davis, of course, was snubbed by many of the NFL glitterati because he challenged their agreement not to move franchises in 1981, taking his Raiders from a successful home in Oakland to a potential-filled place in Los Angeles. Sometimes Parcells would talk to Davis for hours. They'd begun a relationship when Davis, then a coach, coached Parcells, then a player, in a postseason all-star game in 1963. Parcells called Davis regularly for advice over the years, and they liked to hang around together—even though this was something that Giants' management frowned upon. Parcells didn't care. He learned from Davis, and he loved Davis's fuck-what-everybody-else-thinks attitude.

At breakfast one morning in Arizona, Parcells smoked and drank coffee and talked about Al, his pal.

"People ask me, 'What happened last year? How'd you go six and nine?' It doesn't matter. I learned this from Al: Nobody cares. Nobody gives a shit what the circumstances are. Winning is all that counts. The important thing is, find a way to win. Until you get to the mentality that no one cares what the reasons are and start eliminating that sense of self-doubt yourself, you're not doing a good job coaching. And I would say that's what happened to us the last month of last season, when we started playing better."

Life was good for Parcells right now. He'd been a coaching gypsy all his life, moving eleven times in his first nineteen years in the business until finally, three miles from the house where he grew up, he got one of the biggest jobs in the coaching world. He got the job coaching his hometown team, the Giants. And he hit the coaching lottery, too. For four years, he was going to be paid like a star player. Finally, money wasn't a worry to him. In addition to his coach's salary, he had two coach's shows—which took a total of seventy-five painless minutes a week—which paid him, according to New York media industry sources, a total of about $225,000 a year. Parcells was making more than Lawrence Taylor in a year. (And he didn't mind telling the players all about it either. Several said Parcells told them all about his new contract when the club's off-season workouts began in March.) And why shouldn't he enjoy it?

In Avanti's, one of Arizona's nicest restaurants, Parcells ate one night with Tim Mara, the coowner of the franchise.

"What's the biggest tip you ever got before?" he asked the kid waiting his table.

"Fifty bucks," the kid said.

"From who?" Parcells said.

"Chuck Norris," the kid said.

Parcells handed the kid a $100 bill.

Parcells handed the piano player a $100 bill.

Life was good. But life was also life.

"We're going to have a better team out there this year," Parcells said before he left Arizona. "Or there ain't gonna be anybody left standing. Including me."

—36—
The George Young School of Thought

May 1988
East Rutherford, New Jersey

George Young went to see the Mets play one night at Shea Stadium, and he sat with Joe DiMaggio and a mutual friend of theirs, a scout for the Baltimore Orioles.

The scout said he thought free agency was undermining the team quality of the sport, and he noticed free agency was beginning to be a factor in professional football now. He said he didn't think that was a good thing.

DiMaggio agreed. He said finding and cultivating one's own players was the key to winning.

Young, who is not shy when it comes to opinions, said, "The key to sports is developing your own players, your own team. I believe in that as strongly as I believe in the Ten Commandments. Mercenaries aren't your best soldiers."

Times were changing a bit in football, it seemed, what with the Redskins' signing of Wilber Marshall and the San Francisco 49ers' trades for key players (Fred Dean, Russ Francis, Wendell Tyler, Steve Young) in the eighties. But the Giants wouldn't join the dealers. They would do what they always did —build their team from the draft almost exclusively, and develop their own identity.

"Look at the great dynasties in football," Young told his ball-game companions. "Green Bay, Pittsburgh, Dallas, Miami—they weren't big trade teams. They were big developmental teams."

Young was so ruled by history. It fascinated him. He taught high school history and political science (to, among others, Baltimore mayor Kurt Schmoke and Kansas City Royals general manager John Schuerholz) for fifteen years. "I never read anything that doesn't have a bibliography," he said a few days after the DiMaggio encounter. "I don't like fiction. In fact, I think the last fiction book I read was *The Godfather*, which wasn't really all fiction if you know anything about it. I don't like sport books either. I don't read 'em."

"Not even the books after you guys won?" he was asked.

"And especially not those!" he thundered.

Young was a largely intractable man, a man who railed at the modern distractions to the games, then calmly sat down and figured a way to deal with them. In reality, to the Giants, he'd been a godsend. In 1979, the two Mara families were feuding over how the team was being run. For years, Wellington Mara, the president and seventy-one-year-old patriarch, had made decisions for the franchise, and through the late sixties and seventies many of them were wrong ones. In 1978, two things happened to bring the control of Wellington Mara to an end. The fans, in general, rose up and said they were mad as heck and weren't going to take it anymore. These fans, some of them, hired a plane that flew over Giants Stadium during a 1978 game that read:

15 YRS OF LOUSY FOOTBALL WE'VE HAD ENOUGH.

The Giants won fifteen games in the five seasons from 1973 to 1977. In November 1978, the fans watched in horror as the Giants, with a 17–12 lead over Philadelphia at home and thirty seconds to play, tried to run a running play instead of quarterback Joe Pisarcik's just falling on the ball. In the huddle before the play, the players realized that all Pisarcik had to do was take the snap from center and fall to the ground. But Pisarcik was in a battle for his job, and he didn't want to do anything to alienate the coaching staff. So he called the play. "No!" a couple of teammates yelled in the huddle. "Fall on it, Joe!" He didn't. His handoff to Larry Csonka, the fullback, hit him in the hip, and Herman Edwards of the Eagles scooped up the fumble and ran it in for the winning touchdown. The next day, offensive coordinator Bob Gibson, who'd called the idiotic play, was fired. After the season, the director of football operations for the team, Andy Robustelli, and general manager John McVay were fired. Tim Mara, who didn't get along with his godfather but had tacitly allowed him to run the club over the years, said he would challenge any move Wellington made if Tim didn't feel it was a good one. Wellington tried to hire Terry Bledsoe, Robustelli's assistant, to take the job as head of football operations. Tim stopped the move. There the real family bitterness started. Since they both owned 50 percent of the club, the problem was going to be—well, let's just say Tim and Wellington, in 1978 and early 1979, got so pissed off at what the other was doing that they stopped talking to each other. To this day they speak only perfunctorily to each other, pass in the halls at the stadium as if the other were invisible, and sit separately at games. Into this breach, on Valentine's Day 1979, came George Young, making $35,000 at the time as the doer of the Miami Dolphins' dirty work. He scouted. He planned travel. He was seated at the right hand of Don Shula, and he did whatever Don Shula thought would make the club better.

In 1979, he was a compromise candidate for the Maras. In his first meeting with Wellington, he asked, "Is there going to be a fence around my office, and a gate that locks?" He was kidding. He was serious.

A decade later, Young would say, "When you come into a franchise that's been down a long time, you say, 'Have patience,' and the fans say, 'We've been patient enough.' But if you're going to develop a winning football franchise, you do it with the thought of doing it in a decade. This had been such a great franchise for years, but it was down for so long that I came in at the right time. They were ready for a change in the cycle. My goal was to avoid major blunders."

He hired Ray Perkins, a taskmaster of a coach, and the first draft pick ever under Young was Phil Simms, a decision that was roundly booed and cursed by Giants fans at draft headquarters in New York. Fourteen players in his first eight seasons as general manager made the NFL's all-rookie team. Young also plucked four starters from the United States Football League when it was in its demise in the mideighties.

Young was very big on continuity. He hoped his coaches would give players the chance to prove themselves, then give them the benefit of every doubt before cutting them or demoting them. (Parcells, in this regard, fit well with Young. Example: Elvis Patterson, 1987. Parcells stuck with the guy through many problems in the previous two years.) This is why, although the signing of players and protracted negotiations dragged him down emotionally, he rarely allowed personal differences with agents or players to affect his thought process. He just wanted to get everybody signed and playing.

Young often angered agents and players by his negotiating tactics. He railed against holdouts, but in 1986 he didn't give first-round draft pick Eric Dorsey a contract offer until six days after the opening of camp. Same thing with Carl Banks and Mark Bavaro and Sean Landeta this year. Here it was May, and their contracts had expired in February, and Young hadn't fired the first volley in salary talks with their agents. "I'm doing the same thing I always do," Young said. "This is moonshot time for the agent. This isn't talk-turkey time." Young almost always waited until he thought the market was right for a deal and then made an offer very close to the final offer that he would ever make. Then, if there was no agreement, he'd improve the offer once. Usually, almost invariably, that was it. One offer, one slight improvement.

"I like George," Phil McConkey said once. "And the Giants have been fair to me. But so much of this stuff could be avoided if he'd just make an effort to get guys in and be fair."

Young's theory: He didn't want to offer player X, who was seeking $100,000, a contract for $55,000 when he knew the market said player X should get at least $80,000. He didn't want to get into a back-and-forth, you-come-down-$10,000-and-we'll-go-up-$10,000 thing. And he didn't want player X to be insulted by the offer. This was a point that made Young shake his head, although he did get a kick out of players' saying they were insulted by offers of big money.

"Football must be the only business in the world where you can offer to pay somebody $2.6 million and he says, 'They don't respect me,' " he said.

He was getting ready for a lot of that this off-season. He knew he'd staved off some renegotiating and some extensions of contracts in 1987 by pleading

for togetherness. It didn't matter that the Giants were 6-9 in 1987. He
thought: Am I the only guy around here who had a bad year last year? Am
I the guy who made us 6-9? None of this mattered. Money mattered. And
Young knew this was going to be a trying off-season.

"These contracts will get done," Young said with a sigh one May day in
his office. "Those guys won't go to work in a bank."

Then Young said he planned to read the Bible on vacation in the summer.
"For inspiration," he said. "We seem to need it."

But the team seems like a team this spring. Parcells buried the hatchet
with the players. When the team gathered in May at Giants Stadium for its
annual minicamp—a coach's check on who's in shape, and a coach's way to
send messages for the coming season—Parcells wanted to wipe the mental
slate clean with his team. When he addressed them for the first time since
December, he said, "I don't think I held up my end of the deal last year. I
just want to make sure that doesn't happen again."

A mea culpa. From Parcells. It surprised a few players.

"All football players want is consistency," said Harry Carson, the linebacker.
"What Bill said is important because he's going to be more consistent this
year."

The players seemed to be more serious at this minicamp than they'd been
in 1987. It was as if they'd been to the heights of their game, they liked
what they saw, and they were so bitter at having all of it taken away from
them last year that they were determined not to let it happen again. The
signs for a return to prominence were there. Forty-three players were working
in the four-times-weekly off-season workout program. And those who weren't
working out with the team were working by themselves. Carson, who went
his own way in every off-season, was working at a gym in north Jersey. And
Taylor—yes, Lawrence Taylor—had $18,000 worth of weight-training equip-
ment installed in the basement of his off-season home, which was just off a
golf-course fairway in Houston.

"That kind of scares me," Taylor said of his seriousness. "But I want to
be a better player this year. I want to be a better all-around player. I don't
just want to be able to rush the quarterback. I think I need to be better at
stopping the run. That's what I'm going to work on this year."

Lawrence Taylor. Working on something. Thinking about being a better
football player.

This was serious.

"We are going to kick ass this year," Carson said. "I mean it. Kick ass.
Take prisoners. Take names. We're back."

──37──

The Residue

June 1988
Flemington, New Jersey

Publicly, the Giants' players were still smarting over getting their asses handed to them on so many platters during the 1987 strike. But this didn't make them any different from any other NFL team. And most of them cursed their own leadership for getting them into this no-win mess in the first place.

Would it be a factor in how they played in 1988? Probably not. But they were bitter about it nonetheless, and several players said they'd never feel the same about their benevolent owners, the Maras, again. (Even though their walkout cost the Maras $2.5 million in 1987.)

"Nobody has brought this up yet," said McConkey, sitting in his restaurant. "But the story of the NFL last year was the story of some of the most competitive people in the world. They're taught for years to compete, to win, to stay together as a team against an enemy. It's always been us versus them. So this was us, the players, versus them, the management. We're some of the most competitive people in the world, and those were the qualities that came out during the strike."

But, McConkey was told, most of you guys are smart. Most of you are reasonable. Why couldn't you see free agency was unattainable through negotiation and just go to court right away to try to get it?

"Forget about reason," McConkey said. He was an emotional guy, and his voice rose an octave just then. "I'm telling you that this is what we've been taught, to be competitive. That's all we know. There's a battle to be fought and we follow what our leaders say and we go out there and fight it."

And there it is.

What many football players are, in a way, are physically aggressive sheep. The very good ones, at a young age, start to have everything done for them, and many fall into the mode of letting people do things for them and not doing much for themselves. There was Authority to tell them what to do, and they did it, and they were rewarded with a college scholarship or a pro football bonus or later, a big pro football salary. And so it wasn't very surprising when the Giants cut a journeyman defensive lineman named Curtis

McGriff in 1987, and gave him a plane ticket home to Alabama. Curtis McGriff, who had never been cut before, had to ask an office aide with the Giants how to use the plane ticket. All he'd ever done before is take charters or been ushered onto a plane by Authority. (And when the Giants cut the man who fell asleep on national TV in the first strike game, Reggie "I Was Just Resting" Carr, Carr asked for a plane ticket home to Jackson, Mississippi. He got the ticket, worth $330, on Delta Airlines, paid for by a Giants' credit card, with the words "REFUND TO GIANTS ONLY" clearly on the front of the ticket. He tried to cash it in and get the money. When the airline told him he couldn't get the money because it was the Giants' ticket, he huffed and he puffed and he couldn't understand why something worth $330 was not worth $330 to him.)

This is not meant to demean the players, calling them sheep. But most players took no time to actually learn what the issues were in the strike. On the picket line the previous fall, outside the stadium during a strike game, the players kept saying the owners wanted to reduce all their benefits and send them back into the 1970s of collective-bargaining agreements. This was clearly not true, but by this time there was such an us-versus-them fervor whipped up that players just hated management and didn't want to hear anything about it. They didn't want to hear about one of the great benefits in any union in the eighties, severance, whereby a ten-year veteran who was cut or who retired was handed $130,000 in the two years after he left the sport, as a means, ideally, of adjusting to life after football as painlessly as possible. They put blind trust in their union, and they suffered for it. "Now," Cincinnati Bengal Cris Collinsworth said, "it's like Sherman's gone through us, Atlanta's burned and we don't have any furniture." Strange allegory, but that's the way many players entered the 1988 season: with lingering bitterness. Against something, somebody, that cost them a quarter of their 1987 income that they'd never get back. It was, in layman's terms, making $60,000 a year and being near the top of a trade, and the union for this trade, which collects $1,000 a year from its members, asks membership to strike to gain major concessions from management, concessions management had steadfastly refused to give in two previous contract negotiations that ended up in court. There was a three-month strike. There were no concessions. The union told membership to go back to work while it went to court trying to force the concessions again. The member of the union at the top of his trade lost $15,000. The union member wonders if he will still be with the company whenever the situation with management is settled. This is exactly how the 1,570 NFL veterans felt as they went to training camp this summer.

"There will be some malcontents in football this year, mad because they pulled a total blunder last year by striking," said New Orleans general manager Jim Finks, the league's executive of the year in 1987 for guiding the Saints through the strike storm. "They realize now they could have done the same thing—go to court—without losing twenty-five percent of their income. Really, they should be mad at themselves."

At a charity roast for a hospital, Leonard Marshall said he thought that, if he played five or six more years with reasonable production and a few more Pro Bowl appearances, he could make the Pro Football Hall of Fame when he retired.

—38—

What Makes Joe Go

July 1988
Parsippany, New Jersey

At a charity roast for a children's cancer fund, Tom Boisture, the Giants' bright director of player personnel, was buttering a dinner roll and talking about Joe Morris, whose performance was quite possibly the most important factor in whether the Giants got good again.

Before he bit into the roll, Tom Boisture said, "Joe Morris will have a big year this year, just to prove Bill Parcells wrong."

This was quite a statement. In the previous few months, the *New York Post* reported that Parcells questioned Morris's heart because he kept getting injured, Morris stormed up to Parcells and seethingly asked if it was true, Parcells denied it, there were reports that the Giants were shopping Morris around the league, Parcells denied those, and Morris reportedly was very unhappy about being a Giant. "Rumors and whispers" is what Parcells called all the negative Morris stuff in the papers.

But there was no denying a couple of things. Morris was angry that he was being made the scapegoat for the Giants' horrible showing in 1987. And Morris resented Parcells's double standard in the locker room, the standard he set with Lawrence Taylor.

Morris was an intriguing person. At five foot seven, he was one of the three or four shortest players in the league. He might also have been one of the three or four most hard-driving. All his life he'd had to show people he was good enough to be on the team, whatever team he was on. As a starry high school player in Massachusetts, friends told him not to play major-college football, that he'd get lost in the shuffle there because of his size, that he should go somewhere nice, near home, like the University of Massachusetts. Morris remembers. "If I'd gone to UMass," he said in his quick-and-nervous-and-quiet-all-at-once voice, "I'd have always said, 'What if?' "

He was this always-something-to-prove guy because of a couple of things that happened to him very young. His father, Earl Morris, was away in Vietnam most of the time while Joe grew up, and the Morris family spent several formative years moving around. In Southern Pines, North Carolina, the family discipline fell to Addie Morris, Joe's mom, much of the time, and she had her hands full. Joe was constantly in fights, starting in the third grade. The four-foot-six kids chided him because he was four-foot-two, and as Joe recalls, he'd just pop them one. In his neighborhood, there were rock fights. With real rocks. In one-on-one rock fights, if you pelted the other guy first, you won. "At one time, I had guys bringing me quarters. 'You bring me the money or else,' I'd say. Nobody could beat me up."

But he respected his father so much that when his mother asked him one day, "How do you think your father would feel if he knew what you were doing?" he stopped doing it.

And when his father came home from the Army, Joe had a job. His job was to clean the kitchen, and to keep his room spotless. Sometimes, Earl Morris would jostle Joe out of bed at 3:00 in the morning and tell him, "The kitchen's not right. Do it over."

This is why Joe Morris was so fiercely defensive about his skills and why he was unforgiving of writers who wrote him off soon after the Giants chose him in the second round of the 1982 draft and why he still works the way he does. On Monday mornings following Sunday road games, Morris is in the weight room by 9:30. After he suffered a concussion in New Orleans in 1985, he went up to Parcells on the sidelines, still a little fuzzy but claiming he was ready to play. "Rest awhile," Parcells told him. Morris, pacing, went behind the bench and started screaming, "PUT ME BACK IN THE GAME! PUT ME BACK IN THE GAME!"

"Even now," Morris said just before training camp started, "I can never have a bad game. There's never going to be a day where I can relax. Hey, I'll take some of the blame for what happened last year. But not for all of it. If they don't want me, I'll sell my house. Move. Somebody wants me. I just want people to know I'm not dead yet."

══ 39 ══

New Home, More Problems

July 1988
Madison, New Jersey

On the first defensive play of this new training camp in this new town—
the Giants moved from New York because of better facilities in this central
Jersey college town—versatile defensive back Herb Welch planted his foot
on a slippery patch of grass. His cleats didn't take hold. His knee flew out
at an awkward angle, and the ligaments inside the knee shredded.

The Giants' team surgeon, Russell Warren, said it was one of the worst
knee injuries he'd ever seen. Welch was out for the year.

Parcells was acting like a tyrant. "He's more intense than I've ever seen
him. This is the toughest camp I've ever been in," Hill said.

Karl Nelson's comeback from cancer wasn't going as well as Parcells had
hoped, and the coach thought Nelson might be ready for the season but not
be the same player he was before he was hit with forty-three shots of radiation.

Redskins' interlude:
Bobby Beathard is one of the brightest guys in football. He is also one of the most
realistic. Sitting in his training-camp dorm suite at Dickinson College in Carlisle,
Pennsylvania, Beathard is drinking some fresh-squeezed juice (he was a health fanatic)
and keeping half an eye on ABC's World News Tonight *because he wants to see*
what Michael Dukakis is saying at the Democratic National Convention in Atlanta.

Repeating as champions, though, is never far from his thoughts. Beathard is normally
a worrying type, and his brow is in full furrow on this hot early evening in central
Pennsylvania.

"I don't think it's only the Wilber Marshall thing that presents problems for us.
There's problems for any team that wins the Super Bowl. Signing a player like Wilber
Marshall just compounds the problems," Beathard says, stretching out on his couch.

"This time of the year, I really have no idea how we'll play. Were the Giants
ready last year to defend? Were the Bears ready the year before? I don't know. But
I do know that what you've seen happen is that it's very difficult to come back to play
at that very high level of intensity that you need to win. I really believe it's true what
they say. It's tougher to win again, because you have to play better. We didn't play

194

well for a long time last year. For a while, we were just scraping by. But when the playoffs came, we played very well, fortunately for us.

"I don't know how we'll react. It's scary, because you really don't know. I remember getting a feeling of what it's like to try to repeat last year. My wife, Christine, said to me, 'What's wrong? You don't look happy.' I'm saying, 'Golleeee, what's next year gonna be like? We could hit the skids, go down the tubes.' I start thinking about what holes we have to fill, what problems we have. Two days later, I'm at the scouting combine looking at players, thinking the old saying is true: 'It's harder to stay on top than it is to get on top.' "

Beathard's visitor says, "Last year, George Young was saying he thinks people feel bound to celebrate so much after they win. He said it's like when somebody at Ford designs a great car and it's a big sensation and everybody wants to go out and buy it right away, and the guy goes out and celebrates with a big dinner and champagne. But the guy's back at work the next day, working on the next design. He doesn't take six months to go out and revel in it. George says he thinks it's unnatural to celebrate for so long."

"Yeah," Beathard says. "Maybe we enjoy it too much. I don't know if the players can really look back and know what it took the previous off-season, how they came to camp hungry because the Giants beat us three times the previous year. The feeling is: 'Hey, we've gotta do something to beat these guys. We have to win.' Now we win it, beat the Giants, and you have to just hope there aren't too many guys on your team that aren't satisfied. Give you an example. Donnie Warren. {He's a Redskins' tight end.} If you could just find out what makes him tick . . . He's an incredible worker. He's been here nine years and has always been afraid of losing his job. He's had no competition, but he works every year like he's got to beat out all the competition in the world to keep his job. But we've got guys who, I think, are oblivious to competition and don't get the most out of their ability."

The worrier worries.

"I don't know how affected we are. The tough thing is, you never know what's going on in their heads. You never know, truly, what they're thinking."

One week later, Pro Bowl defensive end Dexter Manley was suspended for thirty days for violating the league's substance-abuse policy.

"He's always been afraid of losing his job."

That's what Bobby Beathard said. And Bill Parcells, too, believed a little pressure was a good thing for a player. Right away, Parcells put the pressure on some veterans—Harry Carson, Kenny Hill, Chris Godfrey, George Martin. Perform well in camp, or lose starting jobs. Perform in a mediocre way, and get cut. Put the fear of God into 'em, Parcells thought. Parcells had twelve offensive linemen in camp, and only two—Billy Ard and Bart Oates—had assured jobs. Carson, the everlasting Carson, felt the brunt of Parcells's prods continually. "God takes it away from all of us," Parcells told Carson before camp started. "If your heart's not in it, then we're going to sack up the bats."

That was a Parcellsism for packing it up and going home.

"Our number one goal in camp is to reestablish the winning attitude that made us successful," Parcells pronounced on the first day of camp.

At least they would try to do it in a quieter way. Comparing the first day of camp 1987 to the first day of camp 1988, in numbers:

1987		1988
9	TV crews	2
35	Reporters	15
11	Books by or about Giants	0
50	Kids bugging players for autographs	6

"I'm glad it's pretty normal now," Simms said. "Last year I felt like I was running for president."

But a normal camp in the eighties, in any sport, included a general manager holed up in his office talking on the telephone with agents or standing by the fax machine waiting for a new contract proposal, and it included a lot of unhappy people. Annually, it seemed, players in all sports got more and more powerful. The reason for this is a complex one. For years, there was a pronounced imbalance in the negotiating process. When defensive lineman Jerry Shay was the top draft choice of the Minnesota Vikings in 1966, he didn't have an agent. "I didn't know what the hell I was doing," said Shay, now the director of scouting for the Giants. "I just went in there and basically took what they gave me." In 1972, Shay's last year in football, he signed for $37,000. It was in the early seventies when most players began getting agents, and by late in the decade, everybody had one. So now the agent was doing the contract, telling the player, "You let me negotiate. Don't get involved." The agent and club would often get antagonistic during contract talks, with the player staying clear of it except to get reports back from the agent and to cheer him on as he tried to get the extra few thousand bucks. It was easy for a player to tell an agent to go in there and fight for a few thousand, whereas a player negotiating directly with a team would probably feel uneasy making demands to his boss when in many cases he'd never even stepped on the field yet.

"It's not the fault of the players today," said Sam Huff, the former Giants' and Redskins' linebacker. "The owners offer you the money and what are you going to do, turn it down? I remember walking into Wellington Mara's office after being the NFL defensive player of the year [in 1958], and I had absolutely no chance. He gave you what he wanted to give you. He said, 'Here's the contract. It's for $9,000. We think it's a good contract for you.' What am I going to say? I don't have an agent. Wellington Mara was like a father to me. I loved him like a father. But that's just the way it was in those days, and the player was powerless to do anything. Although I get mad at it sometimes—I can't stand guys making a million bucks who don't even know how many zeroes are in a million—it's great to see them finally getting the fair share."

Four other things caused salaries to jump: the competition from the World Football League in the midseventies, the competition from the United States Football League in the eighties, the proliferation of salary information so that every player knew what all his teammates and every other player at his position in the league were making, and the power of the holdout.

A look at Landeta's approach to his contract included many of these factors. Landeta came to the Giants from the United States Football League in 1985, and he benefited from the competition of several teams' bidding on him when the league was in trouble. He chose the Giants because they had an aging punter, Dave Jennings, whom the Giants were looking to replace. In his first three seasons in New Jersey, Landeta had some of the best punting numbers in the league, and he looked to become the league's highest-paid punter when he entered negotiations with the Giants.

Landeta was the Pete Rose of punters. As Rose knew every meaningful statistic from his career, Landeta knew his. And Landeta wasn't shy about telling people his numbers either. This helped him tremendously in putting together his contract proposal in the spring and summer of 1988. It also helped that Landeta had a bright agent, Tony Agnone, who worked tirelessly for his clients but not with any vindictiveness toward the clubs he dealt with. Landeta, Agnone, and a statistician compiled a twenty-two-page proposal for George Young's perusal. Landeta signed a three-year, $535,000 contract with the Giants in 1985. The bottom line this time: Landeta wanted a three-year contract worth $900,000.

"We're negotiating a contract for a damn punter, not for Salt Talks II," Young groused to Landeta when he saw the twenty-two-page document.

Landeta said he did it because he wanted to show the Giants clearly why he thought he should make more than any punter. He began the proposal with a quote from then-Cleveland-coach Marty Schottenheimer: "Field position in the NFL is directly responsible for whether you win or lose." Then he came up with one of his beloved stats: "Seventy percent of the time in the three years with the Giants, opponents have had to travel seventy-five yards or more to score after a punt."

Then Landeta listed the top five punters in salary in the NFL, with their stats of the previous three years. Only Rohn Stark, with Indianapolis, led Landeta in gross average.

Then Landeta showed his punting average for the previous three years until December 1 each year. The point: Giants Stadium weather is often windy and horrible late in the season, leading to some awful punting, and league stars Reggie Roby (in Miami) and Stark (in the Hoosier Dome) punted in nicer places. Landeta figured that his average, before December, was 44.5 yards per punt in his three seasons, which was more than the full-season numbers of both Stark and Roby.

Then ("You're going to love this one," Landeta said) he had a weather chart that told Young the average temperature in the New York area in December was thirty-seven degrees with a windchill of about twenty.

Then, Agnone brought placekickers into the argument, theorizing that placekickers are specialists just like punters. But it was clear why, really, Agnone brought in placekickers. As a rule, for some reason, they were higher paid than punters, and Agnone tried to show how punters were as valuable to teams as placekickers.

Then they brought up incentive clauses. Denver's punter, Mike Horan, had more than $100,000 in incentives in his contract, and Landeta had an incentive package modeled somewhat after Horan's. There would be bonuses for punts that landed inside the opponents' 20-yard line, a bigger bonus for punts landing inside the 10, and a bigger bonus for punts landing inside the 5. (In an average year, this proposed placement-of-punts bonus would bring Landeta about $17,000. In all, a good year for Landeta would bring about $80,000 to $100,000 in bonuses, all told.)

Young said, "I never read those proposals. They have no effect on me."

"Numbers motivate me," Landeta said. "If your numbers are good, your life is good. Think about it. If you can perform well for sixteen weeks, for ten years, in the sport of football, that's about one hundred and sixty weeks of work—maybe three years of your life—and then the rest of your whole life will be wonderful. If I perform well for sixteen weeks, the other thirty-six weeks of the year will be wonderful. You better damn well believe you get motivated to produce big stats because they count big time in your life."

The Giants never came up with the $900,000. Finally, on August 22, they came up with $455,000 over two years, which would make Landeta the league's second-highest-paid punter, behind Stark, who was working on a four-year, $1-million contract.

Landeta signed the contract in the afternoon. The Giants said they would ask the league for a two-week roster exemption for Landeta, meaning using him in the final preseason game against Cleveland wouldn't mean he would count on the Giants' roster when they made their final cuts.

That evening, while it was still light, Landeta went out onto the Giants Stadium AstroTurf and began punting. He had been punting during his holdout. But on this night, he tried to put everything into his punting, so that he would be able to kick in the final preseason game at Cleveland four nights later.

On about his fiftieth punt, he felt something pull in his back. Then he felt pain. Then he tried to punt some more, and he felt some more pain.

Landeta would punt in one game in 1988.

He would earn none of the bonuses.

In December, looking glum, he would pull aside a writer and say, "Do you realize how much money I've missed out on this year? A hundred thousand bucks. One hundred thousand bucks. Can you believe that?"

• • •

There was still enough talent here to win. The Giants looked pretty good in the preseason, winning three and losing one, and only the running game was still highly suspect. Confidence was high.

"I feel strongly we're back," Lawrence Taylor said in truly great anticipation just after the last preseason game in Cleveland.

But three big problems would haunt this preseason. By the time the Giants would break camp in late August, they would have:

1. Two unsigned important players sitting in Michigan (Carl Banks) and New Jersey (Mark Bavaro).

2. Serious questions about their offensive line.

3. The results of a very important drug test sitting on the desk of the NFL's drug adviser in West Covina, California.

40

Vintage LT

August 1988
Cleveland, Ohio

The fog was just starting to settle into one of the great old stadiums in America, Cleveland Stadium on the shores of Lake Erie. At 12:15 on Saturday morning in late August, that's what usually happens in this archaic bowl of a place. The fog made the chewed-up grass on the field slick in spots where it was already wet from some rain earlier in the week. And it was starting to get cool, so that, on some players who were perspiring heavily, steam was rising from their heads when they took their helmets off. The effect, standing down on the field, a halo of lights ringing the field and focused on the dirt-caked players, was to make it seem like the fifties again. Otto Graham versus Andy Robustelli. Jim Brown and Sam Huff.

Lawrence Taylor belonged here.

Taylor's greatness has been well-documented, and it is well-deserved. He is one of the three or four best defensive players in the seventy years the National Football League has been playing. Even the people who hate him for his off-field excesses admire him for his football greatness and his incredible pain threshold. In many ways, Lawrence Taylor is the Sammy Baugh of his day. Legend (confirmed legend, really, which then makes it not a legend) has it that Sammy Baugh, the Washington Redskins' quarterback of the forties, spent many Saturday nights drinking, stayed up, and went straight to the ballpark for Sunday's game. Stories about his hatred of losing and loving of boozing get richer every year. But Baugh set the National Football League's completion-percentage record in 1945, and it stood for thirty-seven years. And he won. So his off-the-field stuff was tolerated. Same thing with Taylor, who said in his book that he did cocaine and crack during the 1985 season and didn't play up to his standard but still played well enough to go to the Pro Bowl.

Taylor was almost everything coaches didn't want a player to be. Parcells was a fanatic about his players' participating in the off-season conditioning program, but Taylor never did. Taylor loved to sleep in team meetings. Taylor, in his early Giants years, would never tiptoe down the hall after training-camp curfew and then sneak out; he would walk right past the coaches in the lobby of the team dormitory at camp after the appointed time, say hi to them, and go out through the front door. It cost him $100 nightly, but he wasn't going to go slinking around. He was Lawrence Taylor. When all of the drug stuff hit the papers in 1987 with the release of his book, Taylor was consistent. He'd be damned if he was ever going to apologize for it, and given the opportunity, he'd tell kids: Look, I made a mistake, and I don't want you to make a mistake, but I'm not going to tell you what to do or how to live your life. Do what you think is right.

His biggest ally in the world was Parcells. Now, Parcells knew the other players thought he bent over too far in Taylor's behalf. The players knew that Parcells had gotten rid of a number of drug users in his twenty-three-player purge of the Giants' 3-12-1 team in his first year as coach in 1983. And here was Taylor, flaunting his drug use in a book. And even flaunting getting away with the testing by taking a non-drug-using teammate's urine, putting it into a Visine bottle, then holding it next to his penis while he pretended to urinate. So the team actually was testing a teammate's clean urine in 1985 and thought Taylor, acting tired, was clean. Parcells justified his treatment of Taylor by pointing to his play on the field. "He's got to be the best linebacker ever to play the game," Parcells said. Most recently, there was his incredible strike game at Buffalo in 1987, and several other great performances playing with torn shoulder cartilage and a hamstring injury late in 1987.

The Giants were 2-6 and playing at Philadelphia in November 1987. The Eagles had the game's best running quarterback, young Randall Cunningham. The Giants had the game's best quarterback-chaser, Taylor. Before the game, Philadelphia coach Buddy Ryan said the Eagles, who for seven years had been tormented by Taylor, might finally have a quarterback who could outrun him. This motivated Taylor, who thought he could catch anybody. With twenty-five seconds left in the game, and the Giants ahead by 3 points, and the Eagles with a third-and-4 at the Giants' 26, Cunningham tried to run for the first down. Taylor, from behind, took off after Cunningham, conscious of the fact that he couldn't let Cunningham get to the first down at the 22-yard line. Taylor, running full speed, leaped after Cunningham, popping the hamstring muscle when he took the powerful lunge. Taylor tackled Cunningham. At the 23. A yard short of the first down. The Giants won the game.

Lying on the trainer's table after the game, getting the hamstring treated, Taylor looked up at Parcells.

"I guess I can still do it," Taylor said.

"I guess you can," Parcells said back.

On this night in Cleveland, during the Giants' final preseason game, Taylor showed again his love for the sport, and his distaste for losing. He'd left the game late in the third quarter, like most of the veterans, to allow the younger players the chance to gain some experience. But the Browns, at the Giants' 3-yard line, called a time-out with seven seconds left in the game. This angered the Giants, because the Browns led 17–13 and only had to let the clock run out to win the game. Taylor, sitting on the bench, saw what was happening. He put his helmet on and ran past the coaches, not saying a word, onto the field.

"Andy! Andy!" Taylor yelled to reserve linebacker Andy Headen.

Taylor meant to take Headen out of the game and insert himself. Headen looked at him with an expression of: What the hell you doing? Headen gave Taylor a look of disgust—it wasn't often he got to play—and started to jog off the field. A couple of Giants looked at Taylor with quizzical faces.

"Head man sent me in," Taylor said.

"Right," said linebacker Pepper Johnson suspiciously. "You the head man."

On the sidelines, with Headen approaching, Giants defensive coordinator Bill Belichick yelled at Headen, "Get LT out of there!"

Headen jogged back toward the huddle—by this time, the Browns had finished their time-out and were huddling, getting ready to run a play—but Taylor waved toward the sidelines and hollered, "No! No! No!"

Headen turned around and started toward the sidelines. Belichick waved him back to the field.

Headen turned around and started toward the huddle. Taylor waved him back to the sidelines.

This all happened in about six seconds.

Headen stretched his arms out, shrugged, and jogged to the sidelines. But he came sprinting back to the field as the Browns came to the line of scrimmage and took cornerback Perry Williams's place in the goal-line defense. Taylor played safety. As the ball was snapped, Taylor ran into the middle of the line of scrimmage and helped plug a hole that the Browns' short-yardage running back, Tim Manoa, couldn't get through.

Taylor, after the game, was surprised to hear a writer make a big deal of the play. It was the play. It was the significance. When does Layrence Taylor play football? Whenever he wants to.

"I saw 'em bring in one of their big backs," Taylor said in explanation. "I said, 'The hell with that shit.' I can take losing by four—well, I can't take losing by four because I hate losing—but I won't take losing by eleven if we don't have to. The hell with that losing by eleven shit. I ain't gonna take that shit."

Lawrence Taylor was ready to play a football season. He said so that night.

"I do believe I've never been in condition as much as I am now," Taylor said.

The Giants' charter got back to Newark at 3:25 in the morning. Taylor made an 11 A.M. tee time.

He didn't know about the drug-test results sitting on the desk of the NFL's drug adviser in West Covina, California.

That weekend, in the offices of the Giants' coaching staff, the defensive coaches met to decide whether they should go from a defense with four linebackers to one with three. For eight years they'd employed the 3-4 defense (three defensive linemen, four linebackers), but the combination of the continuing holdout of Carl Banks and the drug-test report on the desk of the NFL's drug adviser in West Covina, California, made the staff consider changing to the 4-3.

On Sunday, two days after the Cleveland game, eight days before the Monday night season-opener with the Redskins, the writers were all worried about the state of the offensive line. The perennially disappointing William Roberts was just recently put at left tackle after missing three weeks with a sprained ankle. Karl Nelson, who wasn't the same Karl Nelson, was at right tackle. How this team was going to run the ball well no one knew. But Parcells said he wasn't that worried about the offensive line.

"There's something else more important on my mind right now," Parcells said.

More important than the offensive line, which he thought so important? The writers all thought this was a very significant thing to puzzle about this late in the preseason. Were the Giants about to make a trade for a big tackle? Were they about to cut an established player with a big New York name? Was there some deep dark secret the team was trying to hide? Or was Parcells trying to throw the sniffers off a trail, which he often joked about doing?

About the time Parcells was saying that, Taylor was on the phone with Ed Croke, his friend and the Giants' publicist. Taylor was breathless when Croke picked up the phone.

"Eddie, this is an emergency," Taylor said. "Can you help me?"

Croke feared the worst, but it was just Taylor saying that he and Simms were stranded without a tee time in Alpine, New Jersey, and could Croke please get on the phone and get them one? Croke got him a game.

Later that day, George Young called the agent for Carl Banks in Lansing, Michigan. The agent, Charles Tucker, was stuck on getting Banks $3.8 million over four years. The Giants were offering $3.2 million. But the Giants were fighting the losing battle here, just days after finally getting Bavaro to sign for three years for a total package of $3 million. Young had isolated the contract of Wilber Marshall ($1.2 million a year) with the Redskins as an aberration, but he had been sickened, almost literally, a couple of weeks into camp when the Indianapolis Colts, bending to the wishes of one-time Pro Bowl linebacker Duane Bickett, had the Marshall contract thrown in their face during negotiations; Bickett signed with the Colts for $1,125,000 annually. So Young cursed his fortune. And he cursed the timing of the drug-test report on the desk of the NFL's drug adviser in West Covina, California.

Young and Tucker were at loggerheads over the money. Five times before midnight they spoke, with Young in a high state of agitation.

"Something's going on," said Tucker close to midnight. "I can just feel it. Something's bothering George. I know people, and I know when something's bothering them. I can't quite figure it out."

It had something to do with the drug-test results on the desk of the NFL's drug adviser in West Covina, California.

At 1:20 A.M., after a final eighty-minute conversation by phone, Tucker and Young reached a tentative agreement on a four-year contract that would make Banks the second-highest-paid player on the club. In the next four years, he would make $3.6 million.

Four hours later, news would hit the New York streets about why George Young was so agitated that night.

The back-page headline in Monday's editions of *Newsday*:

DRUG CRISIS
SIDELINES LT

——41——

Vintage LT, Part II

August 1988
East Rutherford, New Jersey

Lawrence Taylor was driving the eleven miles he drives to work every day on a bright, hot Monday morning, the twenty-ninth of August. From his two-story home in Upper Saddle River—not far from the homes of Bill Parcells and George Young—it took Taylor no longer than twenty minutes to reach the parking lot at Giants Stadium.

It was time enough to hear that he was about to be suspended for a month later in the day because his midmonth league drug test turned up positive.

He turned the car around. He went home. At some point that day, perhaps immediately, he started crying.

Boy, this guy was in trouble.

Taylor never addressed the subject about exactly what happened, but his friends suspected he fell off the cocaine wagon once during training camp, apparently very close to August 15, which is when, with wide but quiet warning, the Giants had the league's mandatory drug screening for all players. (A demeaning thing, several players said of the new, foolproof test. "It was one of the most degrading things that ever happened to me in my life," one player said. A tent was set up in front of the players' dormitory. Players filed into the tent one at a time and were told to take off all their clothes. Each player, after he stripped, was given a Gatorade cup and told to urinate in the cup. Five feet in front of the player, staring directly at the player's penis as he urinated, was a representative of a testing lab designated by the National Football League. If a player couldn't fill the cup, he went to the side of the tent and drank liquids until he could urinate.)

Taylor apparently thought the drug was free and clear of his system, because he was so shocked when he heard the thing on the radio that morning, the report quoting the *Newsday* story that Taylor would be suspended for at least the first four months of the season.

He went home and cried. Friends came to console him, friends from the Giants and friends from life, all passing through the gauntlet of television cameras and reporters in front of the house. For a while he was inconsolable. Then something made him get some of his LT wit back.

"At least I'll keep Dan Quayle off the front pages for a while, huh?" Taylor said.

Quayle was George Bush's vice-presidential nominee whose candidacy was in trouble because of his spotty military record.

Taylor, NFL rules said, would be suspended until at least the week before the Giants' fifth game of the year, at Washington. The Giants would withhold his pay for the four weeks, which amounted to $250,000. He would be treated as an outpatient during his suspension. George Young said this wasn't a four-week hiatus to play golf. Wellington Mara said he didn't care if it took longer than four weeks; he wanted to make sure Taylor was ready to cope with life without drugs when he returned to the sport.

Conceivably, but not probably, the Giants thought on the morning Lawrence Taylor took the fall that he could be out for the season.

"This is a life-and-death situation," George Young said after lunch that day.

"We'll be okay," Bill Parcells countered, in the privacy of his office. "Don't worry about us."

Parcells wasn't much of a motivational speaker. He did his motivational prodding in other, more private ways. But in this week, he tried to say something meaningful about the Taylor mess.

On August 31, in a fifteen-minute team meeting, he asked the players how much they knew of the filth and degradation of Vietnam. He told them he knew of a commander who once led his troops into battle just after getting to Vietnam, and the squad lost eighteen men that day. He said, then, that this was "small potatoes" compared to real life. He told them that four coaches had already called that week in sympathy with him for losing Taylor to drugs and having Bavaro and Banks report to the team so late. In his best Al Davis, he told the coaches that none of that mattered, that all anyone cared about the morning after the game was whether you won or lost. He told them that all that mattered now was to go out Monday night against the defending Super Bowl champions, the Redskins, and show them that they were in for one of the toughest struggles of their lives.

Parcells seemed remarkably unaffected by it all. He kept the defense the same, plugging in Andy Headen for Lawrence Taylor. He decided to show some faith in Karl Nelson at right tackle, starting him though knowing he wasn't fully ready to play in games.

The team did, too. Except for a fifteen-minute wildcat walkout by Harry Carson over the inequities of his contract versus Carl Banks's deal, these Giants were harmonious and kept trying to convince the writers of that.

"Look," McConkey said. "Everybody wants to know what's going on in this locker room. Fine. I'll tell them. Taylor's story is not a topic of conversation in this room. Nobody's crying about it. I guarantee nobody's preoccupied with it."

— 42 —

The Season Begins, Mercifully

September 1988
East Rutherford, New Jersey

A football season can usually be pretty neatly divided into chapters. For these Giants, this is how this season was compartmentalized:

The Killer Section—In the first six weeks, the Giants would face five games against strong playoff contenders and a sixth at traditional nemesis Dallas; the Giants were 1-11 in Dallas since 1975. And they now would face the first four, at least, without their 1986 NFL most valuable player, Taylor.

The Catch-a-Breath Section—in the next four weeks, the Giants would play Detroit at home, at Atlanta, at Detroit, and Dallas at home. Combined 1987 record: 18-42.

The Playoff-Drive Section—Three bitch games (at Phoenix in the heat, pesky Philadelphia at home, at New Orleans in a killer place to play) followed by a relatively wonderful December of Phoenix, Kansas City, and the Jets at Giants Stadium.

Their realistic hopes: The pragmatists in the locker room thought they'd be in good playoff condition if they went 3-3 in the Killer games, followed by 4-0 in the Catch-a-Breath games, and 4-2 or at worst, 3-3 in the Playoff-Drive stretch. After the 6-9 season of 1987, 10-6 or 11-5 in 1988 sounded pretty good to these guys.

Redskins' interlude:
In coach Joe Gibbs's smallish office at Redskin Park in Herndon, Virginia, there is a saying he has posted on a wall. "Longevity is a measure of success," it says.

In the first two weeks, the Giants won one they should have lost, and vice versa, without Taylor. The Giants scored on two turnovers to beat the Redskins 27–20 after being badly outplayed for most of the game. The next week, up 17–13 against the 49ers with a minute to play, the Giants single-covered Jerry Rice (cornerback Mark Collins was beaten, then knocked off the play by Kenny Hill) and watched him catch a 78-yard touchdown pass.

The next two weeks were more of the inconsistent same. The Giants won at Dallas 12–10, benefiting from an official's bad call on a safety, and were blown out by the Rams at home 45–31.

They were without Taylor, granted. But there was something else missing. It was emotion. The Giants were this kind of team emotionally: If a couple of plays happened that fired them up, great, they'd be fired up. But they were such a businesslike group of people (Kenny Hill, Terry Kinard, Gary Reasons) that the extra effort that comes with being excited about the job just wasn't there. Before the Rams game, Phil Simms, who almost always keeps to himself, was going around prodding players to get up, to get ready, to show some excitement, because they looked so flat. The young players, especially, were so stern, so downright serious. Rookie offensive linemen Eric Moore and John Elliott, who the Giants hoped would be fixtures on the line for years, were probably lovers of high jinks at some points of their lives, but they were absolute rocks here. It just didn't seem natural. The Giants didn't blow their cool during tight games—this was obviously a plus—but they also didn't get revved up in other times either.

There was one bit of excitement early. In Dallas for the third game of the season, Elliott, the rookie from Michigan, was about to start his first professional game. He was stone silent. In the tunnel at Texas Stadium, the Giants' offensive team lined up, ready to go out for introductions. Simms, as he usually did, was going around, shaking hands with everybody and telling them, "Have a good game, big guy," or "Let's get 'em, big un," (short for "big one") when he came to Elliott. Elliott weighs 305 pounds.

"Nervous, big guy?" Simms asked.

A spray of hot vomit shot out from between Elliott's face mask. Simms dodged the stream, then turned to guard Billy Ard.

"Hey, Billy," said Simms. "Guess the big guy's pretty nervous."

(That really happened, by the way.)

There's no question that the Giants had a shortage of enthusiasm, and what they had was sometimes manufactured. When Phil McConkey raced out of the tunnel before the Super Bowl, waving a white towel and running up and down the Giants' sideline toward the end zone, where he whipped down an end-zone cone with the towel and got half the place roaring, it was under direction from Parcells. "Go out and get people going," Parcells had said.

And when Jim Burt waded into the stands that season after the playoff win over the 49ers, it wasn't without premeditation. Although it was portrayed at the time as a spontaneous act of enthusiasm and glee, it was actually well-planned by Burt. Now, Jim Burt was an enthusiastic guy, and he was one of the guys who kept the Giants up. But he wasn't well-known to anyone outside Giants fandom. He asked his agent, David Fishof, how he could change this. Fishof told him that he needed what in the business was called a "point of recognition," or a way for the business world to distinguish Jim Burt from all the other beefy look-alike hulks who clogged up the middle of lines of scrimmage on Sunday afternoons. Burt thought about it for a while. He went back to Fishof and asked what would the reaction be if he went up into the stands to mingle with the fans if the Giants won a playoff game. Great idea, Fishof said. So Burt did it, and the reaction was terrific. Blue-collar star mingles with fans, film at 11:00. The image worked for Burt, who, just behind Simms, was the team's most commercially attractive player of the late decade. But it was fitting, in a way, that some of the great enthusiasm around the Giants' great season didn't happen. It was invented.

Dynasties don't die because teams don't have cheerleaders. The Celtics and Yankees were stone-faced, too. But there's a good argument that football players need to be more prepared to play mentally than in other sports because there's so much of an edge to be won or lost through constant effort. Early in the 1988 season, the Bears were making news because they had lost two Pro Bowl line-backers, Marshall and Otis Wilson, to free agency and a knee injury respectively, and they had inserted a bunch of low-round guys in the defense. Fiery low-round guys, it should be noted. And the Bears started the year 7-1.

"You can never underestimate the value of enthusiasm and attitude and aggressiveness," said Bill Tobin, the Chicago Bears' vice president for player personnel. "We do not make our team up on a stopwatch and a tape measure. Intelligence, aggressiveness, and personality are big factors in the makeup of our team."

The Giants got Taylor back in time to play at Washington on October 2. On the third play of the game, he burst in from his right outside linebacker spot, slammed into Washington quarterback Mark Rypien, and forced a fumble. The Giants went on to score, and went on to win 24–23.

Redskins' interlude:
Thirty minutes after the Redskins fell to 2-3, defensive end Dexter Manley walked to his locker, picked up the wooden folding chair in front of it, and slammed it against the side of his locker, sending shards of wood in every direction.
"We've dug ourselves into a very deep hole," Washington tackle Joe Jacoby said.

The Giants were 3-2 now, with two wins over the defending Super Bowl champions. But was it a mirage? Parcells and offensive coordinator Ron Erhardt still were determined to win with the run. "It worked before," Erhardt told the players one day. "Just keep doing it. It'll work again." The players had their doubts. Someday, when Moore and Elliott and Doug Riesenberg got enmeshed and learned to block well together, it might. But the running game was in this kind of disarray, compared to the good times:

Year	Won-Lost	Average Gain per Carry	NFL Rank
1988	3-2	3.2 yards	24th
1987	6-9	3.3 yards	24th
1986	14-2	4.0 yards	6th
1985	10-6	4.2 yards	4th

This is one of the primary reasons in football why greatness hasn't been sustained recently. What did the great recent teams have in common? A good rushing game. Pittsburgh for years would have Franco Harris among the league leaders. So would Miami with Larry Csonka, and Green Bay with Paul Hornung and Jim Taylor. The Giants needed Joe Morris to be a very big player for them, but the transient nature of the line made that an impossible dream.

After the Giants lost at Philadelphia the following week, they were 3-3 and embarrassed. For the first time in Parcells's five years as coach, they were last in the league in team defense.

After six games in 1986, the Giants were the top-rated defense. After six games in 1988, they were number twenty-eight.

They were going crazy trying to figure out their deficiencies, on both sides of the ball. Sixteen of the twenty-two starters were the same in the two seasons. Simms was still handing to Morris, and fullback Maurice Carthon was still blocking for him. Taylor and Banks were still there, and Harry Carson was still filling the middle of the line.

So why was George Young thinking to himself—and telling some colleagues—almost daily, "Is it going to take an act of divine Providence for Bill to make some lineup changes?" Why, the organization wondered, was this following chart a reality:

Span of games	Years	Won	Lost
Giants' last eighteen games	1987–1988	9	9
Giants' eighteen previous games	1986	17	1

Count the physical reasons. Taylor missed four weeks in drug rehabilitation. Banks and Bavaro had nagging injuries that wouldn't go away, and Parcells privately was grumbling that players who hold out always end up getting hurt. (By January, Bavaro would have a cast on his foot and surgery on his shoulder.) The offensive line was in flux. Three key defensive players—Marshall and safeties Hill and Terry Kinard—continued to disappoint the staff.

Count the competitive ones. "Two years is an eternity in football," Phil McConkey said. "But more important than what happens to your team sometimes is what happens to the teams around you. They can get better or worse, and in our case, the teams around us have gotten better." Dallas hadn't. But . Philadelphia had the best new quarterback in the game, Randall Cunningham, and a feared defensive end who ate up the Giants, Reggie White. Phoenix had the disadvantage of a mediocre front office but the advantage of huge money because of their move from St. Louis. Washington had a new Super Bowl trophy in the showcase. No question it was a better division. And no question the Giants had been helped less than they'd liked through the draft in the last couple of years, picking so low in each round.

Count the emotional ones. Everyone in the locker room knew the team was in trouble in the next two weeks when, first, Harry Carson had to go absolutely bonkers in a halftime tirade to make the Giants start playing, and second, when they were lifeless in surviving a trip to Atlanta.

On October 16, the Giants trailed a lousy Detroit team 10–7 at halftime. In the defensive team's meeting room, someone had written on the blackboard, "Do you take pride in NY Giants defense and play like it?" Carson stood in front of the group and for the first time in an organized group of people in his life committed mayhem. He threw a chair. It broke. It scared a couple of the offensive players nearby. Hell, it scared some guys in the next room. Defensive end Eric Dorsey thought to himself as it was happening, "Look at that look in his eyes!" Carson threw everything he could get his hands on, and when it was over, two chairs were broken in the meeting room. In the third quarter, the Lions gained − 12 yards. The Giants won 30–10. Quarterback Rusty Hilger of the Lions said the Giants in the second half were playing as hard as any team he'd ever seen.

Chair-throwing can't work every week.

The next week, in Atlanta, the Giants trailed 1-7 Atlanta 16–6 with four minutes to go. Midway through the third quarter, with the Giants allowing the Falcons to run at will, Carson burst through the line and stopped running back John Settle for a one-yard loss on a big play. It was the Giants' best individual play of the day to that point, and it helped to turn the game in the Giants' favor.

As Carson walked off the field, none of his defensive teammates ran to him and slapped him on the helmet or butt or shoulders. He got to the sidelines, and no one congratulated him. Finally, near the bench, center Bart Oates gave him a feeble handshake.

The Giants won a game they had no business winning, 23–16. So here were the Giants halfway through the season, 5-3, and respectable, in good position to win their division. Their motivation? It might have been written on the blackboard of their defensive meeting room.

The message on the blackboard read:

10 in a row will get us some dough

13-3. That's the ticket.

"Truth is truth," said Kenny Hill. "We aren't as good as we were in 1986. We're a long way from it."

The Super Bowl winners in 1986 and 1987, Chicago and New York, had much in common entering the season. The Bears were missing Marshall and Wilson. The Giants were without Taylor. The Bears' defense rivaled their Super Bowl numbers. The Giants' defense plummeted.

"A lot of defense is the 'want' factor," Chicago cornerback Vestee Jackson said at the season's midpoint. "We've got a bunch of new guys who are pushing us to be better, fitting into our system and doing exactly what they're supposed to do on the field."

Said Carson, "The way I see it, it's very difficult to maintain that same high level of intensity we had in 1986. When you're world champs, people bring more to play you every week; it's always like a playoff game. But when we were getting there, the intensity we felt going into the playoffs was just incredible. If you could match the way we felt in the last couple of weeks of the season and heading into the playoffs, it'd be incredible. You'd have an incredible team. We couldn't believe how everything was going so right. But if you maintained that level, you'd also have to be pretty sick, because you'd have to be thinking about it every minute, every day."

Carson was asked about how emotionless the team seemed at times.

"We haven't had a coach who can go out and get his guys inspired," said Carson. Parcells was stolid, and he urged his players to be hardened and not to allow themselves to be shaken late in games by pressure situations.

"Our young players are talked to like it's a business," Carson said. "They go out on the field not fully emotionally ready to play."

────43────
The Struggle

October 1988
Northfield, Michigan

Look. Parcells didn't like this team more than any of the fans or the sports writers. He knew it was struggling, and he knew against a schedule like Washington's he'd be looking up at .500 right now. He knew safeties Terry Kinard and Kenny Hill and linebacker Carl Banks and defensive end Leonard Marshall were playing well below their 1986 levels, and he thought constantly about what he should do about it.

On Sunday morning, October 30, Parcells was in the lobby of the Northfield Hilton by about 6:00. Couldn't sleep. So he sat there with Whitey Wagner, the club's equipment manager, and drank coffee and smoked cigarettes.

Parcells, though, was a pragmatist. If he changed the lineup now—say, if he put in second-year player Adrian White for Hill at strong safety, and sub John Washington in full-time for Marshall at defensive end, and went out and looked for a replacement for Kinard—then he'd risk losing these players for the rest of the season. Not literally. But veteran longtime starters don't take kindly to being replaced in the middle of a season, and they probably wouldn't be very helpful coming off the bench if needed because they'd be in a mental snit about their demotion.

"I'm thinking about it," he said.

But you could tell that, with the Giants 5-3 and still in the playoff race seriously, making big changes could do more harm than good at this point. So it seemed as if he'd sink or swim with these same players this year, then wait until the off-season to make whatever changes he'd make.

"If we win this division this year," Parcells said, blowing smoke out at predawn Michigan, sitting in the Hilton lobby, "it'll be my best coaching job."

A win is a win. The Giants were forced to overtime by one of the bad teams of their time, the Lions, who could play some defense but had no teeth for the offensive side of the ball. They won on a Paul McFadden field goal after number three quarterback John Witkowski fumbled in overtime deep

213

in his own territory. "We're six and three and ugly," said Joe Morris. Make that 7-3 the next week after a win over Dallas at home, the first easy win they'd had in a year. It was an embittering win in some ways, though. The Giants were ahead 26–0 at halftime, went conservative on offense in the second half, and were roundly booed at a couple of points. In general, the players thought the fans were big front-runners.

So the Giants had beaten teams in four straight weeks who would finish the season a combined 16-48. Now what would happen when they faced a good team playing well, at home, in adverse weather? A disaster. The defense gave up 485 yards, the most by a Giants' defense since 1980, and Phoenix, in the heat, won 24–17. The Giants were 7-4, a game in front of the division. The next week's game was crucial, at home against Philadelphia.

So crucial, in fact, that God-fearing George Martin, the elder defensive statesman and one of Parcells's unofficially designated team leaders, went nuts in the locker room before the game.

"Forgive me, Lord Father, for what I'm about to say," Martin said.

Martin had been a Giant since 1975. Those who had been with the team for much of Martin's time said they'd never heard him curse before this afternoon. But he sensed the team wasn't properly ready for the game (wow, isn't that something new?), and he lit into them to try to get them prepared.

The Giants lost in overtime. And Phil Simms hurt his knee. (Dynasty factor number 493, from Los Angeles Dodgers manager Tom Lasorda: "In this day and age, I don't care what sport you're in, there's not the depth to cover up for the big injuries.")

Here's how it happened: The Giants were protecting a 7-point lead in the third quarter, and Simms was back to pass. From his blind side steamed Reggie White, the best pass rusher the Giants saw every year. Referee Tom Dooley saw the disaster waiting to happen.

Simms released.

Dooley yelled, "Leavehimaloneleavehimalone!"

Too late. White hurled his 285 pounds into Simm's left shoulder, driving his right shoulder into the hard Astroturf.

Simms said, *"Ooooooooooohaaaaaaaaghhhhhhhhhhh."*

Losing Simms, with a game at powerful New Orleans the next week, would be devastating.

But they lost him. They lost Simms and Banks (neck, knee) for the game at the Superdome. The Giants, in the game against the Saints, had 8 first downs. They had 14 rushing yards. They held the ball for a third of the game. They had 5 turnovers; Joe Morris fumbled twice without being hit. Eric Dorsey threw up on Bill Parcells's shoes on the sidelines.

They won 13–12.

They won because their defense played some defense. Lawrence Taylor had to keep coming out of the game with a torn deltoid muscle, and he kept getting his shoulder strapped tighter so the deltoid muscle wouldn't rip more, and he was in so much pain. He had three sacks and seven tackles, and Phil Simms said, "That was the best fuckin' game Lawrence Taylor ever played."

They looked good in each of the next two weeks, beating Phoenix 44–7 and Kansas City 28–12 at home. They were 10-5, and they must have been pretty good, because they had all kinds of new fans now. Richard Nixon came in the locker room after the Kansas City game.

"I notice that some of the sports writers haven't given the Giants a very good chance of winning [the Super Bowl]," Nixon said. "But they'll have a chance if they play like they did today."

Redskins' interlude:
The Redskins were out of it now. It was December, and they were 6-8, and mathematically they had no chance to win the NFC East or a wild card berth in the playoffs.

It was contract-padding time for Washington defensive end Dexter Manley.

"For me," said Manley before the fifteenth game of the sixteen-game season, "it means I can build up my stats. It's a stats performance. It's incentive clauses. It's every man for himself. In fact, if we get real selfish, we'll win the ball game. That's my philosophy."

Manley earned $405,000 in base salary in 1988. Here is what he was eligible to earn in incentives:

- *For each sack up to ten in a season, he got $2,000.*
- *For each sack over ten but less than seventeen, he got $3,000.*
- *For each sack over seventeen, he got $4,500.*
- *Each time he pressured the quarterback, he got $1,500.*
- *Each time he batted down a pass, he got $1,500.*

The Giants had to beat the Jets in the final regular-season game to be assured of making the playoffs. They could also make the postseason tournament if either Philadelphia or the Rams lost. But the fact that there was an if involved was not lost on the Giants. They knew this could be their last game.

And not just the last game of the season either.

"If we lose," said Jim Burt, "this could be the last time you see the real Giants. You know, the Super Bowl Giants. I think Parcells is going to make some heavy changes."

It was fitting they lost, and fitting they lost the way they did, and fitting the Rams and Eagles both won, meaning they missed out on the playoffs. The loss typified two seasons. Factor number one: Phil Simms played heroically. He was sacked 8 times and belted after he threw 6 other times, but he still led the Giants back from a 20–7 deficit to a 21–20 lead with four minutes left. Factor number two: Something crazy happened. Phil McConkey, the return specialist with the most reliable hands in the division, muffed a third-quarter punt, leading to a 20–7 Jets lead. Factor number three: The defense died late. The Jets drove 52 yards for the winning touchdown with thirty-seven seconds left, and they won on a ridiculous mismatch. Pro Bowler Al Toon caught a rainbow touchdown pass from Ken O'Brien in single coverage over safety Tom Flynn.

After the game, a coach was doused with Gatorade. It was Joe Walton of the Jets. Bill Parcells went to the locker room dry.

The Giants finished the season 10-6. Philadelphia finished the season 10-6. The Rams finished 10-6. Philadelphia won the playoff tiebreaker with the Giants because the Eagles swept the Giants two games to none during the regular season. The Rams won the tiebreaker with the Giants because of the Los Angeles rout of New York in September.

Seven teams went 10-6 in the NFL in 1988.

Wasting away in parityville.

It ended ingloriously, inconsistently. On the final day the Giants would play football this season, in the second quarter, with the Giants trailing 13–0, here was the Giants' series:

First down—Simms throws to Maurice Carthon, who drops it.

Second down—Simms is sacked by Ken Rose, and Eric Moore is called for holding. The Jets decline the penalty.

Third down—Simms is sacked by Rose, and John Elliott is called for holding. The Jets decline the penalty.

Fourth down—Punt.

As Simms watched television that night at his home, his season down the toilet for the second straight year, he thought to himself: We'll be a different team next year.

⎯ 44 ⎯

The Simms Theory

Phil Simms had one eye on Daryl Hannah on HBO and the other in space, trying to think about the lack of dynasties in pro football these days.

"I think the obvious things, that everybody gets up to play you, that teams you've beaten one year might be better the next year and you might not be, that all the factors in the league are designed not to have one team win all the time.

"But here's one for you: Look at all the guys in our locker room. How many guys in our locker room come from middle-class backgrounds or better? Think of it. Not me. Not Burt, not Taylor, not McConkey, not Carson, not Marshall . . . We all struggled. We had to work for everything. So now that we've made some money, do we change? I don't know. But think about it."

"Wait a minute," a visitor said. "You still play like you've got ten dollars in the bank."

"I still play like that," he said, "because people treat me like I've got ten dollars. People still think I can't play. For me, it's a never-ending battle for respect. There's probably nothing I can do about what people think of me, but I think I probably get some motivation out of the fact that nobody thinks I'm one of the best quarterbacks. So for whatever reason, I keep trying to prove I am."

Simms took his kids to the movies in the afternoon. Then he came home and lifted weights for a couple of hours in the new weight room he'd had built on to his house.

217

45

Young Ideas

Each winter, a week or so after the Super Bowl, the three hundred or so best football-playing college seniors travel to a domed stadium in the United States to be timed and tested and examined by pro scouts, coaches, and doctors. This past February, general manager George Young of the Giants went to the Hoosier Dome in Indianapolis, where he encountered a college prospect who was very excited at the thought of playing in the National Football League, and in particular, for the New York Giants.

"Mr. Young," the player began, speaking earnestly, "I would love to have the opportunity to play for the Giants . . ."

Young has lots of experience listening to young people talk; he spent fifteen years teaching history and political science and coaching high school football in Baltimore before getting into pro football. But the rest of what the young prospect said in Indianapolis Young doesn't readily recall, because his mind had turned it off. As the kid spoke and Young stood there looking very interested in what the kid was saying, Young thought to himself, "How long will it take this kid to get screwed up? In five years, he'll be carrying a picket sign saying, 'Management's a bunch of cockroaches.' "

Back in his office, Young wondered aloud about his life, and the lives of the people in his sport.

"I came out of education to get here," he began. "In education, you're used to having a positive effect on someone's life, you know, making a life better in some small way. The most difficult thing about this job is you get used to seeing people come into the sport all bright-eyed and bushy-tailed. Then—and I'm not saying all of them, but some of them, a lot of them— deteriorate in front of your very eyes. Nothing is good enough anymore.

"It's no fun anymore. I know that sounds ridiculous, but when I was a player, the important thing was how you were able to compete on the level you played in. Now, the only thing that matters is dollars. There's such a preoccupation with it. And not only isn't it fun for us with the clubs, I don't think it's any fun for the players either. I don't think dollar bills have ever made anyone happy."

The Green Bay Packers signed the starting left guard on the Giants' Super Bowl team, Billy Ard, as part of the NFL's new free-agency system on February 27. The league put in the system to avoid losing a free-agency lawsuit to the players' association, and to afford players on good teams the chance to move to poor teams and play and make more money.

Twenty-five months after they ran behind a dominant line to triumph in Pasadena, the Giants had one of their offensive linemen left.

Epilogue

The hotel was the Westin Galleria Hotel in Houston, the kind where you could get lost for a week and have a lot of different choices for brunch and dinner, and pay $4 for a gin and tonic with lime in the lobby bar, and then pay $6.35 to watch a second-run movie or a tenth-run European soft-porn movie in the privacy of your thick-carpeted room with the windows that don't open. This was the comfy hotel where Bob Cousy realized with finality why no team in any sport today or tomorrow will ever win championships the way his Boston Celtics dynasty won championships.

Cousy knew this kind of dynasty was dead soon after the Celtics' incredible streak of eight consecutive championships and eleven in thirteen years ended. The whys have accumulated to him over the years since.

But on this day in the Westin Galleria Hotel—where Cousy was because he was going to be the color man on the Rockets-Celtics game that night—it all came together for Cousy while he spoke and thought about the old Celtics. Like this:

a. Dynasty equals single-minded great talent.
b. Single-minded great talent does not equal today.
c. Dynasty does not equal today.

"Today's jock," Cousy said, "is bigger, better, stronger. Today's jock is also smarter. I read recently that Kevin McHale's priorities have been re-arranged since he's been in basketball. He said last summer they'd been rearranged. Now for him the priorities are family, kids, and basketball, in that order. Kevin McHale's got great security. And I realized then when I read that, and I'm realizing right now, that my biggest regret about my life is that I was so one-dimensional in my dedication to a child's game."

Then Bob Cousy called himself a stupid ass.

"Why didn't I reach the conclusion that Kevin McHale reached last summer? I missed the formative years of my two daughters, and that's something I'll never, never be able to get back. That I regret. But to be honest with you, with the money we were making, we almost had no choice. We had to work year-round."

Cousy's teammate, Tom Heinsohn, told me that Cousy and Bill Russell were single-minded in their devotion to basketball greatness, almost to the point of being neurotic. Heinsohn was on the next rung of that dedication, and he was there with John Havlicek, Bill Sharman, and K.C. Jones. And they were coached by Red Auerbach, who was as focused as they come, "the ringmaster with the whip," as Cousy called him.

This is not to say that Cousy would have been any different with money. But had he gotten the big dough—a $125,000 bonus, say, with escalating salaries starting at, say, $175,000 a year—coming into the league as a rookie, he probably wouldn't have been a driver's ed teacher in the summer after his rookie year, when he averaged 15.6 points per game. And he probably wouldn't have gone into the woods of New Hampshire looking for a boys' camp to co-own after his second year, when he averaged 21.7 points a game. "I had to go out and get jobs," Cousy said. "It was purely based on finances, what I had to do."

Cousy is not at all sure what kind of player he would have been with big money. But he knows it affects today's players.

"I think it's just a basic reflection of human nature," he said. "I think the one- or two-year contract for a lot of money is fine, and it makes every player continue to play hard. What I raise my voice against is when you tie a no-cut guarantee to one of those ten-year, $33-million deals. That tells the athlete: Here's all this money, and the best part about it is it's not based on performance; whatever you do, good, mediocre, or bad, you get the dough. The athlete says, 'Hey, I've got a lot of pride. I'll do the best I can no matter what I get paid.' Of course. What else is he going to say? I'm saying, when you wake up with a hangover, it's harder to motivate yourself on a consistent basis. There's nothing most athletes can do about it. It's an insidious thing that grows and there's nothing you can do about it. There's some son of a bitch across the blue line or the center line or the diamond who's trying to stop you, and you've got to go out there and beat him. Money doesn't matter out there.

"Today's jock will fight every bit as aggressively to get to the top of the hill. But the conditions I just talked about are why they will never fight as hard to stay there. You will win once, and you will win back-to-back occasionally. But never much more."

There was no regret in Cousy's voice about all of this nondynasty talk. In many ways, he thinks it's fine.

"I admire McHale," he said. "The financial security allows you to be a better person, a better all-around person. I know that doesn't help the manager or the coach, who's looking for one hundred and twenty percent from the player every year. But that's the way it is. All that's left for today's jock is pride. That will take you so far. But for dynasties, it's not enough.

"We were motivated to play well by fear and pride. Your primal instincts for survival came out in every training camp," Cousy said.

The Boston Celtics of the sixties couldn't exist today. Bob Cousy, sitting right there in the Westin Galleria Hotel, says so.

"You will never see the dynasty in team sports that you saw in Boston, Montreal, or Green Bay again," he said with finality.

The Montreal Canadiens of the fifties couldn't exist today. Sam Pollock says so.

"A dynasty," Pollock, the former Canadiens managing director said in Montreal in 1988, "is not impossible in basketball or hockey because a smaller group of great players can carry you a lot further. But the conditions in sports today—the money, the draft, the parity—make me think it's impossible for a team to be on top as long as the Canadiens were."

The Green Bay Packers of the sixties couldn't exist today. Ray Nitschke says so.

"I'd say it couldn't be done," the former Green Bay linebacker said in Wisconsin in 1989. "The structure of football, the parity, the dilution of talent, the lack of incentive to win year after year because of what players are making . . . You've got to be really hungry to be a champion, and I don't see the modern athlete as being as hungry. I think, if we were playing today, all the outside stuff would definitely have been a factor with us."

The New York Yankees of the fifties and sixties couldn't exist today. Phil Rizzuto says so.

"There will be no more dynasties in baseball. None," said Rizzuto, the shortstop on ten pennant-winning Yankees' teams in the forties and fifties, in 1989. "There's so much parity. And I just think the players today are like people anywhere would be with great security. Subconsciously, they don't put out a hundred percent. You can see it."

For the sporting purist, life was so much better in The Good Ol' Days. For the sporting realist, the brave new world is better. Well, maybe not better. More real, though. And why should sports be any different from society, really? Sports have no business being a false economy, in giving the owners 60 or 70 percent of the house, which the successful ones used to get. The pendulum, in 1989, has swung too far the other way, because ticket prices are getting to be like New York real estate. Sure, people are still paying. But the resentment grows. The Giants have raised their prices $8 in twenty-three months. New England just raised its best seat in Foxboro from $30 to $43. Both of those teams have finished out of the playoffs for two years in a row. Fans will curse quietly and pay the tab. Here's betting that the Giants and Patriots, combined, will sell 90 percent of their tickets this season.

The dynasty is not dead because ticket prices keep going up and players keep raking it in. This is a symptom. The dynasty is dead for three reasons:

1. More franchises.
2. More equality, because of more drafts and more free player movement.
3. More money and less true motivation.

"The circumstances are different today from my era," former great linebacker Sam Huff said. "It's a free world."

It's a real world. And in a real world, nothing is static. The real world doesn't have room for dynasties any longer.

PETER KING
Bloomfield, New Jersey
March 1989

Appendix I

The Dynasties

1. The Boston Celtics, 1957–1969
2. The New York Yankees, 1949–1964
3. The Montreal Canadiens, 1953–1969
4. The New York Yankees, 1921–1943
5. The Green Bay Packers, 1960–1968

The Dynasties

The five greatest sports teams of all time:

1. The Boston Celtics
1957–1969

National Basketball Association championships:

1957, 1959, 1960, 1961, 1962, 1963, 1964, 1965, 1966, 1968, 1969.

NBA Eastern Division championships:

1957, 1958, 1959, 1960, 1961, 1962, 1963, 1964, 1965.

The greatness: Boston won eight consecutive NBA titles and eleven in thirteen years. From 1951 to 1969, the Celtics didn't have a losing season.

They had talent that turned into greatness that turned into endurance that turned into the greatest team ever to play any professional sport.

It started when Red Auerbach, thirty-four then, was hired to coach the Celtics in 1950. He coached sixteen seasons, and all were nonlosing seasons.

Bob Cousy came out of Holy Cross in 1950, Bill Sharman in a deal with Fort Wayne in 1951. Bill Russell came in a trade with St. Louis in 1956, and Tom Heinsohn and K.C. Jones in the 1956 draft, Sam Jones in the 1957 draft, Satch Sanders in the 1960 draft, and John Havlicek in the 1962 draft. Don Nelson came when the Lakers released him in 1965.

"We never got tired of winning from what I saw," Cousy said. "We'd come back for training camp every year after three months off with the saliva dripping off our lips, saying, 'Kill, kill, kill, I want another title.' "

The testimony to their greatness came with their last title, in 1969. Russell was the player-coach by then, having taken over after the 1966 championship.

Boston finished 48-34 in the 1968–'69 season, good for only fourth place in the Eastern Division. Sixth man John Havlicek was twenty-nine, but each of the other six main contributors to the team were thirty or older. Russell and guard Sam Jones were thirty-five. In each of the playoff series they would play, the Celtics would have one more road game in the best-of-seven rounds, because their record was inferior to the opposition. First they beat Philadelphia, four games to one, winning three times at Philadelphia. Next they beat the New York Knicks, four games to two, winning the series opener at Madison Square Garden. Then they played Los Angeles, the winner of the West, for the NBA championship. The Lakers had acquired Wilt Chamberlain before the season, and teaming him with Jerry West and Elgin Baylor, they were roundly expected to rout the Celtics in the finals.

The home team won the first six games, sending the series back to The Forum in Inglewood, California, for game seven. Lakers owner Jack Kent Cooke put a huge net high above the court and filled it with balloons before the game, anticipating a seventh-game victory. The balloons would float down on the celebration after the Lakers' big win, Cooke figured.

With ninety seconds left in the game, Boston led 103–102. Jerry West and Keith Erickson missed shots for the Lakers that would have put them ahead. When the Celtics got the ball back, with seventy-seven seconds left, Don Nelson, cut by the Lakers four years earlier, shot a 15-foot jump shot that hit the back of the rim. It bounced six feet up in the air. It came down. It swished through the basket.

The Celtics won, 108–106.

"It's fun," said Cousy, "to sit back and have a couple of beers and be able to say, 'I played on the greatest sports dynasty in history.' "

2. The New York Yankees
1949–1964

World Series titles:

1949, 1950, 1951, 1952, 1953, 1956, 1958, 1961, 1962.

American League pennants:

1949, 1950, 1951, 1952, 1953, 1955, 1956, 1957, 1958, 1960, 1961, 1962, 1963, 1964.

The greatness: In sixteen seasons, the Yankees won fourteen pennants and nine World Series championships.

From before the Korean War to after the assassination of President Kennedy, the Yankees failed to win the American League twice.

From 1949 to 1957, the Yankees won between 95 and 103 games each year. The key: Talent, obviously. But acquisition, and tying players to their original teams, were more important. There was no draft in this era. From the thirties until about 1960, there were three teams that scouted and committed the most energy to young talent in baseball. These teams were the Yankees, the Dodgers, and the Cardinals.

In the 1930s, some of the best minor-league talent played for independent minor-league teams, and the sixteen major-league teams scouted them heavily. Yankees scout Bill Essicks, who scouted the West Coast in the thirties, saw a lot of the minor-league San Francisco Seals, and he spotted a nineteen-year-old right fielder that he and a lot of other scouts started to follow religiously. In 1933, at nineteen, Joe DiMaggio batted .340, drove in 169 runs, and hit safely in 61 consecutive games. The next season he hit well but tore a left-knee cartilage, causing a few of the scouting hounds to lose the DiMaggio scent. He was still well-regarded, though, and the Yankees liked him enough to outbid any other major-league suitors. In 1934, general manager Ed Barrow of the Yankees told San Francisco owner Charlie Graham to name his price for DiMaggio. The price: five minor-league players, $25,000, and the Yankees not taking possession of DiMaggio until 1936. The Yankees snarled. The Yankees agreed.

The same year DiMaggio came, a five-foot-six shortstop from Brooklyn was using hook and crook to get tryouts with any team he could. Phil Rizzuto wanted to play with the Dodgers, but he showed up at Ebbetts Field for a trial and Dodger manager Casey Stengel told him, "Kid, you better get a shoeshine box. You can't play big-league ball." The New York Giants turned him down. Finally, he got into a one-week camp at Yankee Stadium while the big club was on the road, and he wowed them. They signed Rizzuto and sent him to a Yankee farm team in Bassett, Virginia. He made $75 per month.

Scouts were so critical to a team's success, and the Yankees had good ones, and in abundance. In the sixties, DiMaggio was named the greatest living baseball player. And in 1950, Rizzuto was the American League's most valuable player.

"It was an era where everyone wanted to be a Yankee or go to Notre Dame," said Rizzuto, who lives in New Jersey and does the Yankees' games on television now and doesn't confine his "holy cow" to the TV only. "And because there was no draft, we got a lot of guys just for that reason. People would always ask me, 'How can it be that you guys go out every year and get a Johnny Mize or a Ewell Blackwell right around World Series time?' Holy cow, it was amazing, the way we used to get the missing ingredient like that."

With the homegrown and dealt-for talent, the Yankees won five consecutive Series, from 1949 to 1954. No baseball team before or since has done that.

3. The Montreal Canadiens
1953–1969

Stanley Cup championships:

1953, 1956, 1957, 1958, 1959, 1960, 1965, 1966, 1968, 1969.

The greatness: In seventeen seasons, the Canadiens won ten Stanley Cups. In the other seven seasons, they played in the Stanley Cup finals five times.

This could have been an almost Celtics-like dynasty had Montreal won in 1954 and 1955. In 1954, an overtime goal in game seven of the best-of-seven series lifted Detroit over the Canadiens. In 1955, Maurice Richard missed the finals because he was suspended for stick-swinging (a suspension by NHL president Clarence Campbell that caused Montreal fans to riot at The Forum), and Detroit won the series four games to three again.

The Canadiens had won only two Cups in fifteen seasons when, in the summer of 1946, the board of directors hired a man named Frank Selke to turn the franchise around. On his first day at work, he told office to have the toilets cleaned, because The Forum smelled so bad, and Frank Selke, fifty-six, who had been playing with and managing hockey teams for thirty-nine years, believed every aspect of an organization must be first class for the team on the ice to be a champion. Then Frank Selke went around to every employee in The Forum—from the house plumber to front-office honchos—and told them the Canadiens would do things the right way and be a championship team soon.

There was no player draft then, so Selke took the club's money and put hockey man Sam Pollock in charge of building a farm system. Selke, through Pollock, begin sprinkling the money all over Canada, building feeder teams to produce players who would eventually be Canadiens, or to produce players who would be traded to bring better players or cash to continue the work of the system. It took six years for the first Stanley Cup to come, in 1953. Then, after the two disappointing final-series losses to Detroit, Montreal did something no hockey team in the ninety-seven-year history of Stanley Cup play has done: The Canadiens won five Cups in a row. In those five Stanley Cup finals, Montreal won twenty games and the opposition five.

"When I was a kid," Pollock remembers now, "I followed baseball more than hockey, even though I was from Montreal. You take the Cardinals, and they'd have farm teams in Rochester, Columbus, Houston, Sacramento, and it went on and on through a huge minor-league system. Baseball had a system very much like the one we built.

"There's no doubt about it: Out of quantity comes quality, and we had quantity. A great deal of success was the development of our system. Look what came out of it—Maurice Richard, Dickie Moore, Jean Beliveau, Bernie

Geoffrion, Doug Harvey. We were great in the fifties and sixties because of the seeds we had sown in the farm system."

The system produced four more Cups as expansion and the draft began pushing parity on the NHL. And the Canadiens had a solid base as the seventies opened, so they were able to deal from strength with the new teams that were dying for early respectability.

"It's interesting," said Pollock, "how that investment in the system a long time ago kept paying off."

The winners of the Stanley Cup from 1953 to 1969:

Team	Cups won
1. Montreal	10
2. Toronto	4
3. Detroit	2
4. Chicago	1

4. The New York Yankees
1921–1943

World Series titles:

1923, 1927, 1928, 1932, 1936, 1937, 1938, 1939, 1941, 1943.

American League pennants:

1921, 1922, 1923, 1926, 1927, 1928, 1932, 1936, 1937, 1938, 1939, 1941, 1942, 1943.

The greatness: In twenty-three seasons spanning the Gehrig-Ruth era, the Yankees won ten World Series titles and fourteen pennants. Eight times in twenty-three years these Yankees won more than one hundred games.

They just mashed people. The Yankees found Lou Gehrig playing at Columbia and bought Babe Ruth from the Red Sox and filled in with some very good players of their time (Earle Combs, Tony Lazzeri, Bob Meusel). And they could pitch, too. Look at what they did to the poor American League in 1927:

	Won	Lost	Percentage
New York Yankees	110	44	.714

Hitting

	Average	Home runs	RBI
Ruth	.356	60	164
Gehrig	.373	47	175

Pitching

	Wins	Losses	ERA
Hoyt	22	7	2.63
Moore	19	7	2.28
Pennock	19	8	3.00
Shocker	18	6	2.84

World Series: New York defeated Pittsburgh, 4–0.

In 1932, the Yankees beat the Cubs in four straight, scoring 37 runs in 34 innings. Ruth's last Yankees season was 1934. But Joe DiMaggio arrived in 1936, and the Yankees promptly won four World Series in a row.

By 1939, Gehrig had been sick for a while, for most of the winter before the 1939 baseball season in fact. But he began that season playing. His eighth game of 1939 was his 2,130th in succession, against Washington at Yankee Stadium. But he felt weak, and he left five runners on base in four times at bat, and he felt he was letting the team down. The Yankees' next game, on May 2, 1939, was at Briggs Stadium in Detroit, and Gehrig told manager Joe McCarthy that morning, "I think it would be the best thing for the club if I took myself out of the lineup." He never played baseball again.

The New York writers scurried around to players for both teams, asking them how they felt about the great Gehrig's finally missing a game after fourteen years of playing every day. Now Gehrig and Ruth were gone, and the rest of the league was starting to see some cracks in the damn Yankees. "Maybe," Detroit first baseman Hank Greenberg said, "that Yankee dynasty is beginning to crumble."

The Yankees won three of the next five Series.

5. The Green Bay Packers
1960–1968

National Football League championships:

1961, 1962, 1965, 1966, 1967.

NFL Western Conference championships:

1960, 1961, 1962, 1965, 1966, 1967.

The greatness: The Packers won five NFL championships in the seven seasons from 1961 to 1967. In the two years they didn't win, their combined record was 19-7-2.

Between 1948 and 1958, the Packers didn't have a winning season. The 1958 season was the worst: one win in twelve games, following a training camp during which the players drank and played poker with coach Scooter McLean. In January 1959 the Packers set out to find a new coach and general manager, and they found him in New York, coaching for the Giants. Vince Lombardi was an unknown assistant with the Giants, and his appointment was greeted with skepticism by a team and a town. "Who the heck is that?" guard Jerry Kramer remembers asking when Lombardi was named. "They really screwed up."

"In 1958, I remember going home to Idaho after the season and telling my friends, 'Pro football's not all that tough,' " Kramer said. "The quest for a championship wasn't there. Our fundamental thought was that it was great to be pro football players. In my first year in the pros, I gained seventeen pounds. It was a good life."

The Packers hadn't coached well, but they had drafted well. On that horrible 1958 team were fifteen players who would go on to be named all-pro or be installed in the Pro Football Hall of Fame, or both. It was Lombardi's job to get production out of them. Kramer and quarterback Joe Francis drove to Green Bay from the West Coast in the summer of 1959 for training camp, and they arrived three days early. The Packers allowed them to check into their training-camp rooms early. Kramer and Francis were headed out to play golf one morning, before the veterans were due to report, when Lombardi spied them.

"Where're you guys going?" Lombardi demanded.

"To play golf," Kramer said.

"GOLF?!!! No you're not! You're in training camp! You will make all meetings, you will make all meals, you will make all bedchecks!"

Kramer says now, "There's been a lot of discussion over the years about how much of our success was talent and how much was Lombardi. We had talent, no question about it. But Lombardi had this incredible burning drive inside him. It had been smoldering for years, just waiting for the right outlet. This was perfect for him."

The Packers, using a relentless rushing game and a defense that was among the two or three best of its day, won their first four NFL championships by 37, 9, 11, and 25 points. In the fall of 1967, they tried to win their third title in a row. They were getting old, and they weren't steamrolling teams the way they had in the past, and they'd lost their final two regular-season games. Lombardi, always a fire-and-brimstone speaker, told the players before the playoffs, "Run not to be in the race. Run to win."

"The first one's tough, obviously," Kramer said. "The second one's tougher exponentially, because everyone wants to knock you off. The third one—how can I describe it?—the third one is just a bitch."

The Packers won the championship that season, over Oakland, by 19 points.

Only one team before or since—the Packers of 1929, 1930, and 1931—won NFL championships in three successive seasons.

Appendix II

The New Age:
The Class of Sub-Dynasties

1. The Pittsburgh Steelers, 1974–1980
2. The Oakland A's, 1971–1975
3. The Montreal Canadiens, 1970–1979
4. The New York Islanders, 1979–1984
5. The Los Angeles Lakers, 1979–present
6. The Edmonton Oilers, 1983–present
7. The Cincinnati Reds, 1970–1976
8. The Oakland/Los Angeles Raiders, 1972–1984
9. The New York Yankees, 1976–1981
10. (tie) The Miami Dolphins, 1971–1975
    The San Francisco 49ers, 1981–present

The New Age:
The Class of Sub-Dynasties

They're not dynasties, not in the way we know dynasties. They are teams battling the socialism in all sports and the problems that million-dollar contracts present to motivation to stay great. A few do. Rarely for long.

"It's useless to compare us with the old Yankees," New York Mets journeyman Lee Mazzilli said in 1989. "It's fantasyland. Apples and oranges. Sports is different, with different rules."

We set 1970 as a line of demarcation between the old and the new, between real dynasties and the new-age dynasties. That's the year the National Football League and the American Football League merged, and the year Curt Flood challenged major-league baseball for the right to choose his employer rather than have it be forced on him. All the forces of equality were nearly in place then. Every sport had a draft by then. Every sport had at least a dozen teams competing for players in the annual draft, with the worst teams picking first. By 1976, free agency was happening.

Hockey is clearly the exception to the maintenance of greatness. Since the advent of baseball's free agency, only two teams in major sports—the Montreal Canadiens and New York Islanders—have won three or more titles in succession. A third, the Edmonton Oilers, won four in five years in the late eighties. Hockey's union hasn't been as strident in seeking the big-money changes other sports have, and there still seems to be room for some industry in scouting players, especially in Europe. Edmonton, for instance, took very low risks in drafting European forwards Jari Jurri and Esa Tikkanen, and they become valuable players in the Oilers' rise to success.

Baseball has been a good lab experiment in the free-market influence on sports. Emboldened by the challenge of Flood in 1970, pitchers Andy Messersmith and Dave McNally played without contracts in 1975, claiming that they would be free agents after this because ownership could renew a veteran player's contract for only one year without his permission before losing him. Management said it could continually renew a player's contract if the two sides couldn't annually reach agreement on terms. Arbitrator Peter Seitz ruled in favor of the players and said, "I am not an Abraham Lincoln signing the Emancipation Proclamation . . . The decision does not destroy baseball. But if the club owners think it will ruin baseball, they have it in their power to prevent the damage."

The Yankees bought Catfish Hunter and Reggie Jackson and thus the keys to world championships in 1977 and 1978. But in the decade and a half of the Free Agency Era, where is the ruination of baseball? Where is the domination? Where is the Yankee or Angel dynasty, bought by George Steinbrenner or Gene Autry? Nowhere. Because free agents didn't all go to the same team. Free agents went, usually, where the money was best. And as the Yankees proved with the willy-nilly buying of anybody on the market (Ken Griffey, Dave Collins, Omar Moreno, etc.), team chemistry and logic still count for something in baseball. Only nine guys could play at once, and career-long starters not only didn't often adjust well to playing part-time but also often became divisive forces because of their own situations.

Free agency, then, didn't lead to a new dynasty in baseball. It did the opposite.

"Baseball," said veteran player Darrell Evans in 1988, "has never been healthier. We've got more teams in more pennant races, we've got record attendance every year, and we've got all the teams benefiting from free agency because any team can fill almost any need any year—if it wants to. And that's the key."

Check out the division winners in baseball from 1982 to 1984:

Year	American League		National League	
	East	West	East	West
1982	Milwaukee	California	St. Louis	Atlanta
1983	Baltimore	Chicago	Philadelphia	Los Angeles
1984	Detroit	Kansas City	Chicago	San Diego

Twelve division championships, twelve different champions.
Check out the American League East winners from 1981 to 1986:

1981—New York
1982—Milwaukee
1983—Baltimore
1984—Detroit
1985—Toronto
1986—Boston

In 1987, *Sports Illustrated* picked the seventh team in the seven-team division, Cleveland, to win the division.

In baseball, football, and basketball in the eighties, no team won consecutive titles until the Lakers at the close of the decade. In the face of this mounting parity in sports, here are the best teams in the four major sports since 1970, the class of sub-dynasties:

1. The Pittsburgh Steelers
1974–1980

Super Bowl championships:

1975, 1976, 1979, 1980.

American Football Conference Central Division titles:

1974, 1975, 1976, 1977, 1978, 1979.

The greatness: The Steelers are one of only two NFL teams in the league's seventy-year history to have won as many as four titles in six seasons. They are also the only team since 1974 to have won back-to-back Super Bowls, and they've done that twice.

No team in football history drafted as wisely as Pittsburgh did in a six-year period beginning in 1969, which, not coincidentally, is when the very underrated Chuck Noll (twenty-one coaching seasons, four Super Bowl titles, never coach of the year) took over as Steelers coach. The Steelers had a great base of perhaps eight or nine future Hall of Fame players mature as a team together because they were drafted so close together. Will any football team, with the absurdly expensive and expansive scouting systems of today, ever have a draft class like the Swann-Lambert-Stallworth-Webster one the Steelers had in 1974? And will any perspective-preaching organization, led by the selfless Noll, ever be able to motivate its players away from selfish goals and toward team goals again when players can make $75,000 for looking into a camera and yelling, "I'm going to Disneyland!"?

"Things change," said Pittsburgh president Dan Rooney. "Society changes."

The Steelers, Rooney thinks, may have been the last team to be a true family. "This is going to sound strange," he said, "but the Steelers sold love—playing together and love. We had some holdouts, but even they realized when it was time to come to camp, they'd better be there. The money was played down, because the players realized the team success would benefit us all. We've lost some of that now. What football has gotten away from is togetherness. Agents' influence is really strong. Influences from salaries in other sports is really strong. Players see what other athletes are getting and they say, 'My career's short, I've got to get it now.' "

The Steelers should be getting something now. Their due. This is an example of what they did to teams during their greatness, from the last nine games of the 1976 regular season:

Opponent	Win/ Loss	Score
Cincinnati	W	23–6
at New York Giants	W	27–0
San Diego	W	23–0
at Kansas City	W	45–0
Miami	W	14–3
Houston	W	32–16
at Cincinnati	W	7–3
Tampa Bay	W	42–0
at Houston	W	21–0
TOTAL	9–0	234–28

Average score of game: Pittsburgh 26, Opponents 3.

2. The Oakland A's
1971–1975

World Series titles:

1972, 1973, 1974.

American League West titles:

1971, 1972, 1973, 1974, 1975.

The greatness: Since 1953, the A's are the only team to have won three consecutive World Series.

The A's should go down in history not only for their greatness. They were also the first team in history to be ruined by money and free agency. The A's won three straight world championships, and at the end of the third they were primed for continued greatness. Well, twenty years earlier they might have been. They had three premier starting pitchers—Vida Blue, Catfish Hunter, and Ken Holtzman—and the best reliever in the game, Rollie Fingers. They had two of the game's best sluggers, Reggie Jackson and Sal Bando. These six players were twenty-five, twenty-eight, twenty-eight, twenty-eight, twenty-eight, and twenty-nine when the A's beat the Dodgers four games to one in the 1974 Series. That was three in a row.

"We could have won five," said Phil Garner, a bit player in 1974, a regular thereafter. "That was easily within our reach."

Their disintegration began the following New Year's Eve, when Hunter, 7-1 in the three previous postseasons, signed a $3.2-million contract with the Yankees. He won his freedom from owner Charles O. Finley when an arbitrator ruled that Finley wrongfully withheld $50,000 from Hunter and declared him a free agent. Finley didn't want to pay the going rate for free agents, so he tried to sell them off. In 1976, he dealt Joe Rudi and Fingers to Boston for $2 million and Blue to the Yankees for $1.5 million. Rudi and Fingers were in Boston uniforms the next day, ready to play for the Red Sox, when commissioner Bowie Kuhn voided the deals, saying they weren't in the best interest of baseball. Kuhn beat Finley in a bitter court battle that enforced the commissioner's powers.

Finley dealt Jackson and Holtzman in April 1976 before losing them to free agency. Then, in thirty days in late 1976, Don Baylor, Bert Campaneris, Bando, Fingers, and Gene Tenace all left as free agents. The A's were a last-place team in 1977. What Finley had made, a new reality had torn asunder.

"I can remember how quickly it changed," said Garner. "Our catcher, Gene Tenace, was making $50,000 in 1976, and his contract was up. He was looking for something like $80,000, and they wouldn't give it to him. So he went out on the market."

San Diego gave him a six-year contract, worth an average of $266,666.66 annually.

Said Garner, "I remember him coming back to clean out his locker. The look on his face was total shock."

Ditto baseball, and all of sports.

3. The Montreal Canadiens
1970–1979

Stanley Cup championships:

1971, 1973, 1976, 1977, 1978, 1979.

The greatness: While adjusting to expansion, a new draft, and the financial pressure of the rival World Hockey Association, the Canadiens became the only hockey team in the ninety-seven-year history of Stanley Cup play to win six Cups in the same decade.

It wasn't supposed to happen this way. When the league expanded to Philadelphia, Minnesota, St. Louis, Pittsburgh, Los Angeles, and Oakland in 1967, talent was supposed to be diluted and the best teams were supposed to be beaten down by picking so late in the draft each year. Ditto with the expansion to Buffalo and Vancouver in 1970, and to Atlanta and Long Island in 1972. And when the WHA came into being in 1972, the best players in the NHL were supposed to flock to the new league for bigger paydays.

Some of that happened to every team. Montreal, though, because of the shrewdness of managing director Sam Pollock, rose above it. The Canadiens were at the end of a dynasty in 1970—they'd won Cups in 1965, 1966, 1968, and 1969—when Pollock started making deals with the expansion teams for draft choices. He stocked the best early expansion teams, St. Louis and Minnesota. He dealt for three of the top eight picks in the 1972 draft. But his best trade was dealing a low-round choice plus above-average forward Ernie Hicke to Oakland for its first-round pick in 1971. That pick: Guy Lafleur. Expansion trades yielded Lafleur in 1971, future all-star left wing Steve Shutt in 1972, and perhaps the best defensive forward of all time, Bob Gainey, in 1973. The 1973 draft was classic Pollock. The Canadiens had the second overall pick in the first round but wanted to take Gainey, who was perhaps the eighth- or tenth-best player in the draft. Pollock traded the second overall pick to Atlanta for the fifth overall pick plus a future first-round draft choice. Then he traded that fifth overall pick to St. Louis for the seventh overall pick plus a future first-round pick. With the seventh overall pick, the Canadiens took Gainey, the man they wanted all along. Plus they'd picked up two future first-round picks.

Eventually, though, the business aspect of hockey wore Pollock down. "In the last six or seven years, running a sports team became very, very, very hard," said Pollock, who retired from the Canadiens in 1978 and now is an equity banker in Montreal. "Every situation was a panic situation or an immediate situation. You could never plan anything because things changed so fast."

Pollock planned one thing before he quit. In 1975, he signed a Hall of Fame player, Lafleur, to a ten-year contract, keeping him away from the rival league for life.

4. The New York Islanders
1979–1984

Stanley Cup championships:

1980, 1981, 1982, 1983.

The greatness: The Islanders became the only team besides Montreal in National Hockey League history to win four Cups in a row, and they were the first hockey expansion team to have a string of greatness.

What has held the Islanders back from being considered a truly great franchise are their neighbors in hockey history. Immediately preceding them were the Montreal Canadiens, winners of four straight Stanley Cups and six in the seventies. Immediately after them are the Edmonton Oilers, who won four of the next five Cups. Bob Bourne, a forward on the great Islander teams, sits up in British Columbia at his home these days and chuckles about this.

"Everyone looks at what's happened in hockey in recent years and says, 'Four in a row. Hmm. Must not be very hard. The Canadiens did it. The Oilers are doing it,' " said Bourne, a stockbroker today. "But maybe in twenty years, we might really realize how good we were."

And how good they were. With right wing Mike Bossy (never fewer than 51 goals in the four championship years) scoring, defenseman Denis Potvin defending, goalie Billy Smith playing an aggressive goalie position, and a selfless cast contributing, the Islanders dominated the sport as well as the Canadiens ever did. From the playoffs of 1980 to the playoffs of 1983, the Islanders won sixteen straight playoff series. "Sixteen straight playoff series!" Bourne marveled. "I don't think that can ever be duplicated." Their record in the four Stanley Cup finals series is almost as stunning. Here it is:

Year	Best-of-seven final series outcome (number of games won)	
1980	Islanders 4,	Philadelphia 2
1981	Islanders 4,	Minnesota 1
1982	Islanders 4,	Vancouver 0
1983	Islanders 4,	Edmonton 0
Total	Islanders 16,	Opposition 3

In 1983, New York headed into the finals against the Gretzkys with the series rated a toss-up. This burned the Islanders, who couldn't understand why they wouldn't have earned more respect by then. In 240 minutes of hockey in that series, Edmonton had a lead for a total of 5 minutes.

General manager Bill Torrey, the architect of this 1972 expansion team, was born in a hospital across the street from The Forum in Montreal, and the Canadien way rubbed off on him. He drafted for character and talent, not just the latter. The Islanders liked western Canadian players because they kept getting western Canadians with great work ethics.

"Winning meant so much to us," Bourne said. "I remember how hard it was, and how hard we worked for it. The night before we played our first Stanley Cup final game, I went out to dinner with (teammates) Clark Gillies, Lorne Henning, and Gordy Lane. We all ordered dinner, and when the food came, none of us could eat. Nothing! We didn't have an appetite. We just wanted to get out there and play. It just grew on us. All your life you think how great it would be just to win one championship, but what happened with us is we had so many players who wouldn't settle for that."

5. The Los Angeles Lakers
1979–present

National Basketball Association championships:

1980, 1982, 1985, 1987, 1988.

Pacific Division championships:

1980, 1982, 1983, 1984, 1985, 1986, 1987, 1988, 1989.

The greatness: The Lakers in 1988 became the first NBA team in nineteen years to win consecutive championships, and they became the only basketball team besides the Celtics to win five titles in the same decade.

In 1975, the Lakers traded for the best center in the game, Kareem Abdul-Jabbar. In 1979, they drafted a franchise player, Magic Johnson, with a pick acquired from Utah. In 1982, they picked James Worthy, with a draft choice fleeced from Cleveland. In 1987, needing backup help for Abdul-Jabbar, they traded with San Antonio for Mychal Thompson.

All four were first overall picks in the draft when they came out of college.

They had the talent, without question. And talent is the prime reason why the Lakers were the team of the eighties in the NBA. But talent never seemed to be enough in the NBA. They needed a focus, and a man to focus them. That job fell to Pat Riley, who soothed, cajoled, froze out, hugged, and motivated great basketball out of great players. "I've heard people say you can roll the ball out there and the Lakers will win championships, but that's a bunch of bullshit," said Denver coach Doug Moe, who's not very friendly with Riley. "Riley's done a great job keeping them up for this long."

"We can talk about greatness and all that stuff," Riley said after the 1988 title. "But that's what we were playing for, more than just winning. We were playing to leave footprints, to leave a legacy."

6. The Edmonton Oilers
1983–present

Stanley Cup championships:

1984, 1985, 1987, 1988.

The greatness: While setting themselves up to be in constant contention in the nineties through a series of largely unpopular trades, the Oilers won four Stanley Cups in five seasons.

On a June morning in 1987, the day after the Oilers won their third Stanley Cup in just their eighth NHL season, coach Glen Sather opened the morning paper and read that, in the midst of the celebration the previous night, star defenseman Paul Coffey took time to grouse about his contract. It was then that Sather knew even the greatest things, in modern sports, can't last forever.

"You can't be afraid to make a deal," Sather said, "or your stay on top will be a short one."

The Oilers won their first three Cups with the greatest player in the world, Wayne Gretzky, and four all-star scoring forwards. Coffey was the best offensive defenseman in the world, and goalie Grant Fuhr among the best goaltenders in the world. In 1987, the Oilers traded Coffey to Pittsburgh. In 1988, they traded Gretzky to Los Angeles. For the two stars, Edmonton got two young scoring stars, Jimmy Carson and Craig Simpson; two high draft choices, Martin Gelinas and Craig Joseph; and three top draft choices. Beginning with the 1989 draft, the Oilers would have eight first-round picks in the next five years, more than any team in hockey. Owner Peter Pocklington, who also got $18 million (Canadian) in the Gretzky deal, had his likeness hung in effigy by Albertans the day after the trade, and the anger hadn't subsided months later. The fans thought Pocklington selfishly gave away greatness to line his own pockets.

But let's make that judgment around 1993. If the Oilers win a couple of Cups before 1995 and are in contention until the end every year, they could turn out to be the greatest dynasty of all these sub-dynasties.

7. The Cincinnati Reds
1970–1976

World Series titles:

1975, 1976.

National League West titles:

1970, 1972, 1973, 1975, 1976.

The greatness: The Reds, the last baseball championship team built exclusively through trades and the draft, won 108 games in 1975, more games than any National League team since Pittsburgh won 110 in 1909.

Imagine if this team had had a great pitching staff.

The Reds' worst offensive starter, center fielder Cesar Geronimo, hit .307 in 1976.

Each infielder—catcher Johnny Bench, first baseman Tony Perez, second baseman Joe Morgan, shortstop Dave Concepcion, and third baseman Pete Rose—would get serious Hall of Fame consideration when his career ended.

Bench hit 40 home runs one year. The left fielder, George Foster, hit 52 in another. Rose won three batting championships. The second baseman, Joe Morgan, hit 27 homers and knocked in 111 runs in 1976.

Morgan and Geronimo came to Cincinnati in a big 1971 trade with Houston. Foster came in a minor trade with San Francisco in 1971. The other five everyday players grew up in the Reds' system. It was a system of rules. The Reds were the last bastion of disciplined greatness in baseball history, forbidding facial hair, ordering players to wear black shoes with no insignia showing, and mandating that the stirrup socks be cut low so most of the red showed. This bunch of business suits would have continued to beat the leisure-suited major leagues if free agency didn't begin to chip away at them.

"We were the last real organization team," Rose said. "We were the last team built entirely from within, and I don't think in today's baseball you'll see it again."

8. The Oakland/Los Angeles Raiders
1972–1984

Super Bowl championships:

1977, 1981, 1984.

American Football Conference Western Division titles:

1972, 1973, 1974, 1975, 1976, 1982, 1983.

The greatness: In twelve seasons, the Raiders won three Super Bowls and qualified for the playoffs nine times.

There was this us-against-them thing about the Raiders that they did nothing to discourage. Pete Rozelle is against us because he hates Al Davis; that was one firing-up tool. Another: The other owners are out to get us because we're mean and rough on the field. And another: We broke the rules of the men's club by moving from Oakland to Los Angeles without league permission, so we'll never get a break from the league.

But it was hard to deny the Raiders their rightful spot among sports' great modern teams. From 1963 to 1984, here were the winningest teams in each sport, and their winning percentages:

Team	Winning percentage	Sport
1. Oakland/L.A. Raiders	.714	Football
2. Montreal Canadiens	.666	Hockey
3. Boston Celtics	.656	Basketball
4. Baltimore Orioles	.583	Baseball

"This Raiders team is one of the best in the history of pro football," said Davis, the managing general partner of the Raiders, after the third Super Bowl championship.

What distinguished the Raiders was their ability to go from one era to another—until the late eighties—and continue to win. They went 16-1 in 1976 and won a Super Bowl under the fiery John Madden. They went 15-4 in 1983 and won a Super Bowl under the collected Tom Flores. They won with Ken Stabler, and when he got too old, they won with Jim Plunkett, and when he slumped, they won with Marc Wilson—for a while at least. They won anchored in Oakland, and in the first two tumultuous years after their move to Los Angeles, they won 24 and lost 6.

They won, consistently, with a defense of angry young men. "The Raiders' defense," Matt Millen said in 1983, "is based on the three Ps—pointing, pushing, and punching." Millen once said about Curt Warner, the great Seattle runner, "Curt's a great one. You can't just tackle him. You've got to punch him."

"Just win, baby" was Davis's motto, and that's all they did.

9. The New York Yankees
1976–1981

World Series titles:

1977, 1978.

American League East titles:

1976, 1977, 1978, 1980, 1981.

The greatness: The Yankees begged, borrowed, and stole to build the best team of the late seventies, becoming the first team to use free agency and win. No team since has repeated as World Series champion.

On the Yankees team of 1978 that won the World Series, catcher Thurman Munson, Roy White, and Ron Guidry were the only Series starters to come up through the Yankees' system. In that series, which ended four games for the Yankees and two for Los Angeles, the starting infielders were Chris Chambliss (trade) at first, Brian Doyle (trade) at second, Bucky Dent (trade) at shortstop, Graig Nettles (trade) at third, and Munson catching. The four outfielder/designated hitters were White, Reggie Jackson (free agency), Lou Piniella (trade), and Mickey Rivers (trade). The three solid starters were Guidry, Catfish Hunter (free agency), Ed Figueroa (trade). The bullpen ace was Rich Gossage (trade). The developmental tally:

How acquired	Number of key players
From the Yankees' system	3
From trades	8
From free agency	2

Now, five years can be an eternity in many sports. But usually in baseball, five years isn't an era. With the Yankees—with owner George Steinbrenner's schizophrenic Yankees—five years was eternity. How the 1978 playoff lineup and the 1983 regular lineup compared:

1978		1983
Chris Chambliss	1B	Ken Griffey
Brian Doyle	2B	Willie Randolph
Bucky Dent	ss	Roy Smalley
Graig Nettles	3B	Graig Nettles
Thurman Munson	c	Butch Wynegar
Lou Piniella	LF	Dave Winfield
Mickey Rivers	CF	Jerry Mumphrey
Reggie Jackson	RF	Steve Kemp
Roy White	dh	Don Baylor
Ron Guidry	Pitchers	Ron Guidry
Catfish Hunter		Shane Rawley
Ed Figueroa		Dave Righetti
Goose Gossage		Goose Gossage

Same starters: three.

10. (tie) The Miami Dolphins
1971–1975

Super Bowl championships:

1973, 1974.

American Football Conference Eastern Division titles:

1971, 1972, 1973, 1974.

The greatness: In seventy years, the National Football League has had one perfect season, and it was Miami's. The 1972 Dolphins were 14-0 in the regular season and 3-0 in the playoffs.

Don Shula played for Paul Brown, and he learned the game well. Run the ball, and run it some more, and when you're tired of doing that, run it. In 1972, the Dolphins sent Larry Csonka, Jim Kiick, and Mercury Morris behind an offensive line that would send two of its own to the Hall of Fame, and they responded with 211.4 rushing yards a game, a league record.

In the first Super Bowl win, quarterback Bob Griese threw 11 passes. Miami beat Washington by 7.

In the second Super Bowl win, Griese threw 7. Miami beat Minnesota by 17.

In the 1972 and 1973 seasons, the Dolphins went 32-2.

Prosperity beckoned. At the same time the World Hockey Association was trying to steal credibility from the National Hockey League, the World Football League made a huge splash. Ten weeks after winning the second Super Bowl, three of the Dolphins' biggest stars, Csonka, Kiick, and wide receiver Paul Warfield, signed a $3-million package deal to jump to the World Football League in 1975. The Dolphins, with their starry lame ducks, won eleven games in 1974 but lost in the first round of the playoffs. They haven't won a Super Bowl since.

"I think a dynasty can happen again," Shula said a decade and a half after the Dolphins' run at greatness. "But you have to have the best players and you have to be lucky with injuries. It's more competitive now than it's ever been."

10. (tie) The San Francisco 49ers
1981–present

Super Bowl championships:

1982, 1985, 1989.

National Football Conference Western Division titles:

1981, 1983, 1984, 1986, 1987, 1988.

The greatness: The 49ers are the second NFL team to win three Super Bowls in the same decade. Only the Steelers, at 4-0, are better than the 49ers (3-0) in Super Bowl history.

"The Steelers had the greatest players, the greatest coach, the greatest everything," 49ers coach Bill Walsh said after the third Super Bowl win. "It'd be awfully tough for anyone ever to beat their record. The only difference between ours and theirs, really, is that we've sort of done ours with three different teams."

Except for the money of owner Eddie DeBartolo, the coaching of Walsh, the quarterbacking of Joe Montana, and the defensive direction of safety Ronnie Lott.

In the first championship season, Montana threw to Dwight Clark. In the second championship season, Montana threw to Roger Craig and handed to Wendell Tyler and Craig. In the third championship season, Montana handed to Craig and threw to Craig and Jerry Rice. A partially new defensive face was on each team, with Lott the spirit keeping it together. "I remember when we were getting ready to play in our first Super Bowl how we didn't get caught up in all the hype," Lott said. "We just loved football so much that all we wanted to do was go out and play another game."

But how difficult it was for the 49ers to keep climbing the ladder. "This is the team of the eighties," safety Carlton Williamson predicted after the second Super Bowl win. "We're mature, we're talented, and we're still hungry." They were also losers—in the first round of the playoffs in each of the next three seasons.

Like every great sub-dynasty, staying great was a great struggle for the 49ers. And it never lasted for long.